EDUCATION IN INDIA : A Tree Without Roots?

Shitangshu Kumar Chakraborty

Mentor Emeritus
Rabindranath Tagore Centre for Human Values

Third Edition: 2013

Himalaya Publishing House

MUMBAI • NEW DELHI • NAGPUR • BENGALURU • HYDERABAD • CHENNAI • PUNE • LUCKNOW • AHMEDABAD • ERNAKULAM • BHUBANESWAR • INDORE • KOLKATA • GUWAHATI

First Edition : 2010
Second Edition : 2011
Third Edition : 2013

Published by : Mrs. Meena Pandey for **Himalaya Publishing House Pvt. Ltd.,** "Ramdoot", Dr. Bhalerao Marg, Girgaon, **Mumbai - 400 004**. Phone: 022-23860170/23863863, Fax: 022-23877178
E-mail: himpub@vsnl.com; Website: www.himpub.com

Branch Offices :

New Delhi : "Pooja Apartments", 4-B, Murari Lal Street, Ansari Road, Darya Ganj, New Delhi - 110 002. Phone: 011-23270392, 23278631; Fax: 011-23256286

Nagpur : Kundanlal Chandak Industrial Estate, Ghat Road, Nagpur - 440 018. Phone: 0712-2738731, 3296733; Telefax: 0712-2721215

Bengaluru : No. 16/1 (Old 12/1), 1st Floor, Next to Hotel Highlands, Madhava Nagar, Race Course Road, Bengaluru - 560 001. Phone: 080-32919385; Telefax: 080-22286611

Hyderabad : No. 3-4-184, Lingampally, Besides Raghavendra Swamy Matham, Kachiguda, Hyderabad - 500 027. Phone: 040-27560041, 27550139; Mobile: 09390905282

Chennai : No. 8/2, Madley 2nd Street, Ground Floor, T. Nagar, Chennai - 600 017. Phone: 044-28144004/28144005; Mobile: 09345345051

Pune : First Floor, "Laksha" Apartment, No. 527, Mehunpura, Shaniwarpeth (Near Prabhat Theatre), Pune - 411 030. Phone: 020-24496323/24496333; Mobile: 09370579333

Lucknow : House No 731, Shekhupura Colony, Near B.D. Convent School, Aliganj, Lucknow - 226 022. Mobile: 09307501549

Ahmedabad : 114, "SHAIL", 1st Floor, Opp. Madhu Sudan House, C.G. Road, Navrang Pura, Ahmedabad - 380 009. Phone: 079-26560126; Mobile: 09377088847

Ernakulam : 39/176 (New No: 60/251) 1st Floor, Karikkamuri Road, Ernakulam, Kochi - 682011, Phone: 0484-2378012, 2378016; Mobile: 09344199799

Bhubaneswar: 5 Station Square, Bhubaneswar - 751 001 (Odisha). Phone: 0674-2532129, Mobile: 09338746007

Indore : Kesardeep Avenue Extension, 73, Narayan Bagh, Flat No. 302, IIIrd Floor, Near Humpty Dumpty School, Indore - 452 007 (M.P.). Mobile: 09301386468

Kolkata : 108/4, Beliaghata Main Road, Near ID Hospital, Opp. SBI Bank, Kolkata - 700 010, Phone: 033-32449649, Mobile: 09883055590, 07439040301

Guwahati : House No. 15, Behind Pragjyotish College, Near Sharma Printing Press, P.O. Bharalumukh, Guwahati - 781009, (Assam). Mobile: 09883055590, 09883055536

DTP by : HPH, Editorial Office, Bhandup **(Krunali)**

Printed at : M/s. Aditya Offset Process (I) Pvt. Ltd., Hyderabad. On behalf of HPH.

Chalati ekena padam,
Tisthati ekena buddhiman;
Asamikshya param sthanam
Na purvam ayatanam tyajet.

– Hitopadesa, Mitralabha.

[The wise one pauseth before moving a single step. Without careful scrutiny of even a glorious destination, he does not forsake his previous ground.]

To The Late Sashadhar Ganguly:
Twameva Bandhuscha, Sakha Twameva
[Friend, philosopher and guide in my early youth.]

Nabh kamal mein hai kasturi,
Kaise bharam mitey pashuka re?

– Sant Kabir Das

[The musk is lodged in the navel within, How, alas, can the deer get rid of the illusion that it is without in the forest.]

Foreword

This book — ***EDUCATION IN INDIA : A TREE WITHOUT ROOTS?*** — is a product of exceptional erudition. With keen insight in draws attention to the deep-rooted malaise that has overpowered the education system of India, its aims and directions.

The author is an internationally reputed thinker and is a true lover of India. With his immense learning and wide experience as a teacher, and his association with various organizations about proper dissemination of human values, he has marshalled irrefutable facts to challenge those who are defining the sacred temple of Education in India with materialistic and iconoclastic attitudes, as also by pursuing a policy of commercialisation of the education system for spinning easy money.

He has also given a clarion call to all right-thinking persons to pause and ponder whether the educational policy of India is proceeding with the Right Temper and is on the right track, and what should be our real goal.

It is a pity that India — *Bharatvarsha* — has fallen on evil times and on evil tongues. There was a time when the entire world looked up to *Bharatvarsha* for true knowledge and proper guidance in all matters, material and spiritual, so as to build character to stand up in the world with the head high.

Unfortunately however, bewildered by the dazzling feats of modern science and the ever-increasing allurement of consumerism, a progeny of the globalization of industries, people are forgetting the true goal of human life. As a natural consequence, greed, passion and lust for newer and newer fleshly comforts are rising steadily. International terrorism is also another manifestation of the weird outlook towards basic human values.

We have forgotten that in this glorious land of ours, where a Nachiketa had asserted — *Na vittena tarpaniyo manushya,* or a Maitreyee could solemnly declare — *Yenaham namritam syam kimaham tena kuryam,* character of a human being was of prime importance, and the attainment of proper knowledge of Truth was the highest goal. The ignorance and apathy of modern policy-makers and so-called intellectuals about the infinite treasures contained in our resplendent intellectual and spiritual heritage are appalling. This has given rise to shameful corruption in every sphere of life in a country which was once highly acclaimed as the Land of Truth.

This book also draws attention to the precious opinions of many world-renowned scholars and thinkers who sincerely believe that the future of civilization is not safe along the path of extreme technology of the West, but in the human values and the spiritual insights of the invaluable tradition of India.

It has been a privilege to read this courageous book containing immensely valuable information and proposing a proper orientation of ideas for setting right the Educational Policy of India.

Subir Kumar Sen

Editor — *TRUTH*

Kolkata

Preface

This book is likely to prove to be a 'cry in the wilderness'. But it is not a, 'crying wolf'. In early April this year the author was standing in front of 'Swamiji's mango tree' at Belur Math for the umpteenth time perhaps. This grand old sentinel had been standing there even before Swami Vivekananda had acquired the land for the Ramakrishna Math and Mission on the Western bank of the Ganga. This was in 1898. It has thus been a witness to Divine events, and is perhaps now at least one hundred and twenty-five years old, still bearing mangoes and giving shade.

In silence an image flashed across the author's mind: Suppose this venerable 'senior citizen' of Nature, in a sudden spell of 'enlightenment', were to begin to loathe and deny its roots as a mass of dirty, uncouth tangle. It wanted to wrench itself off from this filthy bondage, and to stand free on fresh ground. What might happen then? The tall, concrete pillars supporting some of its decrepit trunks would themselves have crashed first, and then the sacred witness itself would be gone for ever — fruits, leaves, branches and all that.

Another image may well complete the one above. Imagine that the river Ganga, flowing past the Math a few metres to the east of the mango tree, were to receive the 'wisdom' that its present course from the Gomukhi to the Bay of Bengal has been a big mistake. It must therefore roll back and carve a new pathway supposedly more meaningful than the one traversed for several millennia. If the Ganga could do that, what results would follow? Comprehensively disastrous in short.* The *Kena Upanishad* called such blight *'mahatih vinashti'*. These two images appear to capture and convey some anxious worries and concerns voiced in this book. Having gathered some experience teaching at various levels. In India

* In fact, Vivekananda, in his unsurpassable treatise on comparative culture. *The East and The West,* had posed this very question and given his emphatic reply by using the word 'river' instead of Ganga. Thus: (a) 'If it ever tries to trace back its course, it will simply dry up by being dissipated in all directions'; (b) 'if our national life of these ten thousand years has been a mistake, then there is no help for it; and if we try now to form a new character, the inevitable result will be that we shall die'; (c) 'I ask in all seriousness — which is easier, to give up our national character evolved out of thousands of centuries, or your grafted character of a few hundred years?' (*Complete Works,* Kolkata: Advaita Ashrama, vol. 5, 2005,.p. 460).

and abroad, for five decades, the author has been irresistibly compelled from within to share some critical thoughts. He has nothing to win, nothing to lose. So, sitting on the fence has been eschewed. The bandwagon has not been joined. Playing to the gallery has been shunned. Every episode, each event, all information recounted below has been personally experienced or gathered by the author. It is a duty to posterity that our fading generation leaves for them somewhere a modicum of honest insights into the educational legacy that is in the making in post-independence India. Not only has our own nation enormous stakes in this endeavour the whole world too has.

This book is appearing at a time when education in India is being treated as a 'business' sector worth ₹ 90 billion per year, when teachers in handsomely remunerative government institutions are resorting to hunger strikes and else for still larger pay packets, etc. It is appearing in a period when heavy-weight opinion-moulders are writing books with titles like – *'Fault Lines of Mind Civilization', 'The Siege Within', 'India Unbound'* and the like. They do not seem to mind advocating, 'compound fracturelines', or 'siege without', or 'borrowed bondages'. They forget, or ignore that this is the land of *'guru-gariba-vasa'* ages ago Vishnusharma (of **Panchatantra** fame) had refused to accept any remuneration for educating a King's children. Education, *sbiksha daan* was not put for sale. These pages are seeing the light of day also when this author had been summarily put down by two senior IAS officers (once at Mussoorie and once at IIM Calcutta) asserting that Vivekananda was not an authority on Indian culture and whatever he had done was outside India, nothing within. Moreover, it is a time when gross national product (GNP) is soaring while gross national character (GNC) is nose-diving. The book is emerging when the world seems to have turned wild. Everything is being made unsustainable: harmony at home, sacred manage, frugal lifestyle, purity of air and water, harmony with Nature, nobility in teacher-student relationships, etc., — Quiet desperation — has yielded to groaning desperation. Yet, ironically, all this is accompanied by the stupid cant of 'sustainable development'. The pervasive tendency now is one of ugly duplicity – which this book has tried to avoid*.

---

* *The one bright ray in this gloom is that the 150th birth anniversaries of Rabindranath Tagore and Swami Vivekananda are being celebrated during 2011-13. Though eleven of Tagore's paintings recently fetched £1.6m. at a London auction in June, yet the country's capital has no major road or statue or art gallery in his name within its glittering hub.*

Yet another inspiration underpins this book. It is a humble token of gratitude to all the ancient and contemporary *risushis* and *savants* of *Bharatvarsha*. They first, realized *Truth* or *Ritam,* and then performed the sacred duty of educating society for the holy and sacred. *Artha* and *Kama* goals were not left 'unbound'. Hence the sustainability of their cultural legacy. No less ample is our gratitude to the numerous thinkers of the West (no, mere researchers or scholars) who have understood our culture both deeply and loftily. They have been able to pick-up the gems, instead of licking the muck, from *sanatan* culture. They all repose high hopes in these treasures and lament that India is educating herself about them. For such thinkers — political distinctions between majority and minority communities have been irrelevant.

Such conscientious Indians outside the establishment harbour a sense of helpless agony at the determined and orchestrated bid to scuttle an entire culture model — evolved over so many thousands of years of high *tapasya* and noble universality. Schemers without and betrayers within seem now to have swooped down on — education — to set fire, for the time-being and apparently at least, to Bhartiya culture's central themes. The prolonged and tragic post-1950 total eclipse of the national mind in India has no parallel in either the East or the West.

Hardly anybody has heard, far less been electrified by these words of Swami Vivekananda, uttered at, Kumbakonam in 1897: in the West they are trying to solve the problem of how much a man can possess, and we are tiding here to solve the problem on how little a man can live. ...if history has any truth in it and if prognostications ever prove true, it must be that those who train themselves to live on the least and control themselves well will in the end gain the battle and that those who run after enjoyment and luxury, however vigorous they may seem for the moment, will have to die and become annihilated (*Complete Works*, vol. 3, p. 181) and Vivekananda was only thirty-four when he delivered this prophecy.

During a Harvard University address in 1913 Rabindranath Tagore had diagnosed: '... we lust, after pleasures not because they are truly desire, but because the red light of passion makes them appear desirable; we long for things not because they are great in themselves but because our greed exaggerates them... These exaggerations, these falsifications... break the harmony of our life at every step; we lose the standard of values and are distracted ...' (*Sadhana* Macmillan, 1988, p.32). In that year Tagore was 44 years old.

Gandhiji had opined thus in 1908: — When I read Mr. Dutt's *Economic History of India* I wept; and as I think of it again my heart sickens. Is machinery that has impoverished India. ... Machinery has begun to desolate Europe. Ruination is now knocking the English gales. 'It" would be folly to assume that an Indian Rockefeller would be better than the American Rockfeller. ...Machinery is like a snake-hole which may contain from one to a hundred snakes', (*The Selected Works*, Navjivan, 1969, vol. IV, pp. 188-91). And Gandhi's age was 39 then.

A few words from Sri Aurobindo (1915-8) are equally apt: Therefore, in a commercial age ... if it persisted too long, life would become clogged and perish of its own plethora or burst in its straining to a gross expansion. Like the too massive Titan it will collapse by its own mass, mole ruet sua and 'Economicsy' etc., may be man's first business, but no, its chief business'. (*The Human Cycle* 1985, p. 73 p. 148). Aurobindo was around 43 then.

It appears that a few courageous writers and thinkers of the West had begun to echo every forecast and warning of the four Indian seers above, but only from after the end of the First World War, e.g., Bertrand Russell, Albert Einstein, Alexis Carrel, Aldous Huxley, Arnold Toynbee, Andre Malraux *et. al.* Of course they have not mentioned any of these Indian names, although once in a while, suddenly, a Sanskrit word or two pops up!

Let us have a few corroborative lines from a 1980-book from the USA: 'The MNC is the dinosaur of our energy environment. Too big, too energy consumptive, and too specialized, they will run to their own evolutionary dead-end as production moves back to a localized, small-scale base. ... In a low-entropy society, big, centralized, energy and capital-intensive techniques will be discarded in favour of what it is called appropriate or intermediate technology.'(Rifkin, J, *Entropy*, Bantam, 1980, p. 21? Mercifully, Gandhi is quoted on p. 210). The Carl Sagan Committee (1990) had accused sci-tech and commerce for 'committing crimes against creation' (See chapter 5 below).

Here is another such honest 1999 appraisal: 'Global corporations are now reaching out to establish the hegemony of the culture of greed and excess in virtually every country of the world in their relentless search for more customers ... devaluing their cultures as backward, boring and poor, and offering in their stead promises of a material paradise of excitement, ease and prosperity for all' (Korten, D, *The Post-corporate World*, Berrett Koehler; 1999, p. 31)

Yet, today, we get to know that 'moon mania' has begun to grip India. The world's richest country is now set (announced in 2010) to usher in 'space tourism' on a commercial basis, each seat priced at $ 2,00,000. This country is reported to be using up (in 1980 or so) as much of the fixed energy resources as 22 billion people (Rifkin, p. 219). Who dares to talk of and educate students about the deepening crisis and chaos of 'unavailable' energy because of the second law of thermodynamics — high entropy. Cosmetic courses on 'environment' are a dampsquib. The rhetoric of sustainability in IIT's and IIM's is a cruel joke. While globalization is proclaimed as 'inevitable', entropy gets buried under the sand. Apparently, Einstein was foolish to assert that of all the physical laws, the entropy law of thermodynamics could never be overthrown (Rifkin, p. 44). Greed and lust have always been there in human society. Now 'speed' has added a fearsome feature to 'greed'. Moon-mania, money-mania and techno-mania are invading the corridors of education at whirlwind speed.

In early 2010 Stephen Hawking had warned that too much of hob-nobbing with other planets might invite raids from more intelligent aliens there to plunder earth's resourses and move on — as it had happened after Columbus had first landed in America (*Truth*, 05.02.2010, p. 106). Hazel Henderson had relabelled global village as a 'global casino', where only 10 per cent of world's wealth was 'real' production, the rest only monetary froth (*Beyond Globalization*, Kumarian, 1999, pp. 2-6). In our 'his-master's-voice' educational outfits books such as these (and others like the *Collapse of Globalise. The Case Against Globalization, etc.,*) seem to be on the banned list. The Juvenile Justice Act of India speaks of the 'age of innocence' up to the age of 18. At the same time, 'life-skills' education is being imparted in schools. Its core appears to be sex education for safe inter-sex mixing. Is this not obliterating the very 'innocence' the Act seems to adumbrate (in a grossly one-sided and immature manner?)

This book is neither negative nor pessimistic. Someone had to do the 'dirty job' as they say. Everything briefly mentioned above and elaborated later is factual and truthful. It often borders on stupid complacency or immature escapism when we merely mouth homilies and platitudes — whether as monks or as ministers, or as teachers. If one has the patience and openness to read the whole book. One should find it positive and hopeful in the real sense. It is consistently urging all to begin redrawing from the roots of our *sanatan* ethos. In this task sometimes striking hard at our 'ostrich' mentality could not be avoided. An obstinately intoxicated fellow may at times require a reluctant dose of thrashing to bring him back to good sense. Should a few like-minded readers wish to take a courageous stand as this book has let all of us then say: *abhih*, no fear; and pray: *tasmin tushtey jagat tushtam,* if O! Lord Thou art pleased then all the rest should be pleased too.

S.K. Chakraborty

Kolkata

First of Baisakh, 1419

(14th April, 2012)

Contents

CHAPTER 1

GOD IN PRISON: Agenda for *Desh Rin*

नमो मात्रे पृथिव्यै
नमो मात्रे पृथिव्यै इयं ते राड्
यन्ताऽसि यमनो ध्रुवोऽसि धरूणः ।
कष्यै त्वा क्षेमाय त्वा रष्यै त्वा पोषाय त्वा । ।
(यः ९/२२)

Obeisance to Mother Earth (Country),
This is thy sovereignty.
Thou art the controller, ruler,
Thou art steady firm.
Thee for culture of the land,
Thee for peace, thee for wealth,
Thee for Nurture.

(Yajurveda 9/22)

[Quoted from **The Call of the Vedas,** by A.C. Bose, Bharatiya Vidya Bhawan, 1970, pp. 277-8. All similar citations at the beginning of each chapter are from this source, except the last two]

I

It was a mellow afternoon in early February, 2009. The Sri Aurobindo International School at Puducherry had given us an opportunity to speak informally to the senior students there. It was nice to see about a hundred of them squatting relaxed on the floorof a large hall. At one stage we requested them to indicate by show of hand how many had seen the cell where Sri Aurobindo was confined in the Alipore prison in Kolkata. About half-a-dozen hands went up. We suggested that they should all visit that cell (now a sort of modest shrine) as early as possible. It would be a pilgrimage, a homage to the pinnacle of *sanatan* Bharatiya ethos personified in Sri Aurobindo. Aurobindo Ghosh had been holed up in that solitary cell for full one year, May 1908– May 1909. This cell, with a circular one-foot diameter opening in the middle of the arched ceiling, had no windows or other source of light or ventilation. It measured a meagre nine feet long and five feet wide, bare floor. His own first instinct about the cell was that of an 'animal cage'. But this initial shock was quickly transmuted into that of an 'ashram' for spiritual discipline where he 'found God'. Parents, teachers and students should fathom this miracle, and be afire. For, we feel this miracle to be a matchless saga of human metamorphosis in the present era.

Most of the factors setting the frame of life for Aurobindo Ackroyd Ghosh till 1893 were antagonistic to the emergence of Sri Aurobindo. His anglicized father had insulated him from all native influences. An English governess was given the charge of 'civilizing' the boy. At seven he was sent Education in India: A Tree Without Roots off to England where he stayed and studied for fourteen years at Manchester, London and Cambridge. He did exceptionally well in his studies. He had qualified for the ICS too, but dodged the horseriding test. When he landed in India (1893) he was twenty-one, and a cipher in both Bengali and Sanskrit. To cap it all, it has been said that Aurobindo's mother was mentally sub-normal. How could then such a person find God in the Alipore 'ashram', under inhuman physical conditions for under-trial prisoners, without falling sick? No 'princely' treatment for him in royal mansions!

In other words, both genetics or heredity and environment or nurture fail to explain the 'phenomenon' of Aurobindo metamorphosing into Sri Aurobindo. No other great leader of India of these times has had to face such enormous hurdles from the spirituo-cultural angle. The only satisfactory rationale for being able to overcome these stubborn negative forces can be found in the psychological theory of *samskaras*. It is an original and indispensable pillar of the holistic Indian theory of human character, ignored by western psychology. This third component of character theory can explain what the two earlier ones fail to do.

The astonishing example of the Seer of Pondicherry illustrates to students and teachers alike that the 'Being' embodied in the 1872–

1950 Sri Aurobindo would have been evolving through many previous existences in other forms and names which were devoted to the cultivation of the God-ward, Divine powers (*daivi sampat*)*. These efforts, *sadhanas*, inclinations, tendencies, impressions, aspirations were being accumulated from birth to birth in the progressing 'subtle being' or entity. Therefore, in the 1872-1950 'gross' existence of this 'being', the cumulative momentum of all previous sacred labours, *tapasya* was so irresistible that all the adverse forces, domestic and external, were vanquished. Even if this were a hypothesis, no superior one is available.

Swami Vivekananda had once written a letter to an Indian devotee saying that he was convinced that 'leaders are born, not made'. This statement is both true and not true. True, because when we observe a Vivekananda or an Aurobindo within our limited timeframe, in a discrete manner, then we are naturally inclined to infer that towering leaders are 'born'. This suggests that there is 'effect' without 'cause'. But when we look into the *samskara* theory (fully supported in chapter 6 of the Gita, verses 41-5) we get a logical and plausible explanation about cumulative causation behind the apparently sudden emergence of truly good and great leaders – from nowhere as it were. This last viewcontradicts human reason. There must be an unbroken continuity – though invisible. Otherwise 'evolution' becomes a meaningless term in the human sphere. Such sound understanding of the *samskara* theory, associated with Patanjali's involution-evolution theory, appears indispensable for young minds in pursuit of character-building education. Now, a rationalist student (or even such a teacher) might turn back to ask: 'What is there in character-making for me?

What did Sri Aurobindo gain from his travails and tribulations?' The answer depends on how one defines 'gain'. In his own words, in the last paragraph of his 'Tales', he said : 'I had tasted a little of Equality, Non-attachment and Peace'. As many readers would know, these three psychological states of *samatwa, anasakti* and *shantih* had constituted the core of education received by Arjuna in the second chapter of the Gita (verses 47, 48, 51, 66, 70 and 71). Are these states not 'gains'? Have we been, are we being educated for such abiding 'subjective' gains within? True, Sri Aurobindo had gained nothing in objective terms. But the composition of *samskaras* was

---

* *The Bhagwad Gita*, chapter 16, verses 1-5

exalted enough to endow him with a character that could shove the so-called objective gains into a wee corner of life's mansion. The technoxicated modern society, and its educational tricks, require this indispensable saving turn towards sanity.

II

Speaking in glowing terms about an entirely innocent, young prison-mate, Ashok Nandi, Sri Aurobindo had himself confirmed the truth of the Gita theory cited above. Let us listen to him:[1] 'After the advent of Sri Ramakrishna and the spread of Vedantic knowledge and the study of the Gita that truth [*samskaras*, rebirth] is being re-established. Just as heredity is the chief truth of the physical world, so, in the subtle world, reincarnation is the chief truth.'

Unfortunately the gross secular mind spurns all subtle truths. Earnest parents and children however, have today the long-term, basic responsibility, born as they are in Bharatvarsha, to return with humility to Sri Aurobindo and ponder over his following words about the Ashok Nandi phenomenon:[2] 'In love and devotion he was inferior to none. His generous character, sober devotion and loving heart charmed everyone. ...Towards the end Ashok's yogic powers developed considerably; on the day of his passing away, absorbed in the power of Lord Vishnu, he spoke of the holy, salvation-inducing Name and gave spiritual advice to others before giving up the body with the Name on his lips. Ashok Nandi had been born to work out the consequences due to a previous incarnation.' Tearful resonance is what every legitimate teacher of this land should be feeling while reading this tribute. In the passage preceding the above depiction, Sri Aurobindo had envisioned a budding, fresh Bharatvarsha, with Ashok Nandi in mind, with the following hopes:[3] 'These new children of Mother India, ...have grown bold, full of power, high souled, self-sacrificing, inspired by the high ideals of helping others and doing good to the country. The youth are sparks born of the Great Energy, *Mahashakti*, eager to build the new... Among the youth is a marvellous sign of manifesting the Age of Gold, a religious bent of mind, and in the hearts of many, a longing for yoga...'

A century ago Sri Aurobindo had etched out the above benchmark blueprint for his beloved Mother India. It is this Bharatvarsha which has been and still is the object of adoration and preservation the world over. Great soul-searching among parents and teachers is called for while assessing their achievements (?) and failures in this duty of nurturing Indian youth for the Age of Gold. Sri Aurobindo's touchstone for Bharat's youth was not arrogant, fashionable, scientific temper. It was enlightened, authentic yogic temper. A huge chasm separates the many spurious present-day 'visions' about India, and those of Sri Aurobindo (Alipore prison 1908-9) and of Swami Vivekananda (Kanya Kumari, 1892). When shall we discriminate, choose, and prioritize?

Early this year, the centenary year of Sri Aurobindo's secret Chandannagore sojourn, we had heard a top notch, elderly Indian technocrat conveying his impression of today's youth in course of his convocation address at a national institute of higher learning: 'They expect a lot more from life'. The Chairman and Director had proudly announced that the highest annual salary secured by the graduating batch was that of a boy with ₹ 6 million per year flowing into his pocket. One of the current standard parameters for judging the relative prestige of such institutions is the size of the highest pay packet offered to a fres graduate, sometimes crossing ₹ 10 million a year. This practice has been around us for about fifteen years so. On the other hand, the average Indian annual per capita income has barely crossed ₹ 36,000 only in the year 2009. None of them had deemed it a duty to tell this fact to the students.

III

Sri Aurobindo, in a 1905–letter to his wife Mrinalini Devi, had repented that he was beginning to feel like a 'thief ' for spending as much as '14 annas out of 16'(i.e., 7/8th of a rupee) on himself. This is the man who had left the big Baroda job (1906) to become the first principal of the National College in Calcutta. He had accepted a paltry monthly salary of ₹ 300/– only, which was one-third of the Baroda remuneration. This again was the man who had to survive for one whole year with the bounties of an all-purpose aluminum plate and a bucket and a smelling blanket and, above all, having to gulp *lufsi* in its Wisdom, Hiranyagarbha and Virat aspects. To these regal facilities got added small-scale floods in the cell during heavy rains. It shall be education in the true sense for today's elite youth, at the hour of *samavartan*, to evaluate the merit and morality of their 'a lot more expectations' against the canvas of Ashok Nandi's and Aurobindo's (and thousands more like them). They had suffered and sacrificed with only one expectation.

The freedom and flowering of authentic Bharatvarsha. Are our parents and teachers conscious of their crowning obligation to rekindle this dying spark?

The Dalai Lama, at one stage in course of a lecture at an IIM in June 2009, had remarked: 'You students here are fortunate to be born in India'. Some mild clapping followed. We wondered whether this response signaled anything really genuine. Or was it a mere mechanical gesture of courtesy? For, when the question-hour came, not a single point was raised by the audience touching even remotely on the above comment from the Dalai Lama, despite the fact that he had briefly stressed later on the duty to revive the learning and wisdom stored in the ancient Bharatiya universities like Nalanda. It was so depressing to listen to for about an hour of irrelevant exchanges centering around Tibet-China political relationships.

And yet, the above observation of the Dalai Lama had recaptured one essential feature which the *drashta rishis* have always been educating us about: An unflinching, intrinsic trust and love for this *deva bhumi*. This is no mere figure of speech. But the lowdensity, shallow character of most of what is called 'education' in India today has inoculated us against such elevating ideas and ideals.

After his release from prison through his magnificent defence by CR Das, at the behest of Vasudeva, Sri Aurobindo had delivered a 'divine' speech at Uttarpara. Among his last words were these:[4] '...it is the Sanatan Dharma which for us is nationalism. This Hindu nation was born with the Sanatan Dharma, with it it moves and with it it grows. When the Sanatan Dharma declines, then the nation declines....'. The 'beating-about-the-bush' disease afflicting post-1950 Indian education is a crime against the legacy of perennial principles we have received from the Vedic Rishis up to the Sri Aurobindo's and his likes. It is an irony of fate that most of this treachery is being perpetrated or abetted by the Hindus themselves.

Sri Aurobindo had assured the world, on the basis of historical evidence, and on the strength of the flawless impulse of the *adesh* from Him: 'Go forth and speak to your nation always this word that it is for the Sanatan Dharma that they arise, it is for the world and not for themselves that they arise' (p.120). So far as we understand, this holds even more true at this hour.

Let us reproduce a few complementary words, from Sir WW Hunter, President, Indian Education Commission, 1883:[5] 'Your [British] state education is producing a revolt against [the] principles...which represent the deepest want of human nature – the principle of discipline, the principle of religion, the principle of contentment. ...What are you to do with this class, forced under a foreign system, without discipline, without contentment and without God?' One hundred and thirty years on, not a syllable or comma in the above quote can be challenged. Certain quarters today lionize the mischief-making Derozio. He was doing exactly the things that Hunter, a contemporary, had grieved about. Those who shout hoarse against imperialism are also the ones who celebrate one of the founders of imperialism in India. Hunter's ominous picture now looms larger than before for such eyes as can see. And Sri Aurobindo's or Swami Vivekananda's luminous visions? Are they lost and gone forever? Dear parents, dear fellow-teachers — please hold your breath and ponder.

IV

There are a few things to be proud of in India today e.g. atomic energy science and technology, space satellite and communication technology, IT, third or fourth largest economy of the world, etc. But what is the substantive fallout of all this? In international diplomacy India appears always on the retreat – whether it is in relation to USA or China, Pakistan or Bangladesh, Nepal or Sri Lanka. Our assessment is: In all these countries faith in their nation and culture is founded on a few firm, basic nationalistic convictions – right or wrong. Strength flows from this source. Post-1950 India has no footing in such convictions. Hence she is weak, she vacillates, she dithers, she capitulates. Seers and savants like Sri Aurobindo, who had crystallized and formulated the most constructive convictions of universal character, have been exiled from the mind of Indian elite. Without recovering and building on them, despite all her superficial achievements, she cannot hope to be treated with genuine honour and respect.

Many noble and understanding Western minds however expect India to hold aloft the Aurobindovian vision, essentially. Some such names may be gratefully recalled: Sister Nivedita, The Mother, H. Thoreau, A. Toynbee, L. Renou, S. Beer, A. Huxley, A. Malraux, K. Raine, Ronald Nixon, Will Durant, JBS Haldane, AL Basham, Lizelle Reymond, D. Frawley, M. Danino, Romain Rolland and so on. Learning from them also is our supreme duty. In effect, collectively, these really 'good Samaritans' are delivering an unflattering message to the educated Indian: You are like a donkey, carrying a big pile of fragrant sandalwood on your back, knowing little how precious it is.* That is why 'Tales of prison Life' and Sri Aurobindo's are becoming a tragic waste for India and the world. No amount of technology and economics can ever fill this void of sacred conviction.

Students should be helped to grasp these indispensable truths – both at home and in formal institutions. But where are the parents, the teachers who will stick out their necks and undertake such a labour of love for man-making, not just money-making ? One small group of Indian citizens, with high education and high status, are positive towards religion, spirituality and indigenous culture. But they nurse a meek despair about the destructive forces of the present. A sort of goody-goody, keep-aloof, table-talk mentality is exhibited by them. The other class of highly-placed Indian citizens goes over-board in praising and lapping up every new-fangled ideology and technology bandied as progress. They have little time or sympathy for the world-saving, enduring principles that Bharat's culture enshrines. Our *acharyas* should not belong to neither of these categories. Rather, they ought to actively confront the second group, equipped with a firm stand on the unique Sanatan Dharma nationalism of Bharatvarsha.

They forget that since Alexander's time almost every culture from the west of Bharatvarsha has been 'problem-creating' and 'problem inflicting' for the world, and especially for India. This tradition continues to this day. Sri Aurobindo is right to assert that (unlike Greece and Rome or Arabia and Germany, etc.) Sanatan Bharat has never risen to crush others. It has been well said that 'The road to hell is paved with good intentions'. Here is a small list of new dehumanizing technologies which are soon going to sweep us all as a huge tidal wave does, but being touted as inevitable advancement:

- Genetic engineering
- Nano technology
- Robotics
- Information super-highway, etc.

The high-speed, high-greed, high-noise, high-deception

---

* *Yatha kharah chandanbharvahi.*
Bharasya vetta na tu chandanasya.
Evam hi shastrani bahuunyadhitya.
Arthesu mudha kharavat vahanti.

explosion of uncontrolled *rajasic* vital which is thus imminent must be anticipated and seen through. The gospel of 'inevitability' has to be jettisoned. Pretty soon such reckless changes prove to be 'problem-creating' interventions, resulting in intractable chaos. The pauranic legend of *Daksha-yajna* without Shiva is again here today: a pompous sacrifice at the altar of evil and chaos without the presiding deity of Common Weal. It is foolish then to take pride in 'problem-solving'. Teachers should realize that Bharat's sanatan culture has always been a 'problem-preventing' adventure. And hence by far the wiser. The Frankestein today has to be met head on and put in its place. India possesses the *sattwic* wealth and spiritual power in her genes to lead this counter-attack. Teachers and parents should at least feel scared for their own children and grandchildren, if for nothing else. It is high time to abandon the present ostrich-like attitude associated with narrow professional allegiances. The *Manusamhita* (verses III – 70-4) had laid down five common debts or *maha-yajnas* or *pancharin* for householder citizens.[6] The author here is convinced that at this hour a sixth rin has to be added to this quintet: *desh rin*. We ought to pray for Manu's pardon and blessing. Books like 'The Tales of Prison Life' should form standard material for continuous studygroup reading and discussion – in homes as well as schools. Let the saving *samskaras* be planted without delay. Those who proclaim themselves as world citizens discharging world-rin, while recoiling from *desh rin,* are wrong. By engaging first in the discharge of *desh rin*, in the authentic spirit of masters like Aurobindo, Tagore, Vivekananda, Gandhi, etc., they will automatically discharge world rin in terms of what is really imperative. Docile acquiescence and blind imitation arise from *tamas*. They demonstrate neither true tolerance nor real dynamism. The culture of *sattwo-rajasic* or *rajaso-sattwic* disposition is 'essential' for the rebirth of intellectual *kshatra-veerya** in India today. Tamas-induced But *sattwo-rajas*-driven 'essential' learning has no substitute.

A couple of urgent imperatives for the latter are

- If individual suicide is among the greatest sins, cultural national suicide is no less.

---

* Chivalry of the warrior class. A public proposal to declare Netaji's birthday (January 23) as 'patriotism day' for the nation was (early in 2011) turned down by the authorities concerned. The message seems to be: India needs neither 'brahminical spirituality', nor 'kshatra veerya'.

• No roots, no fruits.

Education bereft of these 'essential' driving powers cannot be true education for discharging India's world-responsibility with selfassured dignity. There is a double significance of human birth and that too in Bharatvarsha: The fruition of progressively refined and sacred *samskaras* through many births, and the consequent responsibility to manifest them through one's life and vocation. If this essential apex learning can be fixed firmly as our abiding priority, then indeed 'Tales of Prison Life', and similar other sagas would not have gone in vain.

V

In early August 2009, a young teacher of thirty-five had come to visit us at our home with his parents. He has settled in the West coast of the USA where he went some ten years ago after doing his MBA from one of the premier I.I.M's. Now he is a faculty member in a University there, and has a European wife. He was on a brief vacation to India after a few years. Sometime during discussions he alluded to violence and suggested to his father that he should adopt Buddhism. Then he turned specifically to the *Bhagwad Gita*, Sri Krishna, caste system and a few similar other topics. Some pointed questions were put to us. They were briefly responded to. But we later decided to inform him in some detail about a few vital principles and facts related to the issues he had raised. The following letter contains these replies. They are self-explanatory. They reveal a concrete case of the widespread alienation from *sanatan* roots among the present generation of educated Indians. What worth then has been the legacy of Vivekanandas-Aurobindos-Ashok Nandis-Gandhis-CR Das's–Ramanas-Tilaks and thousands more like them till 1947? What worth is de-nationalising education now being imparted? Any parallels elsewhere in the world?

Dear…,

It was good and stimulating to talk with you at our place a few days ago. This letter is a result of that evening's mutual exchanges on a few significant points. The thoughts below are meant generally, not for you in particular.

(A) First, here are a few early and recent quotations from the West on the *Bhagwad Gita (BG)*:[7]

- **Thomas Merton**: 'The Gita can be seen as the main literary support for the great religious civilization of India, the oldest surviving culture of the world .... Our (West) highly activistic and one-sided culture is faced with a crisis that may end in self-destruction because it lacks the inner depth of an authentic metaphysical consciousness. Without such depth... all our protestations are so much verbiage.'

- **E.H. Powell (SUNY)**: '...there must be a kind of truth in the BG, since those who follow its teachings display a joyous serenity usually missing in the bleak and strident lives of contemporary world.'

- **H.D. Thoreau**: 'In the morning I bathe my intellect in the stupendous and cosmogonal philosophy of the BG, in comparison with which our modern world and its literature seem puny and trivial.'

- **R.W. Emerson**: 'I owed a magnificent day to the BG, ... It was as if an empire spoke to us, nothing small and unworthy, but large, serene, consistent: the voice of an old intelligence ... which had pondered and thus disposed of the same questions which exercise us.'

- **Bede Griffiths (Oxford)**: 'The whole of the BG is Krishna's discourse to Arjuna. It is the spirit of God speaking to the spirit of man and teaching him how to conduct his life. That is why it is such a practical book. ...(it) can become a manual of spiritual guidance for the West. It has a universal message.'

One could cite more such appraisals. Quiet, careful reflection of each word above shows that several high class Western minds have not smelt violence in the *BG* and Sri Krishna. But there is also a class of what one may call 'pussy cat scholars'. They cannot but end up seeing the 'mouse' under the chair, though having gone to see the 'queen on the throne'. It is this class which seems to rule the roost today. Axing down the very roots of *sanatan* Hindu culture seems to be their latent agenda.

(B) Buddhism, flowing as a useful and temporary corrective from *sanatan* Hinduism, has been the parent of Christianity. Buddha's *karuna* and *ahimsa* are no doubt among the loftiest human emotions. But that too is one-sided (Merton above). *BG* teaches Arjuna to 'fight' to discharge a self-less social responsibility after exhausting all other options. But immense care has been taken by Krishna about Arjuna's purging of the mind of hatred, jealousy, vindictiveness,vanity, etc., before picking up the *gandiva* (bow) again.

Human society has never consisted of all monks and shramans. Nor will it ever be so. Buddhism, however, ignored this reality. Buddha is unbeatable for steering individuals towards personal peace and salvation. But Krishna's character is immensely more comprehensive than that of Buddha or Christ. Krishna's charter comprises administration and governance for righteousness in an entire society in all aspects. This has to include protection of the good and punishment of the evil. Armchair sentimentalism is futile. But every bit of all this must preserve the spiritual progress of man and society. A most difficult and complex task. Krishna did not baulk from it. If apparent 'violence' becomes incumbent, as a last resort, to curb evil (taking due care of the inner motive), it needs to be employed. Hence, the supreme moral of *mahaprasthan* by the Pandavas after the *dharma yuddha* ended.

The honourable, peace-loving 'pussy cat' intellectuals may be urged to contemplate a Buddha, a Christ, or a Gandhi in Winston Churchill's shoes during the Second World War! Many historians today opine that the great emperor Ashoka may have overdone Buddhism, leaving the boundaries of Bharatvarsha quite porous. Later centuries to date have made this a credible hypothesis.

(C) As for caste system (CS), KD Sethna (Amalkiran), a Parsee and a centenarian disciple of Sri Aurobindo, had once rebuffed the superficial critics of the system declaring that 'Hinduism does not stand or fall by the CS alone' (in *India and The World Scene*). Swami Vivekananda had evaluated the CS as aprotective armour for Hindu society during its darkest days under Muslim rule.[8] Mahatma Gandhi had opined that this system had acted as an insurance against life-corroding competition. Rabindranath Tagore had read into the quardruple CS a ladder for ascent along the social scale (In *Gora*, a Bengali novel).

In any case, the right expression for the quadruple design of society is '*varnashrama dharma*'. CS is a slippery mis-translation. So called castes are based on 'varna' (colour) variations which, in turn, derive from 'guna' differences. Thus we get four varnas + four ashrams+ four purusharthas = 12 pillars of the *sanatan* Hindu social system. The aim is spiritual blossoming for all. There is no such theory and goal behind the quadruple or other functional caste systems in Christianity or Islam. (e.g. Nobles and Lords, Knights and soldiers, merchants and farmers, workers and labourers). And they too contain their own abominations, including white-non-white casteism.

Only the 'untouchability' accretion is abhorrent and dispensable. But even this pales into insignificance in the light of the near-extermination of the Hottentots, Red Indians, Aborigines and others like them by the enlightened races! The ugly aspects of CS would also have naturally died out by now. But post-independence, fractured politicization of CS has blackened the fair and sensible face of society carved by our ancient social legists who were rishis with transcendental insight.

Lastly, if we possess a truly educated 'Indian Mind' in an 'Indian Body' then we may justifiably say this to the nit-picking scholars: "If the vast sacred culture and society of India has lived on for over 5000 years, its CS as you brand it, must have been fundamentally correct. At any rate, your own sci-tech based secular societies are falling apart at the seams. So, it is better to stop attending to Hindu culture and start greasing your own machines. Recently gained material affluence does not confer a Divine right on you to pass judgments on things you do not or will not understand. The CS, etc., are our domestic affairs. We do not cross over and sermonize on your domestic ways. Neither should you. For heaven's sake do not export your social plagues, masking them as modernization, to countries like ours e.g., a certain society, with only five percent of world population but having thirty percent of world's lawyers, teaching us trust. All the major world problems of today – from global warming to extinction of species, from brutal commercialism to ghastly terrorism – have originated in the so-called advanced and modern part of the globe. It makes little sense then to take lessons on responsibility, environment, ethics, etc., from rich countries who, as recently as in 2009, wanted to wriggle out of the Kyoto protocol."

(D) Bharatvarsha had also exchanges with many countries lying to her East. These were all characterized by cultural and peaceful contributions to those societies, the very opposite of what she received from across her western borders. No invasions, conversions, massacres, destructions, etc. But then this historical fact is also twisted and turned 180 degrees: India could not have conquered and ruled because of ceaseless internecine strifes among the countless rajas and rulers of small territories; it is the raiding outsider only who gave India the semblance of a nation. What about Europe then? Countries there had not only fought incessantly among themselves; they had all invaded and colonized most of the world. Yet, all this confers legitimacy to them, but no credit for India's benign cross-border connections.

As for one nation, the unity of Bharatvarsha should be understood outside the frame of modern political discourse on nationalism. Her 'diversity in unity', not 'unity in diversity', as Sri Aurobindo had correctly understood Bharatiya culture, lay in the religio-spiritual plane. The four *dhams* (Rameshwaram, Dwaraka, Puri, Kedar-badri); the *kumbhmela* at Allahabad, Ujjain, Nasik, Hardwar; the fifty one *peethas*, Tirupati, Kanyakumari, Sagar *mela* in Bengal; the Shivratri, Ramanavami, Janmashtami, Ganesh *puja*, Dussehra, Diwali, Hanuman *puja* and many more are the all-India, all-caste, all-age, all-sex institutions and festivals of sacred character. Pilgrims from all corners of India visit these places or join these festivals with great reverence and hardship for a life-time or regular experience. Invaders and colonizers were not required to weave this timeless supra-political fabric of Bharat's nationhood.

I have presented above certain truths because you are a fellow-traveller like me – a *shikshak*, a teacher, born and brought up in *sanatan* Bharat. These thoughts may therefore ring a bell or two in your heart.

Finally, you may wish to keep in mind this aphorism of mine:

Rootless, Fruitless, hence Hopeless

With prayers and best wishes'*

S.K.C.

* (After a few weeks we received a curt, one-line e-mail reply : 'It is nice to know about other viewpoints'.)

References

1. Aurobindo Sri, *Tales of Prison Life,* Pondicherry: Sri Aurobindo Ashram, 1997, pp. 101–5.
2. *Ibid,* p. 104.
3. *Ibid,* p. 102.
4. *Ibid,* p. 121.
5. Quoted by J. Kulkarni, *Truth,* June 26, 2009, p. 211.
6. Buhler, G; *The Laws of Manu,* Oxford : Clarendon Press, 1886. The *Brihadaranyaka Upanishad,* a major *shruti* text, also corroborates this list from the *smriti* text– Madras: Sri Ramakrishna Math, 1979, verse 1.4.16, pp. 71-2.
7. The first four quotes below have been taken from A.C. Bhaktivedanta Swami's *Bhagwad Gita As It Is,* Mumbai: Bhaktivedanta Book Trust, 2003, front inside page and back cover. The fifth one is from Bede griffiths, *The Cosmic Revelation*, London: Collins, 1983, pp. 92-3.
8. Vivekananda Swami; *Complete Works,* Kolkata: Advaita Ashrama, 2005, Vol. 5, p. 214.
9. Gandhi M.K., *Hindu Dharma,* New Delhi: Orient, 2005, pp. 65–6.

CHAPTER 2

COURTING AFFLUENT PENURY:
The Enigma of Education in India

यत्र व्रह्य च क्षत्रं च सम्या चरत: सह ।
तंल्लोकं पुण्यं प्रज्ञेषं यत्र देवा: सहाश्निना ।।
(य: २०/२५)

That holy world I would know where spiritual power (*bahman*) and ruling power (*kshatra*) move together in harmony.

(*Yajurveda 20/25*)
(*Ibid*., p. 281).

I

Once upon a time a poor *fakir* had gone to Emperor Akbar for alms. Akbar was then in his prayer chamber. The *fakir* sat at the open door and waited. A little later he heard and saw the Emperor supplicating to Allah: 'Bestow more wealth, more riches on me, O! Lord.' Hearing such words, his esteem for the King fell, and the *fakir* began to walk away. The Emperor's prayers had just ended. He then looked out and saw the *fakir* going away. Akbar called him back and wanted to know what had happened. The *fakir* replied: "There's no point in begging alms from an Emperor who himself is a beggar." This parable used to be told by Sri Ramakrishna to his devotees.[1] The above story contains the kernel of this and subsequent chapters of this book. Stripped to its essence for our purposes, it conveys the 'beggar-like' mentality of a large and growing population of Indian intelligentsia in the field of education. For, even in the 'soft' spheres of human values, family relationships, yoga, ethics, spirituality, man-making, child-rearing, Consciousness, etc. Indian researchers and scholars commonly seek out and quote mostly from either ignorant or incongruent Western authors — from beginning to end. Despite being heirs to the richest storehouse of timeless concepts and practical processes in these fields, developed and refined to the utmost in

Bharat-varsha, they 'beg' for definitions, terminologies, models, etc., from alien sources which have very little experiential tradition to back up. Even the most brilliant intellectual expositions cannot be substituted for authentic experiences of those who have relentlessly struggled to live the ultimate ideals. To Akbar's credit, he at least was 'begging' from Allah. Who, by contrast, are India's Education in India: A Tree Without Roots educators 'begging' from? A series of personal encounters in this large 'black hole' of the post-1950 educational firmament of India is therefore in order.

But before the series alluded above commences, it is worthwhile to present an important general hypothesis about the above 'begging syndrome': Western countries, and a few Eastern ones too, are materially rich. So, whatever they pronounce must be wholly correct in all matters. India is materially poorer. So, whatever her traditions and seers have realized and advised must be wrong.

This negative, self-undermining psychology, fostered by a dominant class of alien mentors and their faithful Indian protégés, seems to have obliterated the influence of almost equally ample, positive, Western appraisals of the saving richness preserved in this longest surviving culture of the world. Our students do not have access to or acquaintance with this flank. Nor is this capital lesson brought up and unfolded before them: Whatever material affluence has been achieved over three centuries by England or America,

Germany or Japan (by means fair or foul), has been founded upon the respective geniuses of each. They did not beg or borrow ideals or ideas from Bharatvarsha, which was, even materially, far richer than any of them in the earlier millennia. Nor did India, during this long phase of her material affluence, beg or borrow theories or principles from anywhere else.

II

However, let us return to the 'encounters' serial, stretching across 1990-91 to 2008-09.

- It could be 1997 or 1998. An Indian Ph.D research student, studying at a French University, had sent to us the synopsis of his dissertation proposal. The gist of it was: Whereas the Western cultural ethos is generally long-term oriented, the oriental and Indian ethos is relatively short-term oriented. His research was intended to substantiate this proposition. It was a shock to encounter such a viewpoint being seriously entertained even in the late nineties. It was all the more pitiful to see an Indian being engaged in this act of self-disparagement. How much mis-education or non-education about one's own culture must have contributed to the acceptance of this thesis topic by the Indian researcher! Our response was sent, but we heard no more from him.

- It happened in 1996 in Bangalore. A contingent of thirty or so senior European executives of Asea Brown Boveri Ltd., had come to India for a study tour. The Indian CEO of the Indian establishment of ABB had asked us to address them on one forenoon about the enduring contours of the Indian cultural milieu. This group included a German professor who seemed to be unusually attentive during the presentation. At lunch-time we two sat at a small table. Conversation and lunch went together. At a certain moment of deep reflection he said: 'Let me try to express the essence of your session with two images – – the serene *mahaparinirvana* posture of the Buddha during his last hours, and the excruciating crucifixion portrayal of Christ. How do you view this comparative imagery about the essential distinction between the two culture streams in question?' We felt spell-bound by the depth of his comprehension, and the honesty of his articulation. 'I had never contemplated like that' – this was the only gentle reply we could give. May be it was some such compelling flash of profound insight which had prompted Schopenhauer, another German professor-philosopher of the eighteenth century, to characterize the activities of missionaries in India as 'firing bullets at a cliff '. It is worthwhile comparing this encounter with the thesis proposal just mentioned above.
- A team of US high school teachers had come to Kolkata as a part of their educational tour of India. They attended a two-hour lecture exposure by us on a theme similar to the one offered at Bangalore. It took place in the Management Centre for Human Values of IIM Calcutta. During dialogue time a physics teacher asked: 'One thing that puzzles many of us about India is — how come you have so many Gods to worship?' We replied with the help of an analogy : Every organization has a Head, called variously as Managing Director, Chairman, Prime Minister, Chief Minister and so on. This CEO supports himself with a

number of departmental heads, functional directors, regional chiefs, site managers (or their appropriate equivalents), etc. So is the case with the *sanatan*–Hindu conception of many demi-Gods as well as the one Godhead. Thus, *Varun* is the departmental god for water; *Marut* or *Pawan* is the departmental god for air; *Lakshmi* is the demi-goddess for wealth; *Dharitri* is the demi-goddess for earth, etc. Similarly in the trinity of Brahma – Vishnu – Maheshwar, the first god is responsible for creation, the second for preservation, and the third for dissolution. Of course, the One, Impersonal, Eternal and Infinite Godhead too is affirmed which, though embracing all the demi-gods and demi-goddesses, yet transcends them all. Perfect democracy has prevailed in the culture in respect of choice for personal worship from this vast range. Do we not appreciate departmental stores which offer us the widest array of choice for material goods? Just so is the case with our religio-spiritual figures and symbols. Moreover, it is this apparently confusing plurality which has always saved the Hindu culture from indulging in dogmatic and aggressive fanaticism against other belief systems. It has been an inclusive spiritual democracy at its best. At the end of the allotted time the entire group and ourselves were walking back to the hostel. The physics teacher caught up from behind and quietly said: 'Your explanation was eminently logical and rational. We never had any chance before to listen to such a sensible interpretation.' We thanked him for his frankness in recognizing the richness of variety in India's indigenous religio-spiritual ecology. In his case scientific temper did not brush aside the Indian pantheon of numberless gods and goddesses as mere superstition, or imagination run wild.

- While writing this chapter, a monograph on Indian ethos by Justice Rama Jois (retd.) came our way.[2] It was based on his discourses on human rights at Bangalore (1997). The contents present excellent classical material revealing the comprehensive richness of key ideas for human development. While a few more gems from the monograph shall be presented later, here is a quotation by Jois from Kerry Brown[3] (a British social scientist) on the status of women in Indian family relationships, based on his understanding of the *Manusmriti*. 'In Hinduism a woman is looked after (*rakshati*) not because she is inferior or incapable, but on the contrary, because she is treasured. ... No extra burden of earning a living should be placed on women who already bear huge responsibilities in society: childbirth, childcare, domestic well-being and spiritual growth. She is the transmitter of culture to her children.' Justice Jois had himself, preceding this quote, thoroughly refuted the populist rejection of *Manusmriti* by focusing on a single verse, and that too mis-interpreting it. The other complementary positive verses are kept suppressed by malafide critics (III – 56, 57, 58, 62 and 114).

- A senior management professor (70+) had sent us some relevant portions of a manuscript in May, 2009. He had requested us for a Foreword to his forthcoming book which advocated the 'humanization of management'. In lieu of predominantly 'masculine' values, the book was urging for greater emphasis on 'maternalistic' and 'feminine' human values. The long first para contained the word 'divine' quite frequently. It also declared the underlying belief of the author that every human being was nothing other than 'good'. And then came, as the last sentence, a quotation from an 'American spiritual counsellor'. This was the first shock. The second one was: while mentioning holistic approach, masculine-feminine, yin-yang, etc., were readily cited; but our *purusha-prakriti*, or *shiva-shakti* were not. Perhaps Sanskrit and secularism cannot go together. So unsure and Education in India: A Tree Without Roots shaky we are about our standing ground.

The subsequent pages delivered some more such jolts of varied character, including exclusion of references to previous work done on this theme in India by other scholars. The 'Conclusion' carried the title 'Back to Self '. It sounded profound as well as relevant. Here too the lengthy contents completely omitted the entire line of succession and heritage of Indian seers and scholars, ancient or modern, on this supreme theme. The Upanishads, Buddha, Shankara, Vivekananda, Aurobindo, Ramana, Tagore, Radhakrishnan – the whole lot was ignored. Yet the world knows that *Vedanta* and the *Gita* represent the acme of 'realized' exposition and conclusion about lower self v. Higher self. Once more several non-descript writers, barring an out-of-context sudden mention of Confucius in the first sentence, had found their way into the text. Our shock-treatment was complete. One wonders whether any scholar in any other part of the world could show such ingratitude towards his own mother-culture and its ablest exponents while writing a book on such a 'soft' subject. This is what a 'rich pauper' or 'affluent penury' means.*

- The early 19th century American transcendentalist, Henry Thoreau, was a devoted, daily morning reader of the *Gita* in his forest cottage by the side of Walden pond. He was not afraid to declare that compared to the Gita, modern literature seemed 'puny and trivial', and that the book 'referred to a previous state of existence ... so remote (in) its sublimity from our conceptions'.[4] His transcendent imagination wafted him across time and space, to meet the Brahmin priest sitting in the temple on the Ganges and reading the Vedas to Brahma, Vishnu and Indra. The 'affluence' of Bharat liberates and empowers Thoreau at Walden pond, but not our own author sitting right on the Ganga. Nonetheless, a draft Foreword was sent, its last sentence being: 'If the book aims at winning international acclaim, the manner of attempting it is not honourable or dignified'. The author was of course given the liberty to reject the draft sent. All the time that we were engaged with the job, Sri Aurobindo's words kept resounding within:[5]

> 'British rule, Britain's civilizing mission in India has been the recordsuccess in history in the hypnosis of a nation. It persuaded us to live in a death of the will ... and creating in ourselves the condition of morbid weakness the hypnotist desired.'

Even today the West (via America primarily) perpetuates its successful hypnotizing strategy on India, not through direct political conquest, but through a more dangerous cultural subjugation. Swami Vivekananda's call, 'Awake', did initiate a process of de-hypnotization which seems to have petered out by 1950 or so. Since then rehypnotization, whether capitalistic or communistic, has been apace in all walks of life among the educated citizens of the country.

---

* A book titled 'Indian Ethos and Values in Management' (2011) has repeated exactly the same mentality. The first page of the Preface ontains three names — all Western. The last chapter is entirely a biography of a Westerner. We came across the author at a conference in February. When this anomaly was pointed out, he defended it for global appeal. Yet, at the conference itself (at Haridwar) a European Professor had cited all his examples from the West only, not caring at all that he was speaking in India. When this was pointed, our young (30+) author remained unmoved again. Spineless globalism at its peak!

- Sometime during the mid-nineteen nineties Kathleen Raine had delivered a lecture, 'The Voice of the Sacred in Our Time', in New Delhi.[6] She was a reputed British literary critic and writer. Combined with it was her clear intellectual grasp and firm emotional commitment to the 'unifying vision of the "sacred" in "the India of the imagination". Here she found her 'Home at last'. During her address she informed the audience that she had asked twice her chief Indian sponsor (at one time a central minister) the question: 'Does India have to make all the mistakes of the West?' This former minister, herself a well-known exponent of Indian aesthetics and arts, and author of some books, replied on both occasions: "Yes, Education in India: A Tree Without Roots all." Raine was mature enough not to vent any direct reaction to what must have been an astonishing answer from her cultured host. But the curt reply of the latter should be a good proof of the voluntary re-hypnotization the educated Indian is today courting, almost with a vengeance. Raine's lecture was itself, however, an elaborate and well-substantiated rejoinder to the naive 'Yes, all' from her elitist Indian counterpart.* At one stage Raine had uttered these sincere words:

  > 'But while you are adopting Western values along with much- needed Western technology, we look to the Orient to rescue us from a materially affluent but spirituality destitute world. ...It could be questioned whether our modern technological culture is a civilization at all. ...it is a hell, a "nightmare" as Yeats calls it.'

Thus, the thickening paradox of 'penury in affluence' for 21st century India could be understood a degree better from the above thoughts of Raine. Hers is true love for India. If India destroys what the West and the world needs most today from her, then the saving supply line for all will be snapped. The world, and India, will then be denied a minimal platform to float upon — this seems to have been the rebuke of motherly love delivered to India by Raine in her lecture. It is evident that Raine and her ilk in the West, who possess genuine understanding of and goodwill for Bharat's 'real' wealth, do not want her to squander it for borrowed tinsels.

---

* Quite recently she has been awarded the 'Padma Vibhushan' on this person.

- In March 2009 one of the leading management journals of India had sent us a paper for 'blind' review. It dealt with 'Yoga for Emotional Intelligence to Meet Hyper-competition'. The contents were based on a sample size of sixty managers in one company who were given exposure on yoga theory and practice over a period of six weeks. A lot of statistical tools and analysis were employed in handling post-programme, selfreporting, scaled questionnaire responses. The authors claimed at the end of their paper that the statistical results go 'to establish' the contribution of yoga to improved emotional intelligence, and thence to improved performance. For yoga a sort of definition by a Western writer was quoted. The very brief conceptual treatment of yoga was perfunctory. No evidence of studying basic works on yoga like Vivekananda's *Rajyoga*, or Aurobindo's *Bases of Yoga*, or the *Gita* was found. An initial point-wise review was sent, to which the authors sent back a long point-wise reply. Our responses to this elaborate rejoinder are reproduced below. They will clarify all the fundamental issues which surfaced through the review-cum-response process.

III

Dear Chief Editor,

The authors' responses to this reviewer's comments were interesting and revealing. Our respective outlooks, premises and goals seem to be far apart. The north pole and the south pole cannot have a meeting point. Nonetheless, some further reflections follow:

(a) 'Hyper-competition is here to stay', the authors assert. So is terrorism. So is alarming global warming. So is the ever- idening divide between the rich and the poor. And so on and so forth. Accept and accommodate, not challenge or confront them. Can this be the true role of teachers ?

(b) There have been several extra-orbital thinkers, both in the East and West, who have not felt obliged to pay homage even to competition, far less hyper-competition Example: EF Schumacher, Arnold Toynbee, David Korten, Albert Einstein; Tagore, Gandhi Vivekananda, Aurobindo et al. Dictionaries explain competition almost entirely by words conveying negative emotions. One recalls Hamlet's observation: 'There are many more things in heaven and earth, Horatio, than your philosophy can dream of.' One may just use 'business' for 'philosophy'.

(c) TS Eliot, seventy-five years ago, had lamented:

'Where is knowledge lost in information?

'Where is wisdom, lost in knowledge?

In an age which moves progressively backward.'

Since 1985, Rifkin's *Entropy*, Barbara Hudson's *Social Justice in a Risk Society*, DL Spar's *Baby Business*, Rowland's *Greed Inc*, etc. have been just a few latest Western voices who have shown the courage to question the fundamentals of business. But Indian intelligentsia and academics are all mute. Not only this; they are mostly active supporters of these deadly trends. And this muteness and support springs from a culture where Nachiketa, a mere boy, had spurned Yama's *bhoga* enticements by asserting: *na vittena tarpaniyo manushya* (wealth does not make man happy) — a few thousand years ago. He had gone to Yama for seeking knowledge of *yoga* armed with *tyaga*.

(d) The authors are anxious to save business enterprises from 'going bust.' Our 'thinkers' and 'realizers' were however not 'researchers' or 'scholars' in the narrow sense. So, they were hardly concerned about whether a business went bust or not. They have been worried about the earth, about mankind itself going bust. Nor were they career-seekers, constituting a sort of tightly-bonded mutual admiration fraternity.

(e) The paper 'may bring about a complete paradigm shift in the role of yoga in our life'. Such hyper-confidence hardly suggests academic modesty (where N = 60). During almost five decades in management education one has lost count of the 'paradigm shift' claims — each promising a 'golden pot at the end of the rainbow'. Yet the world goes on speedily hurtling down the precipice.

(f) The four prefixes to yoga — *jnana, bhakti, karma* and *raj* — are being omitted these days. This is what happens when the sacred is reduced to the secular. The result is pointless intellectual reductionism.

(g) Speaking somewhat jargonistically, the two polar perspectives mentioned in (a) represent the essentially right brain, qualitative, realizational path at one end; and the primarily left brain, quantitative, research approach at the other. The first involves diving into serious yoga, the second implies a utilitarian view of yoga of sorts — often a fashion.

(h) 'Yoga as a way of life' — the authors declare this several times. Our left-brained research and training efforts will usher this in ? So, forget the ancient founding fathers of yoga. Was not yoga, even for Vivekanandas, Ramanas, Gandhis, Aurobindos *et.al.*, a way of life ? Were they not top performers and leaders too ? What is the import of 'paradigm shift', examined in this light ?

(i) What is the current context of interest in yoga ? *Bhoga* – to be sure. The ultimate aim of hyper-competition in business is anything but stoking the fires of *bhoga*. But control and curtailment of materialistic *bhoga* is the long initial preparation for yoga. Throughout human and spiritual history *yoga* and *tyaga* have gone together. But now business comes and mandates *yoga* and *bhoga* to cohabit. And then, Yoga of what with what? No definition of yoga is available in the paper.

(j) The vital aspect of negative emotions requiring *chittashuddhi* has been dodged. One cannot sow and grow fragrant flower plants on a plot before de-weeding and cleaning it up. This is practical yoga psychology. Sometime in March 2008 the Vatican had to add four more contemporary sins to the long-existing list of seven 'cardinal sins'* . Buddhist psychology calls them 'mental contaminations' (seventeen of them). Hindu or yoga psychology calls them *shadaripus* (six enemies). All these lists comprise negative emotional factors. One wonders how yoga can be 'a way of life' when a truncated psychological model of man leaves out at least fifty per cent of his operative being ? For a needle smeared with mud there can be no yoga with the magnet. If inclined, an attentive manipulation. study of chapter 16 in the *Gita* could be an eye-opener.

(k) It could be safely predicted, however, that as and when the West would begin to employ *chittashuddhi, nishkam karma,* etc. in their works, Indian researchers would quickly follow suit. This has happened earlier e.g., *atman, nirvana, maya, moksha* etc. In contrast, the Japanese and Chinese have persisted with their indigenous terms (e.g. kaizen, ringi, guanxi etc.). Western writers have felt compelled to use them from the start.

---

* Drug pushing, obscene richness, environmental pollution and genetic manipulation.

(1) The proper role of 'yoga' is that of a world-saver. Instead, it is being reduced to a business-server. Even the raging scourge of un-ethicality in business, and the potential remedy of 'yoga as a way of life' against this virus, has been overlooked or not understood. Reductionism all over again. This is both painful and harmful :

i. Painful because, in the process we ignore the pure and prefect sources of yoga psychology, and feel it necessary to go for writings on it from quarters where 'yoga as a way of life' has never been a part of living tradition.

ii. Harmful, because we defend those who have little authority to speak on yoga, spirituality etc. Realized authorities like Patanjali, Vivekananda, Aurobindo, *et.al.*, of course can do well without condescending 'concessions' from seemingly reluctant modern researchers of their own land. These realizers stand taller than the tallest.

iii. Painful also is the absence of courage and originality among our academics. Only when yoga, spirituality, etc., have now begun to be re-exported to India with 'West' stamped on them, we are suddenly waking up and beginning to follow the pied-piper. And playing to the tune composed by them. As far back as in 1985 an Indian management teacher had published a thorough work on Indian concepts and theories, including Patanjali's *Yogasutras*, for integration into Indian management thinking. Twenty-five years on our researchers do not seem to know of its existence. This of course is not surprising. If Aurobindos and their ilk can be forgotten or by-passed with but a patronizing nod, what hope can there be for an ordinary *swadeshi* teacher.

Let no more burden be inflicted on any of you. Given the commitments and compulsions of the authors, the above thoughts may be of no use to them. We respect their stand. But we cannot dis-respect ours. So, the decision has to be made at your end regarding the publication or otherwise of the paper. We should disengage ourselves from this task.

Yours Sincerely

....

IV

- We had visited Stockholm several times during the period 1991-2001. Besides offering a course on Human Values at the Stockholm University Business School in one of those years, about a dozen or so seminars and workshops for industrial and other organizations had also been arranged for us. Of them one striking experience is relevant to recount here. On a certain evening in October, 1994 a Swedish gentleman called on us at the hotel we were staying. We came down to the lobby where the visitor introduced himself as a Deputy Director in the Labour Ministry of the Swedish government. The very same day morning, he informed, he had listened to us at the public seminar in a city auditorium. He wanted to speak to us. As we consented, he asked if we would be inclined to offer a two-day workshop on values, motivation, leadership, etc., to a group of his Labour Ministry officials. Startling indeed! We thought the idea so incredible that our reply was: 'Why me? The USA is just across the ocean from you. They are considered supreme in this field. Our perspectives are primarily those pertaining to the *sanatan** Hindu core of Indian culture. And we are materially a less developed country. So, how could our ideas make sense to your people?'

The Deputy Director's reply came as yet another revelation: 'Frankly, we are tired of American ideas and methods. They do not match with our culture. We are longing for fresher and deeper insights. Hence this request to you.' We needed time to mull over this great evening surprise. He left us at that. Yes, we did humbly agree to respond to this challenge and recognition offered to Indian ethos. The dates for a two-day Workshop during our next visit were decided in a second meeting two days later. This event did materialize as scheduled. The twenty-five participating officials were all decent, patient, receptive listeners. A world-view somewhat different from the one they have been hitherto receiving from America, and the one which they were experiencing in their own land, did not produce frowns in their eyes or faces. They seemed to be more open to Indian thought than the majority of India's own elite professionals and academics are. A probable reason behind the above Swedish request to us could be detected in the following candid confessions of

* Sanatan was duly explained to our visitor.

Osterberg (1994)[8]: 'Despite Sweden's high standard of living ... the Swedish people are very unhappy. ... We have been almost totally secularised. Now there is a growing hankering for spiritual things. ... it is a result of our longing to be where we belong; It is a longing back to God, I think.' These observations clearly point towards a hunger for the identical subjective wealth which Raine too, almost at the same time, had expressed on behalf of the *objectively* rich West. This also is 'affluent penury'– from the material angle. By contrast, India exemplifies today a similar syndrome from the spiritual viewpoint. And remember too that Sweden is included in 'West', and is several thousand miles nearer to USA than India is.

- The Asian-Pacific Regional Conference of Psychology had organised a symposium in 1995 at Guangzhou, China. Its theme was 'Indigenous Behaviours in Effective Management and Organizations.' A collection of selected papers presented there was published in 1999.[9] This book contains seventeen papers, seven of which are by Indian scholars, including one by us. Among the six other papers, only Sinha's contribution was able to shrug off the heavy load of occi-centric managerial lore, and show the courage to mention, for example, the key principle of 'purity of mind' or *chittashuddhi* in Indian psychology.[10] The other five were broadly of two classes: (a) qualitative papers containing little evidence of familiarity with such Indian psychological insights and constructs as could initiate positive changes for the better; (b) quantitative papers using questionnaire data built exclusively on Western models like 'transactional analysis', etc., Except the statistical figures, nothing else was indigenous in them. It should be added, however, that among the (a) group papers the one by Mala did mention about the *rajarshi* and *pancha-rin* models of leadership and human behaviour[11]. This paper also concluded in favour of reinforcing the core or traditional values for the sake of stability.

In contrast to such general self-diffidence and other-dependency in Indian papers, the papers from all the other Asian presenters were expressly anchored in one or more indigenous core concept(s) identified from their respective cultures. For example, from Japan it was *bushido*, from China *bao*, from Thailand *baramee*, from Taiwan *chin shin,* etc. The title of the paper by a Muslim scholar did not hesitate to present 'An Islamic View'. The fairly detailed index at the end of the book contained multiple entries for Confucianism, Taoism,

Shintoism, Buddhism and Islam. This proves that the mainstream religion of each culture has been recognized as the ultimate repository of enduring indigenous values. And yet the word Hindu or Hinduism did not figure in the index at all. Obviously none of the Hindu authors had included these terms in their papers – not even this author. What does this bizarre phenomenon indicate about the drift of education in post-1950 India? Perhaps our hyper-secular policy makers are preparing us for an identity-crisis about our core culture and people only. This process will be simultaneously bringing about incalculable existential crisis too — for all (see Osterberg above).

- The following experience might be of particular interest to the staunch votaries of secularism (i.e., no God, no Spirit, no Divinity, no religion, no metaphysics, etc.). Sometime in the late, 1990s we had received a surprise invitation to speak at a symposium in the Russian Academy of Sciences. It was being organized by the psychology wing of the Academy in Moscow. The formal proceedings appeared listless. The French contingent was most prominent. The afternoon public meeting in the central hall provided an unexpected spectacle: the Archbishop of the Russian Orthodox Church was being accorded almost royal honour. He was the central figure throughout the evening and the Academy people seemed to be rather sycophantic. But the greatest learning was yet in store for us the next morning. An Englishspeaking University student took us out for some sight seeing. Around mid-day we went for the Red Square – an awesome venue during the heydays of communism. While making our way underneath the vaulting front gate, to the right hand fell the erstwhile sentry post. We were guided into this small room which now looked like a mini-church. Scores of pictures and icons of Christian religion were adorning the walls. A continuous stream of men and women entered into it, lit candles, knelt down, and prayed silently with closed eyes. Only thereafter they stepped out into the spacious, blackstone former parade ground. We stood in the shrine, dazed and transfixed for at least ten minutes to let the picture imprint itself in our heart. The education imparted by these two episodes has been this: The opium-like hypnosis of scitech has been waning, yielding room again for the 'opium of religion'. Science is attempting to build bridges with spirituality.
- Let us be educated by Radhakrishnan's prophetic and profound words on this momentous issue:[12] 'When India is said to be a

secular state, it does not mean that we reject the reality of an unseen spirit, or the relevance of religion to life. ... It does not mean that secularism itself becomes a positive religion. ...' 'No unique distinction' to be given to any one religion for preserving 'religious impartiality' these are some of the allied thoughts of Radhakrishnan strung around the above quotation. And of course the sacred, the spiritual is fully admitted, though English dictionaries hold secular to exclude these metaphysical aspects. While concluding his book, Radhakrishnan has quoted Louis Renou, a noted French Professor and thinker from a treatise by the latter on ancient India (1953).[13]

> 'The fact remains that Hinduism provides an incomparable field of study for the historian of religion. ... It combines powers of constant renewal with a firm conservancy of fundamental tradition. In Bhakti, and still more in yoga, it has perfected unrivalled techniques of mystical initiation that contrast sharply with the frequently haphazard methods of spiritual training in the West?'

Equipped with true 'understanding', not mere knowledge, as both Radhakrishnan and Renou have been, they were able to flawlessly capture the kernel of both healthy secularism and rich Hinduism. Phrases like 'composite culture', though politically correct, have however actually been encouraging partiality against *sanatan* Hinduism by playing down its core and magnifying its alleged aberrations. The opposite is happening for the aggressive groups in the 'composite'. No one can object, in principle, to the ideal of composite culture. Yet it should be realized that Chinese culture does not stop at just that geographical expression; soon thereafter it is identified with the 'Confucian' culture. So with Japanese culture — it is effectively and centrally 'Shintoism', and is unhesitatingly recognized as such in all quarters. So is the case with Thailand, Britain, USA, Arabia, Germany, nay everywhere. And yet, most of these cultures too have a broadly composite character today. From this viewpoint, Indian culture has been turned into a solitary and confused exception, a mere geography-centered hotchpotch. To even mention about *sanatan* Hinduism, far less to claim its incomparable richness, has now begun to be treated as a sacrilege by the learned. The road to real 'penury' indeed.

- Danino, a present-day French scholar and lover of India, has arrived at the correct diagnosis of the cause of the Indian malaise of unlimited bending down in the name of non-violence (deriving from Sri Aurobindo's holistic interpretations of the *Gita*): [14]

> '... it seems to me that it (non-violence) has penetrated the collective Indian consciousness deep enough to make it wince at the very thought of force and put a brake on its use even when and where it is patently needed.'

And such effeminacy, in turn, has been the result of ignoring the lessons of 'strength' in the rich holism of Bharat's heritage. *Kshatra veerya* (warrior-like heroism) has been nearly purged from the Indian psyche, rendering it spineless. To many penetrating observers, mechanical harping on phrases like 'composite culture' appears as a mask to hide a signal tragedy of its consciousness — the sub-conscious burden of fear born of nearly a thousand years of sufferings inflicted on it by malafide invasions. If the rich core culture of Bharat is not accorded its legitimate and logical primacy, (as accorded to Confucianism, Christianity, etc., in their respective countries), the very basis and boast of composite culture could then vanish. Permanent cultural, spiritual penury may then be much more dangerous than material penury. For, a huge proportion of humanity might again become second class citizens in their own land. Indian history has shown how aggressive forces can legitimize their malevolent actions and policies. The perennial emperor could thus become an eternal beggar – often aided and abetted by his own people. Sensing this danger, a few sincere foreign well-wishers have sometimes told us: 'If Malaysia symbolises Islamic culture, Singapore Confucian culture, Britain or USA Christian culture and so on, we see nothing parochial or illogical about India symbolizing Hindu culture. For Malaysia, Singapore, Britain, etc., too are composite cultures. Such clarity and frankness will preserve better the integration and richness of your

---

* Sanatan was duly explained to our visitor.

---

* Readers should grasp the following decisive words of Vivekananda with close attention: 'There in Japan you find a fine assimilation of knowledge and not its indigestion as we have here. They have taken everything from the European, but they remain Japanese all the same; ....while in our country, the terrible mania of becoming Westernized has seized upon us like a plague'. So he wanted all the rich and educated Indians to go and see Japan. (Complete Works, vol - 5 p. 372)

culture in the long run. So far as cross-border relationships with other countries are concerned, the record of India's *sanatan* culture has been much nobler than that of Shintoist Japan or Confucian China.' Our teachers and students should acquire a clear grasp of these facts in course of education.

- A recently-established high-profile Business School of India had organized an international conference on Entrepreneurship Development (February 2009). This writer was asked to speak on Indian Values for Lasting Family Business. An American organization had supported the event. Extracts from letters written by Jamshedji Tata to Swami Vivekananda (1898), by G. D. Birla to Basant Birla (1935), and by L. N. Jhunjhuwala to us (2008) were highlighted as first-hand illustrations of Indian values from some pioneering figures of indigenous entrepreneurship.[15] Besides, considerable attention was directed towards the deep-structure educational process Japan* had meticulously conceived and thoroughly executed before and after 1945. It was founded entirely on the Japanese – Shintoist ethos.[16] Thus:

  (a) Nakamura (1960) had stated that propriety and politeness were stressed. Self-assertive, individual independence wasplayed down because this would hurt the feelings of others which, in turn, would hurt himself.

  (b) Yoshino (at MIT, 1968) had written that the stress upon 'familial paternalism', since the second decade of the 20th century, was deliberate, not fortuitous. Compulsory 6-year schooling had become widespread. Ideologial indoctrination about the virtues of family tradition, loyalty to the nation, and diligence was the core of this national endeavour.

  (c) Chie (1970) disclosed that those Japanese who graduated or even received a Ph.D from foreign universities, rather than Japanese, usually failed to secure appointments to good posts in leading Japanese institutions.

  (d) Noda (Berkeley, 1975) informed that both 'ringi' and 'seniority system' were revived in the second half of the 1960s.

  (e) Morishima (1982) argued that the key to Japan's success lay in its central educational gospel: 'Japanese Ethos, Western Technology'. A few of the many characteristics of this indigenous ethos, as explained by Morishima, were: nationalistic Confucianism, total loyalty to one's Lord, the hierarchy of such loyalty leading up to the Emperor, etc.

The above sample of confident self-appraisals about 'local richness' by the Japanese, covering a stretch of nearly a quarter century, triggers a torrent of painful thoughts and questions about India's largely selfdeprecating education. But we must contain ourselves, and leave it to the reader to engage in a personal inner dialogue. Incidentally, and humbly, it may be mentioned that, the down-to-earth audience of entrepreneurs in the aforementioned conference had given an unexpected standing ovation at the end of the above presentation.

- Let us take another similar experience. It was perhaps 1994. A one-week visit to the Curtin University at Perth, Australia, had materialized. One afternoon our local host (an immigrant Indian Professor there) took us and two Japanese visitors for a trip to Fremantle. It is a small port-town on the sea off the Perth coastline. As we walked along the streets in this dreamy little town, we saw small wooden signboards hung on the porticos of several houses. One short sentence appeared on each such board: 'Our Past is Our Future'. This was amazing. The modern white Australian history is barely two centuries old. Its principal actors have been convicts deported from England. And yet, the present generation is so proudly confident of its past. By contrast, a culture whose architects have been *rishis*, and which had excelled in all aspects well before 1000 AD, does not evoke trust and confidence in the people of India. As just seen above, despite their crushing defeat in the Second World War, the Japanese continued to be epitomes of self-confidence. What has gone so grievously wrong, then, for education in India? Getting independence rather cheaply, and thereafter doing no homework at all ?
- In September 2007 a conference on the 'Universal Relevance of the Gita' was held in Singapore. It was organised by the expatriate Hindus of that city-state. We were one of the invited speakers from India. The inaugural lecture was delivered by an expatriate Indian whose ancestors had settled there for several generations. He had occupied several senior posts in the Singaporean government, the last one being that of the country-representative at the WTO. The audience was told that he had

just returned from Bali, where he was deeply moved by the manner in which the Hindu culture and traditions were being faithfully continued by the three million odd Balinese Hindu population. By contrast, he spoke sorrowfully, how in the homeland of Hinduism itself the culture was being cornered or trifled with. He referred specifically to the secularist effrontery then snowballing around the *setubandha* in Rameshwaram. Later in his speech he also informed the delegates how in China for every would-be bureaucrat, the study of Confucian thought was mandatory. Was a similar emphasis, he asked, given in India to the study of Kautilya's *Arthashastra*, for example, by senior IAS people or probationers? Some of us who used to be invited to the IAS Academy at Mussoorie did not indeed get any inkling about Kautilya's ideas figuring in any of the programmes there. However, frothy postmodernism, de-constructionism, syncretism, etc., were sometimes smartly dragged into discussion by some of the learned administrators.

- In September 2000, a 3-day conference on South Asia was organised at the Edinburgh University. After arrival and registration we discovered that the largest contingent of academics hailed form India, Bangladesh occupying the second rank. There was none from Pakistan and Nepal. Of course, many European and American participants were also in attendance. Listening to the larger plenary sessions and the smaller parallel sessions, we gradually sensed some hidden agenda behind the entire act. This uneasy feeling was confirmed during the final plenary presentation. A reputed and elderly American Professor of Sociology was addressing us with the help of slides depicting selected Indian rural and urban scenes. During interpretation he was making condescending or caustic remarks about Indian social customs and rituals. An air of superiority was readily palpable. No Indian academic raised even one question about such nit-picking Readers should grasp the following decisive words of Vivekananda with close attention: 'There in Japan you find a fine assimilation of knowledge and not its indigestion as we have here. They have taken everything from the European, but they remain Japanese all the same; ....while in our country, the terrible mania of becoming Westernized has seized upon us like a plague'. So he wanted all the rich and educated Indians to go and see Japan. (*Complete*

Works, vol - 5 p. 372) But not again imitate her stuff. So, India-baiting, disguised in the garb of impressive jargon of session themes seemed to be the ulterior purpose. We returned hurt. Could Indian academics decide henceforth to boycott such four-yearly anti-India, anti-Hindu events? We went on thinking thus for days together thereafter. Or, an entry in the CV about yet another foreign conference attended would be more relevant for career growth, and so boycotting will not be a practical step?

- Of late a few Indian academics in the field of management are beginning to contribute to the indigenization process. For instance, Subhas Sharma[17] and G. D. Sharma[18]. Both of them are seen to meaningfully refer to the Gita, the Epics, the *rajarshi* model, the subjective and the like. While the epithet 'Indian' is used now and then, the phrase *sanatana* Hindu culture is avoided. They do also challenge many ruling Western concepts or models, and offer useful alternative perspectives. Datta has made a useful entry into Buddhist literature through the Jataka stories, discovering the important concept of 'wisdom power'.[19] G. P. Rao has been advocating the 'maternalistic' approach for humane management.[20] Narayana, a top-level practising manager, adviser and educator, has for long been writing and speaking for and to executives across all levels. His experiential grip over Indian ethos via the *Gita,* the Epics and the Upanishads etc. is evident in what he writes and says.[21] Probably one of the earliest books interpreting the *Gita* for executives by Ramanathan had appeared in 1982. The book is competently done and is succinct. The last chapter is realistic and practically useful.[22] Among the academics, however, Srinivas so far appears to be appreciably more deep and perceptive than the others named above.[23] Sunita Singh Sengupta is the latest scholar who has embarked courageously on the formidable task of integrating *sanatan* spirituality with leadership development. However, all the academics, in varying degrees, reveal shyness or hesitation in getting connected with the enormous corpus of outstanding literature on Indian ethos left for us by the 20th century savants of the land. Allusions to such literature, rare as they are, also appear casual – perhaps to produce a cosmetic aura of Indianness in their writings. Strength of conviction seems feeble. One eagerly awaits the advent of rigorous, independent theoretical frameworks formulated by integrating Indian psychological and social theories and practices. Most other Asian countries, with much lesser materials, have already done so.

- In the early years of our own endeavours in this area (1978-79 onwards) we had earned titles like reactionary, revivalist, or even worse, from the academic fraternity. One day a senior colleague asked us: What you are calling Indian ethos really amounts to Hindu ethos – isn't it ? We were caught off-guard and fumbled. In truth, this issue was never even imagined by us. We had not till then (like the authors above) done enough homework. So the question forced us to think long and hard on this intellectual thorn planted deep within certain sections of our academics. Then another day we gave this reply to that colleague: Our definition of Indian ethos is that corpus of realization, philosophy, social architectures, religious customs and rituals, which had germinated and flourished towards a comprehensive way of life itself, within the landmass of Bharatvarsha. This home-grown quartet of Vedic Hindu, Buddhist, Jaina and Sikh traditions is what we regard as Indian ethos. The solid core and highest common factor of this ethos had crystallized over at least four thousand years prior to 1000 AD. The skeptic, even suspecting, colleague kept quiet, not returning on the subject any more. Whether he liked the definition or not does not really matter. Fact is fact, no prejudice is meant.

V

- What is this highest common factor of Indian ethos so defined? Let us listen to Basham (1975):[24]

  'The theoretical purpose of the whole social and political structure of classical India was to promote *moksha*. ...The complex social order of Hinduism existed primarily to serve this end. ...The Indian quest for *moksha* goes on, and there is no reason why it should not remain the aim of the India of the future. ... this concept ...which has given direction and point to many of (her) best minds ...will not, we believe, disappear whatever be the technological or political forces which affect India ... Few reach that goal – but the secret of the good life is to travel hopefully towards it.' These are the concluding words of Basham in a book on the cultural history of India. The singling out of *moksha* of Hinduism has a message, conscious or unconscious, for all patrons of composite culture. Their professions may be appreciated upto a point, but not at the cost of Bharat's life-line, her core competence as Basham confirms it. The positive echo *moksha* has generated in Basham, had been sounded way back in 1802 in Wordsworth's poem 'The World is Too Much With Us'.[25] '- Great God, I'd rather be a Pagan suckled in a creed outworn'. The poet was familiar with the *Gita*. By 'pagan' he meant the mystical 'Bhagwad Gita culture'.

- Our children and future progeny have the right to know, alongside composite culture, that it was a near-illiterate Hindu-Brahmin priest, Sri Ramakrishna (1836-1886), who had 'realized' the one essential ultimate Truth by himself, practising the core of all religions – Hinduism and its many branches, Islam, Christianity, and indirectly Buddhism as well as Sikhism. It was a *sanatan* Hindu *dharma* follower who alone could demonstrate this unique achievement in world history, through Ramakrishna. It was his chief *shishya*, Vivekananda, students and teachers alike should know, a Hindu again, who had declared in 1897 that India's future vision should be a synthesis of Hindu brain, Buddhist heart and Islamic body. Christmas eve is duly celebrated every year with joy and solemnity in every centre of the Ramakrishna Math. A decorated large portrait of Christ is always there in most of the temples. This event and practice too were initiated by Vivekananda. Any corresponding gestures from the other major streams towards Hindu dharma or culture? And yet we talk of 'national integration'. Since independence this country has had Presidents, Vice- Presidents, Chief Justices, Air Staff Chief, Chief Ministers, Governors, Ambassadors, captains of sports teams, etc., in fairly large numbers from the externally-anchored communities. Whether such broad– minded measures have fostered decency, gratitude and respect in relation to the Mother culture of India, in even a small degree, however, remains an open question. Education needs to inculcate this correct attitude: Junior members of a joint family have a full share of their duties and responsibilities too for the system. The Vedas, the two Epics, the Upanishads, the Gita, the Puranas, the Dhammapada, the Sukrakritanga (Jainism) and a lot more existed in this land much before their arrival. Hence, for all those who are born here this whole corpus is a common heritage. This is no denial of their primary anchorage. Yet, until an open-minded, grateful acceptance of this common heritage is nurtured, national integration will remain a chimera. Education about these facts is indispensable for nurturing strong-minded citizens, instead of weak and apologetic ones. Otherwise, the 'strength' aspect of the nation will tend to be restricted only to one dedicated fringe of the population – our jawans in the defence forces. One even tends to feel at times as to why these all-sacrificing defence forces should continue to do so when the massive civilian population is so unconscious and callous about the stakes. Yet, but for the above undying strengths, there may not have been any 'composite' culture at all. Politically correct verbiage cannot yield such miracles. The goose laying golden eggs is not for killing.

- As we set out to pen down this last paragraph it happened to be May 30. Exactly one hundred years ago, Sri Aurobindo had delivered a divinely empowered oration at Uttarpara in Bengal (on the Ganga) after his release from the Alipore prison. A few of words of the affluence, of real wealth from that speech are offered below. They could very well constitute an all-time benchmark for all of us today who dabble, meddle or quibble with the central foundation of education in India. Without this in steady, clear focus, the sprawling, imitative super-structure, with all its glitter, will be an undoing of Bharat's vision and mission. That will indeed be the grand penury. Anand Coomaraswamy had said as much, way back in 1913.[26] '...all real progress must be based on national ideals, upon intentions already clearly expressed in religion and art.' Now to Sri Aurobindo, after a little, yet pertinent detour[27] 'Then He placed the *Gita* in my hands. His strength entered into me and I was able to do the *sadhana* of the *Gita*. ...I realized what the Hindu religion meant. ...Other religious are preponderatingly religions of faith and profession, but the *Sanatana Dharma* is life itself; it is a thing that has not so much to be believed as lived. ...She (India) does not rise as other countries do, for self; or when she is strong, to trample on the weak. ...India has always existed for humanity and not for herself, and it is for humanity and not for herself that she must be great.' So, the 'enigma' is: How is it that such a supra-mundane vision of India's greatness and responsibility remains beyond the pale of educational thought and practice in India today.

References

1. M. Sri, *Sri Ramakrishna Kathamrita* (in Bengali), Kolkata: Udbodhan, 2004, p. 699.
2. Jois, Justice M. R., *Human Rights and Indian Values*, New Delhi: National Council for Teacher Education, 1997.
3. Brown. K, *The Essential Teachings of Hinduism*, London: Arrow Books, 1990 – quoted in Jois, *Ibid.*, p. 51.
4. Thoreau H. D, *Walden and Other Writings*, New York: Bantam, 1989, p. 325.
5. Aurobindo Sri, quoted by Prema Nandakumar in 'Indian Epic Narrative: Alive and Vibrant' (Mimeo), 2004, p. 4.
6. Raine. K, 'The Voice of the Sacred in Our Time', *Vihangam*, Vol. V, 1997, p. 1 and p. 3.
7. Chakraborty S.K., *Human Response in Organisations*, Calcutta: Vivekananda Nidhi, 1985.
8. Osterberg. R, 'This Mind Stretching Era', in *Merchants of Vision*, ed. JE Liebig, San Francisco: Berrett Koehler, 1994, p. 27.
9. Kao, H. S. R, Sinha. D, B. Wilpert (eds); *Management and Cultural Values*, New Delhi: Sage, 1999.
10. *Ibid., Sinha D., p. 51.*
11. *Ibid., Sinha, Mala, pp. 191-6.*
12. Radhakrishnan. S., *Recovery of Faith*, New Delhi: Orient, 1967, p. 184.
13. Renou. L *Ibid., p. 185.*
14. Danino. M, *Is Indian Culture Obsolete?*, New Delhi: Mother's Institute of Research, 2000, p. 52.
15. Chakraborty S. K and Chakraborty D; *Human Values and Ethics*, Hyderabad: ICFAI University Press, 2006, p. 428 and p. 431.
16. Chakraborty, 1985, pp. 81-90.
17. Sharma Subhas, *Management in New Age – Western Windows and Eastern Doors*, New Delhi: New Age International, 1996, pp. 185-194.
18. Sharma G. D., *Management and The Indian Ethos*, New Delhi: Rupa, 2001, pp. 54-73.
19. Datta T., *Management: Lessons From an Ancient Text*, Kolkata: Jnan Bichitra, 2008, pp. 21-35.
20. Rao G. P., *Human Values in Industrial Organizations: The Feminine Perspective*, Calcutta: Management Centre for Human Values (IIMC), 1997.

21. Narayana G., *Responsible Leadership in the Gita*, Ahmedabad Management Association, 1997.
22. Ramanathan A., *Bhagwad Gita for Executives*, Bombay: Bharatiya Vidya Bhawan, 1982, pp. 218-237.
23. Srinivas K. M., *Pilgrimage To Indian Ethos Management*, Calcutta: Management Centre for Human Values (IIMC), 1999.
24. Basham A. L., (ed.), *A Cultural History of India*, New Delhi: Oxford University Press, (1975), 1999, pp. 498-9.
25. Srivastava K.G., *Bhagwad Gita and the English Romantic Movement*, New Delhi: Macmillan, 2002, p. 163.
26. Nivedita, Sister and Coomaraswamy, A., *Myths and Legands of the Hindus and Buddhists*, Kolkata: Advaita Ashrama, 2006, p. vii.
27. Aurobindo Sri, *All India Magazine*, Puducherry: Sri Aurobindo Society, May 2009, p. 7.

CHAPTER 3

EDUCATION FOR 'NATIONAL MIND': Let Sister Nivedita Teach Us

समाना मन्त्र: समिति:
समानि समान मन:
सह चित्तम् एषाम् ।
सहमानी व आकूति: समाना हृदयानि व:
समानम् अस्तु वो मनो यथा व: सुसीहाति ।।
(ऋ : १०/१९१)

May your aim be common,
Your assembly common,
Common the thoughts and minds of these united.
A common purpose do I lay before you;
And worship with your aim, and your hearts united; Your minds be one so that all may live happily together.

(*Rig Veda* 10/191)
(*Ibid.*, p. 282).

I

Sri Aurobindo, reflecting upon national education for India, had articulated in 1920 a fact of capital significance[1] '... there (is) the peculiar cast as the Indian mind, its psychological tradition, its ancestral capacity, turn, knowledge (which) bring in cultural elements of supreme importance.' Sister Nivedita too, a decade earlier, had struck a remarkably identical note on India's national education[2] '... pre-eminently in this modern age there is a certain characteristic fund of ideas and concepts which is common to society as a whole, and must be imparted to every individual who is to pass in his mature life as efficient.'

Sri Aurobindo had achieved a matchlessly comprehensive grasp of the European ethos over a period of fourteen years. Sister Nivedita was a brilliant and unbiased British woman dedicated to Bharat. Yet both had stressed, respectively, upon the 'peculiar cast' of the 'Indian mind', and 'the characteristic fund of ideas and concepts' created by Indian civilisation. And they both had declared a firm acceptance of this contextual *terra firma* as the starting point of true education for Indians in India.

Disparagement of the 'local' has however been a keynote in most of India's post-independence educational endeavours. The 'global' postures of large segments of academics and intellectuals have been inducing young minds to cast aside their own traditions while espousing, at the same time, unquestioning submission to dictated alien notions. The former is bondage, the latter emancipation! Such persons seem Education in India: A Tree Without Roots to feel that self-hate or self-oblivion is the quickest way to win international acclaim. This implies forgetting that other nations will not respect those who abandon self-respect for their own heritage. Perhaps the best example of this perilous process is the swelling army of young journalists, especially in the English press. 'Cultural dehydration', as we may call it, has been plaguing such minds. Careeristic, moneyspinning education is at the root of their betrayal. May it be asked of those people who incite irreverence in budding minds: How many moments of sympathetic and humble engagement have they devoted to assimilate the inner sense of the deep-structure culture of Bharat? Does it occur to them how a Margaret Noble (our Sister) could bleed herself to death for that culture which so many of our elite tend to despise ? Is it not a similar phenomenon we witness in The Mother, who had settled in Pondicherry after about a decade of the Sister's death? She had uttered these words in 1968[3]. 'The future of India is very clear. India is Guru of the world. The future structure of the world depends on India. India is the living soul, India is incarnating the spiritual knowledge in the world.' Thus, Sri Aurobindo's 'ancestral capacity', the Sister's 'common stock of ideas', and the Mother's 'India is the living soul' – all these expressions converge upon a common message for education in India Abiding *shraddha* for an Indian birth, coupled with tireless striving to live upto the grand responsibility which such a birth confers on students, teachers, parents and other citizen groups. No false pride or empty talk, but a quietly humble *sadhana* to repay our *rishi rin*. This impetus has to be the essential energizing principle for valid education in India. Everything else is incidental or postponable. Sister Nivedita had amplified this imperative in these words[4] '... Germany and America have known how to bring the *national mind* to bear on their respective problems. That is to say, they have organized the common, popular mind and to this organized mind they have presented the riddle... the prosperity and well-being of their respective country and people only.

What is noticed today in India goes to the contrary. Imported ideologies and fashions, vote-based fragmentation, alluring images of false living, vulgar economism, debunking of grassroot ways of looking at life – all such forces are afoot against the crystallization of a common national mind for India. Whatever small attempts are made in this direction get quickly snubbed as the antithesis of 'global mind', 'secular mind', 'progressive mind', etc. The champions of 'global mind' in India cannot or will not see that those very powers which have imposed this treacherous slogan upon us, have done so precisely on the strength of their own 'national minds'. The message from them is clear to those who can see through the dazzle: 'National mind' for us, 'global mind' for you. Our *vishwakavi,* Rabindranath Tagore, must be sighing in his grave at such phoney globalism of today. But, to be sure, without a 'common national mind' as the baseline we cannot achieve social integration and advancement. The tragic truth is that many disunities are being consciously invented or enhanced by political and intellectual forces. This Machiavellian process was perfected by the British to weaken integral Bharat. Such forces necessarily thrive on conflict-creation or aggravation. The apparent social diversity of traditional Indian society (based no doubt on sound original principles), the butt of endless scholarly criticism, has not been able to destroy our *sanatan* cultural fabric, albeit weakening it in some ways. This achievement has been possible because the *rishis* of Bharatvarsha had created a 'national mind' of its own type. Perhaps the most powerful *mantra* which had underpinned this 'national mind' of ours is the following vow in the *Rigveda*:

Samano mantra samitih,
Saman samanam manah,
Saha chittam evaam
Samani va aakutih,
Samana hridayani vah.

The guru administers this oath of common, united purposiveness in the heart of his students. Such a vow contemplates no crusade or aggression or *jihad* directed against others — Indian history is a clear proof of this. The common purposiveness here is aimed at the welfare of *all* and *everything (sarve bhavantu sukhino)* through subordination of egoistic self-assertion – individual or national. Nivedita was able to appreciate this 'universal' temper of the Indian 'national mind'. Yet, she had also wanted such a common mind to embrace civic ideals and responsibilities towards creating a virile society, fit for modern conditions. But she did not strive for this rejuvenation at the cost of its unique, universalist keynote.

II

Where shall such basic educational labour be done? By whom? They are baffling but urgent questions. Mass media, government and private institutions which influence, indirectly or directly, the minds of youth and adults alike, are busy prodding us for a desperate foothold on the bandwagon of so-called 'progress'. Sister Nivedita had anticipated this great hurdle. She knew that centralisers may come and go. But this would hardly matter if the nerve-ends remained strong and alive[5]. This means each home and its parents and adults in the country must perform the task of educating themselves and their children towards a 'common national mind'. Nothing else can equal or replace this role and process. Charity begins at home – as the saying goes. In course of her exposition of an effective psychological theory of education, Nivedita had offered us two major clues[6]:

(a) 'To emancipate the greatest number of people most easily and effectively it is necessary to choose *familiar ideals and forms*...A national education then must be made up of *familiar elements.* The ideals presented must always be first clothed in a form evolved by *our own past*. Our imagination must be first based on *our own heroic literature.* Our hope must be woven out of *our history*' (emphasis here and below added).'

She was all for a high-level common meeting ground for the educated of the world. But such intellectual *mukti* or freedom, she opined, could be attained only by firmly-rooted 'love for the mother and mother-land'[7]. Are such ultimate principles of education obsolete today? They may have been valid when India was a British colony – many might argue that way these days. We feel, however, that every note in the preceding quote from Nivedita is as essential and relevant in 21st century India as it was till 1947. For, in most parts of India almost everything fed to the budding mind is 'unfamiliar'. Our 'own past' has been a futility. There is no 'our history'. 'Our own heroic literature' is merely a chronicle of deceits and violence and hyperboles. Any utterance for *Vedic* Hinduism is dubbed as chauvinism. Debunking it is progressivism. Global love (!), not motherland love, is the sign of emancipation. Until such assaults on the 'national mind' are recognized and repulsed by parents and teachers, India may not again become the true Bharat that she had been. As a pertinent illustration, Sister Nivedita cites how the ideal of supreme holiness in woman is perceived in the betrothed maiden across Europe, while in India it is in the faithful wife. It is futile therefore, she argues, to groom the imagination of an Indian child according to the European conception, at the cost of India's own.[8] She asserts, moreover, that in a 'true' education the place of foreign culture is *never* at the beginning.[9] But it is exactly the opposite of this which is derailing the 'mis-educated literates' of India today. Thus, a young woman was recently heard to tell the interviewer on TV that 'companionship', not 'marriage', is a superior option.

Continuing in the earlier vein, Nivedita holds that an Indian child had far better learn about 'truthfulness' from Yudhisthira than from George Washington.[10] But our liberated educators preach that udhisthira was a liar ! The child in the West is carefully nourished with the lores of Iliad and Odyssey, the battles of Carthage and Sparta, with its civilizing(?) conquests in Asia and Africa, with the victory in Waterloo, with the fruitless military projects of Alexander, and so on. By contrast, Bharat's children are often being told that the *Bhagavad-Gita, the Ramayana, the Mahabharata, etc.,* are but tales of intrigue and violence to be kept at bay. The second major psychological thesis advanced by the Sister is.[11]

(b) 'Unless we train the *feelings* and the *choice* our man is not educated. He is only decked out in certain intellectual tricks that he has learnt to perform. By these tricks he can earn his bread. He cannot appeal to the heart or give life.'

Amazing insight and accurate foresight! This indeed is now a grim reality in modern society. India's professionals in all fields fit this picture in a large measure. This then is what she emphasizes for stemming the rot[12] '....there is nothing so important as the *training of the feelings.* To *feel nobly* and to *choose* loftily and *honestly* is a thousand-fold more important...than any other single aspect of the educational process.' A grand principle is expressed through these words: Wholesome choice depends upon noble feelings cultivated by the 'training of the heart'. Such however is the thick mental fog shrouding many of our scientific-tempered luminaries that they cannot visualize anything else but the biological pumping machine in our body by the word 'heart' Sister Nivedita then goes on to link the theme of 'emotion' with that of the previous one about the 'familiar'[13]: 'Emotion is... entirely a matter of locality. All form is purely local. Every *man's heart has its own country.*'

Thus, her educational theory stands on this foundation: The culture of pure and noble emotions (along with the subduing of the impure and ignoble ones) through local images, characters and processes. But education in India today violates both these basic canons.

What Sri Aurobindo wrote on this aspect, almost at the same time as Nivedita, is remarkably similar[14] 'In the economy of man, the mental nature rests upon the moral, and the education of the intellect divorced from the perfection of the moral and emotional nature is injurious to human progress...the heart is not the mind, and to *instruct the mind does not necessarily improve the heart.*' The word 'mind' in the second part of the quote has been used synonymously with 'intellect'. Thus, exclusively intellect–driven education, neglecting efforts for emotional refinement or purification, is unsound at the very root. Hence flow the severe long-term dangers to individual and social good. Rabindranath Tagore, while attempting to answer the question 'What is Art?' had spoken of emotions from several angles.[15]

- 'Man has a fund of emotional energy which is not all occupied with his self-preservation.'
- 'When a feeling is aroused in our hearts....'
- '(Man) feels his personality more intensely than other creatures....'
- 'The principal creative forces, which transmute things into our living structure, are emotional forces.'

- '(The world) becomes completely our own when it comes within the range of our emotions.'
- 'Our emotions are the gastric juices which transform this world of appearance into the more intimate world of sentiments.'
- 'The things which arouse our emotion arouse our own self feeling.'

Anyone familiar in some measure with Tagorean literature, especially his songs and poems, would know that few can excel him in the authenticity of messages contained in the above quotes. Although Tagore was not speaking about feelings/emotions directly from the standpoint of educational theory, yet the holistic moral/ethical implications of these expressions are self-evident. For, the more intimately and personally one can *feel related* to anything or any one, the more ethical would one's dealings be with the same. The morally educated person must feel *subjectively close* to other wider spheres. The more inclusive our circle of felt closeness can be, the more moral or ethical our conduct will tend to be. At one point however, so it seems, Tagore has voiced his own appreciation of Nivedita's emphasis upon the culture of 'noble emotions'. Thus he says[16] 'We may become powerful by knowledge, but we attain fullness by *sympathy*. The highest education is that which does not merely give us information but makes our life in *harmony* with all existence.' Both sympathy and harmony reside in the human heart as feelings/ emotions. And both are noble since they help towards unity by reducing strife and exploitation. The latter are negative emotions, the former positive. Development of character is essentially a struggle for the desirable or positive emotions against the undesirable or negative ones. Tagore declares thus about character[17]: 'From the life of desire it guides man to the life of purpose. This life is the life of the moral world.' That mounting 'knowledge' or 'information' or 'intellectual' capital' of current times has been dragging us down from a purposeful moral life needs no labouring. Our emotional compass is lost. Sister Nivedita has made passing references to the idea of 'will' also. But it seems to be treated as a synonym for feeling/ emotion[18]:

- 'The nobility of will is the final test of culture., and the watch-towers of the will are in the affections.'
- 'It is not enough to render the will noble; it ought also to be made efficient if the true educational ideal is to be attained ...

But *efficiency without nobility is worse than useless: it is positively destructive.* Infinitely better nobility without efficiency...'* It is possible to view a little more specifically what the Sister says above. Thus, a noble feeling like 'gratitude' may cross one's mind on rare occasions, per chance. But if this pure, lofty emotion is to become a consistent response in all relevant situations, exertion of willpower is needed to assimilate it into one's being. Again, 'patriotism' is a noble emotion. But to make the patriotic feeling so intense as to inspire one (and others) to sacrifice one's all, (e.g. Netaji Subhas), conscious exertion of will is needed. Thus, fleeting, superficial feelings, even if they are positive, may not become practically meaningful and durable unless conscious willing makes them habitual. Sri Aurobindo has of course written amply on/about will while expounding on Integral Yoga. Suffice here to offer just two excerpts which lend completeness to the preceding general statements[19].

- 'The will is perfected when it gets away from and behind its impulses... the will coloured by desire is an impure will and it puts a stamp of distortion....'
- 'There is a will, *tapas, sakti*...the will of the transcendent spirit....'

While Nivedita anchors the human will in the 'watch-towers' of affections (i.e., emotions and feelings), Aurobindo does so in the higher or Divine Will. In both cases feeling and willing are treated as qualities of the heart, not of the head. The head is the source of efficiency as it were, and has an important but secondary role in true education – in Nivedita's opinion. Our own experience fully substantiates this reasoning. And once the nagging phenomenon of negative emotions or *shadaripus* or 'seven deadly sins' is admitted, he role of determination/resolve/will in combating them becomes paramount. In other words, both for sustaining and strengthening noble or pure emotions on the one hand, and for loosening and reducing the hold of ignoble or filthy emotions on the other, exercise of will power is indispensable.

* Witness the unabated high-skill terrorist violences against innocent citizens in India.

III

It is for this vital aspect that the following acute perceptions of Nivedita merit urgent reconsideration today.[20]

- 'Fortunately for the civilisation of India the Hindu has always clearly perceived the *mind behind the method* as the thing with which education has fundamentally to deal.'
- 'Just so long as the Brahminic system of *directly training the minds* of the young to concentration persists, will the Indian people remain potentially equal to the conquest of any difficulty that the changing ages may bring them?'
- '... our forefathers never neglected the culture and development of the mind itself.... Great men have been only as incidents in the tale of this national effort – to achieve control and *self-direction of the mind itself.*'

Such luminous conceptual elucidation makes us see clearly the practical worth of the string of minor and major rituals and processes running through the daily lives of boys and girls in Indian tradition. Ill-motived irreverence, *ashraddha,* masquerading as liberal education, towards them is costing the nation dearly in terms of mounting indiscipline and vulgarity within homes and outside. What Nivedita has so aptly called 'national effort' awaits getting back soon its frontseat. Of course, various psychological disciplines of deep breathing, concentration of mind upon itself or on a deity seated within, silent *japam,* etc., all strengthen the mind's willpower. Purification of emotions (e.g. reduction of vanity and increase of modesty) can be well combined with these processes. Such then is the meaning of 'direct training of the mind' which our Sister had identified as the chief merit of the Brahminical theory of education. Her own conclusive formulation of this whole framework can hardly be bettered[21]. 'In other words, education, finally, works on the *will*, and installs the *heart* and the *intellect* as its loyal and harmonious *servants.*' Rigorous training of the mind by the cultivation of willing and feeling, is thus the foundation of all worthwhile education. Nivedita herself sums up the ideas of the preceding few paragraphs as follows[22] '... a trained power of attention and concentration, an ability to think connectedly and inquire persistently about a given subject and a capacity for willing rightly and efficiently.' This indeed is then the whole truth about education : Concentration, persistence, right willing. All these elements are universal; the third one is *normative* too. But the practical, integral working out of these elements must be congruent with the experiential certitudes and wisdom of Indian culture. And so for others. The role of parents and homes in the education of children has also been addressed by Nivedita with compact eloquence[23]. '*Fathers* and *mothers* must not suppose, when their children go to school, that their own task has ended. Rather must the thought of *dharma increase* daily in the household. *Indian ideals* of family cohesion, of charity, of frugality, of honour; the admiration of national heroes, the fund of poetic legends, must be *daily and hourly* discussed and commented on. All that *makes India India,* must flow through *the Indian home* to make it *Indian*.... the best education of children is the *conversation* of their parents.'

The above desiderata provoke a host of anxious thoughts about the actual picture of homes and parents today. The upper strata of Indian society, especially, are acting in ways which are quite the reverse of what Nivedita had required of us. The urbanized elite tend to scorn *dharma* because of the mistaken notion that it is religion in the institutionalized, dogmatic sense of the English word; or treat it as no more than sterile customs and mechanical rituals. In pursuit of high standard of living, reckless consumerism is becoming the order of the day.* That high *consumption standards* do not mean high *living standards* is not understood by them. There are no Indian heroes; there are only Alexanders and Napoleons, Churchills and Kennedys who pervade their consciousness and of their children. *Alice in Wonderland* is better known than *Panchatantra.* Forget about daily discussion of Indian legends as ideals. The family itself, as a unit, is vanishing. The question of joint family does not arise. Even in nuclear families both parents leave home at 8 a.m. and return at 8 p.m. And then stinking TV garbage is there to feed upon. When parents converse, it is either money matters or quarrels or office politics or neighbourhood gossip. So, the question is: *what is going to be India's future with very little character to go around?* Can the mushrooming of so-called 'international public schools' ever fill this void? Finally, it is also becoming common that the professional father works in the

* Terminal 3 of the Delhi airport, inaugurated in 2010 during the Commonwealth games, is a lurid example to the point. A cup of tea costing ₹ 5 only a year ago now costs ₹ 50 or more! An English female voice 'educates' the Indian announcers in the lounge to speak proper English.

east, the professional mother in the north, and the hapless son gets educated in an expensive boarding school in south India. So, even the nuclear 'family' could be on the way out. What next? As for the learning of history of India by the young mind, Nivedita's approach and methodology is more valid now than it was a century ago. She goes to the heart of the matter along fundamental lines[24].

- 'Only by a gradual and *loving study* of how she came to be can we understand what she is, what is the tendency of her evolution and her potential.'
- 'We are often told that Indian literature includes no histories....we must remember that India *herself is the master-document* of this kind. The country is her own record. *She is the history* we must learn to read.'
- 'It is a characteristic of India that almost every great outstanding thought and doctrine has somewhere or other a place devoted to its maintenance and tradition....*India is at once the occasion, and the explanation* of the web of Indian thought.'
- 'If India itself be the book of Indian history, it follows that travel is the true means of reading that history... (Yet) It is quite possible to *travel* the world over and *see nothing* or only *what is not true.* We see, after all, only *what we are prepared to see.*'
- '... in the pursuit of epochs and parts we must never forget the *Mother* and the *Motherland,* behind them all.'
- '... Indian students will do most to help the growth of knowledge if they begin with the *robust conviction* that in the long tale of their Motherland there can be *nothing to cause them anything but* pride and reverence.'

The prevailing atmosphere in our homes and education alestablishments is a dismal opposite of what Sister Nivedita had so fervently pleaded for. Instead of 'loving', lip-serving or despising is preached; instead of perceiving India as Mother/Motherland, she is portrayed as a mere geographical territory with a certain package of material/natural resources; instead of travelling to understand her, it is commercial tourism or cheap pleasure which is the motive. Consequently, reverence or *shraddha* is today less than a faint beat among the student population. Nothing else can be expected when parents and teachers themselves tend to be destitute of this crowning value. While urging us to think 'strongly' about education for its 'highest results', Sişter Nivedita had pronounced this emphatic declaration[25]. 'Let India *never* tamper with the place that the *Mahabharata* and the *Ramayana* hold in the households of the simple.'

The reason to issue this stern warning lies in the following observation of the Sister[26].

'The great national epics, the *Mahabharata* and *Ramayana*...stand to this day as the type and *standard* of imaginative culture amongst all – save the *English-educated classes.*' Her assessment then about the petty arrogance among many so-called educated elite holds equally true to this day. So, her warning is squarely valid against their periodic pernicious or politicized edicts e.g., these Epics should be banned from primary schools because they allegedly breed violence in the minds of children. This must rank as an unbeatable feat of intellectual terrorism. In these heady days of globalization, we should do well by respectfully listening and adhering to this sagacious policy blueprint from Nivedita[27]. 'It is *not by imitation* of foreigners, but *by renewed apprehension* of their own intention, renewed effort at self-expression...that nations arise. History is *ashirbad* – the promise that the nationality makes to each one of its children.'

This quote has two important components:

(a) 'not imitating foreigners';

(b) 'history is *ashirbad*' (blessing).

In (a) she reiterates that embracing ideas/things foreign can never usher perfection. It is a sin, in her view, to bring up an Indian child on anything else but the *Mahabharata.* This of course will enhance later the student's capacity to appreciate the Odyssey and enjoy Homer. Love for the *Ramayana* must not be tried to be stimulated through Tennyson. Such reversal of priority can only create a 'bastard culture' – so warned Nivedita. Wasn't she prophetic?[28] As for (b), how and when can education in history descend as a shower of blessings? The Sister answers with burning conviction on this issue: Such an outcome can flow only from those who study India's history with the heart; mere 'head-knowledge' will be futile. Such a process, in both writing and teaching India's history, can only be expected of those who are 'lovers of India'[29]. But we often hear high-browed intellectuals sighing about the burden, the curse of Indian history.

IV

Once again, most of us would know by now that in postindependence India both these criteria have been flouted by a certain powerful groups of scholars. They are adept in capturing power and in twisting educational systems, policies and texts to deprecate national ideals and echo borrowed ideologies. The few who dare to challenge such mischief, inspired by Niveditas and her likes, are persecuted or sidelined, stifling the expression of truth, honesty and sincerity. Therefore, back to the task of national self-regeneration, she writes this austere prescription[30]. 'Children will need to *renounce* personal ambition, and parents to make the deeper renunciation of ambition for their children. Yet these *tyagis* of the new time will wear no *gerua*.' Bridging the immense gulf between this saving spirit and the prevailing mercernary craze in homes is the greatest task of educational efforts in India. For, we regularly discover that either the daughter or the son, or both, amongst our acquaintances have settled abroad, chiefly the USA. Heartless careerists as most of them are, Nivedita's dream of *non–gerua tyagis* for Mother India has gone with the winds – for the foreseeable future at least. In August 1907, at the time of leaving Bengal National College as its Principal, these were the words Sri Aurobindo had spoken to the students[31].

'... I wish to see some of you becoming rich, rich not for yourselves but that you may enrich your Mother... I wish to see some of you becoming great, great not for your own sakes,... but to make India great. ...You will earn your living that you may live for her sake. You will go abroad to foreign lands that you may bring back knowledge with which you may do service to her. Work that, she may prosper. Suffer that she may rejoice.' Thus, Nivedita's *non-gerua tyagis* had been concretely blueprinted by Sri Aurobindo almost at the same time. By contrast, what are the calls, for example, sent out to young graduates at IIMs, IITs etc. by India's elite in their convocation addresses hundred years on?*

References

1. Aurobindo Sri and Mother, The; *On Education* Pondicherry: Sri Aurobindo Ashram 1997, p. 10.

* See chapter 10 later

2. Nivedita Sister; *Hints on National Education* Kolkata: Advaita Ashram 1976, p. 15.
3. Mother, The; *India and Her Destiny*, Pondicherry: Sri Aurobindo Society, 1977, pp. 13-14.
4. Nivedita; op. cit. pp 9-10.
5. *Ibid., p. 3.*
6. *Ibid., p. 37.*
7. *Ibid., p. 39.*
8. *Ibid. pp. 35-6.*
9. *Ibid., p. 42.*
10. *Ibid., p. 42.*
11. *Ibid., p. 24.*
12. *Ibid., p. 25.*
13. *Ibid., p. 43.*
14. Aurobindo Sri and Mother, The; op. cit., p. 27.
15. Tagore Rabindranath; *Personality*, New Delhi: Rupa, 2002, pp.10-5.
16. *Ibid., p. 124.*
17. *Ibid., p. 87.*
18. Nivedita Sister; *Complete Works*, Kolkata: Advaita Ashrama, Vol. 5, 1999, p. 73
19. Aurobindo Sri; *The Synthesis of Yoga*, Pondicherry: Sri Aurobindo Ashram, 1988, p. 642, p. 648.
20. *Hints on National Education*, op. cit, p. 7, p. 968.
21. Nivedita, *Complete Works*, op. cit., p 7.
22. *Ibid., p. 51.*
23. Nivedita, *Complete Works* (Vol. 5) pp. 74-5.
24. *Complete Works*, op. cit., Vol.4, pp. 5-19.
25. *Complete Works*, op. cit., Vol-5, p. 73.
26. *Complete Works*, op. cit., Vol.4, p. 164.
27. *Ibid., p. 306.*
28. *Complete Works*, op. cit., Vol.5, p. 69, p. 76.
29. *Ibid., p. 48, p. 50.*
30. Nivedita, Sister, *Dharma and Religion,* Kolkata: Advaita Ashrama, 1994, p. 42.
31. Quoted in *Footprints of God,* Pondicherry: Sri Aurobindo Society, 2010, p. 9.

CHAPTER 4

THE 'BEAR-HUG'* AND CULTURAL DIS-EMPOWERMENT

सं जानामाहे मनसा सं चिकित्वा
मा युष्महि मनसा दैव्येन ।

(अ:७/५२)

May we (ourselves and foreigners) unite in our minds, unite in our purposes. And not fight against the Divine Spirit within us.

(*Atharva Veda* 7/52)

(*Ibid.*, pp. 283–4).

I

For many policy–making educational elite of India dismissing the inexhaustible fund of wisdom born of *tapasya* (ascesis) has tended to become a sign of progressiveness, of emancipation. This is the fate of both ancient and recent wisdom heritage. Valmiki is useless (Rama did so and so ...); Vyasa is confused (Yudhisthira, Bhisma did so and so ...); the Gita is perverse (Krishna teaches violence to Arjuna ...); Manu is abominable (rationalises brahminical craftiness), and so on. That all this amounts to dangerous dis-empowerment is not understood. As indicated in Chapter 1, this contrasts starkly with the determined re-empowering exercises done in Japan and other Asian countries. Just one experience should suffice. About fifteen years ago (perhaps 1996-97) we had called on a learned central finance minister at his New Delhi residence. Impressed by some of his earlier

* This is a special grip employed in freestyle wrestling.

newspapers articles, we had approached him for an essay on leadership power and ethics for a book to be edited by us. He readily gave us time, and a little discussion ensued. The purpose of our book project was to provide a foundation for wise leadership based on indigenous classical works like the *Ramayana, Mahabharata,* etc. As soon as a few such titles were named, the minister interrupted and said: 'What is the use of going to these ancient texts? We are living in modern times.' The fond mental image we had formed of him was shattered. Such nit-picking elite of India often revive the image of the nursery rhyme pussy cat. Instead of seeing the queen on the throne, the poor creature ends up seeing a mouse under the queen's chair! So, let us get back to our trustworthy sacred trail left by the ancient pilgrims of the Eternal. The constellation of seven stars in the northern night sky is known in Bhartavarsha as the *saptarshi mandala* – a sacred assembly of seven *rishis* or sages*. The stable polestar is called the *dhruva nakshatra,* so named after the sage-king Dhruva who had, by *tapasya* as a boy, attained the vision of the Lord of the Universe, Narayana. In English, however, this constellation goes by the name Great Bear. This striking contrast of nomenclatures in the two languages is just one instance of the abiding bent of the Bharatiya mind towards the lofty, the sacred. The secular Great Bear is empty of any transcendental note. These two metaphors constitute a vivid revelation of the characteristic difference between the Western and Indian culture types. The prolific sacred imagination at the base of Indian culture can still be detected in almost every act or object in this land. Just one more example: the rivers Ganga and Narmada are both associated with the vision of their being 'daughters of Shiva'. Both are revered by millions as sacred streams of Divine care and compassion flowing for all creation. They are affectionately addressed as Mother Ganga, Mother Narmada. All this is perhaps without parallel in the world. Such uniqueness has to be recognized and kept alive for many reasons. To put the problem metaphorically, the 'Great Bear' culture today seems to be on the verge of strangulating the '*saptarshi*' culture with a deathly hug. The roaring trumpet of global village has been drowning the gentle flute of the local village. For the benefit of humanity? Of the earth? Not so difficult to divine the answer. A few recent events should suffice to amplify. Kathleen Raine, a reputed British literary

---

* Called 'Human Fathers', headed by Brihaspati.

critic and a positive observer of Indian culture, had commented to this effect:

- On her first visit to India (1969) the beauty of young and old women ... came to her as a revelation. And the dignity above all that the *sari* imparted to its wearers ...
- During her second visit (1994) young women were beginning to adopt the Western unisex uniform of jeans and jerseys, expressing their adoption of Western values. In exchanging the most beautiful and dignified women's dress in the world for the ugliest, they were renouncing the concept of beauty – and with that, love and delight.

Could there be a rebuke sharper, yet more affectionate, than that of Raine to awaken us to the naked truth of the 'bear hug', of cultural disempowerment? In December 2008 we came to know a Japanese woman who was spending a few days of retreat at the Brindavan ashram of the century-old Ramakrishna Mission. Except for *salwar-kameez,* she matched perfectly a Hindu Bengali wife in her bearing: white conch bangles, red lac bangles, a round vermilion mark on the forehead, a vermilion streak along the parting of hair on the head, long braided hair along the back, etc. To cap it all, she could speak fluent Bengali, was married to a Bengali Brahmin, and was living in Kolkata with her mother-in-law. Every morning and evening she could be seen sitting in an *asana* on the floor of the temple of Sri Ramakrishna, meditating for long periods. She also visited most of the ancient temples in the town riding rickshaws or walking on foot. Brief words were exchanged between us at noon and night meal times in the guests' dining room. Once we asked her, how often she went back to visit her homeland? She replied: 'I hardly feel the urge to go there. I feel so much more at ease in all respects in this country.' This was profound and touching. After a few days an Indian visitor came to the ashram. He was on a short holiday to India from Canada. He had retired after serving as a food scientist in a world-wide organization. One evening all three of us were having together our evening meals. The Japanese woman asked the visiting Indian: 'Do you not feel like coming back to India and live here after retirement?' With ill-concealed self-satisfaction the gentleman quickly replied: 'No. I am well-settled there. Life is comfortable. My children work there. They are Canadian citizens'.

Both of us finished our meals in stunned silence. Such 'bearhugs' are aplenty – readily perceived by those who possess a culturally sensitized mind. It was perhaps the end of 2005. An English daily had organized a seminar for college and school principals in a certain state capital. This evening event had invited an all-India celebrity and this author as the two presenters. The multiple awards-winning celebrity arrived late, about half-way through our presentation. When her turn came, the celebrity began to unfold her non-stop success story since childhood – be it in studies or in sports. In course of this narration she asked the audience thrice: 'Is there any 'sacred heart' person in the audience???' Somewhat disappointed at no response, she recounted her great learnings from a missionary school named Sacred Heart. A little later a sudden reference to the 'middle path' of Buddhism was made.

Then a comparative negative comment on Hinduism was just about to follow. But somehow she realized that this might be improper. So the sentence finished abruptly in the middle. Another instance of the 'bearhug' syndrome? During December 2007 we came to know an American woman, wearing saris and working in the Vivekananda Polyclinic of the R.K. Mission at Lucknow. She had left California and settled in India twenty years ago. She lived within the campus of the Polyclinic, alone. Finding no answers to her growing daughter's queries from Western religious thought, she had sought out the Los Angeles Vedanta Centre. So captivated was she (an accomplished student of philosophy) by Vedanta that she decided to burn her boats and come to India. One day we asked her what she thought and felt about India after two decades of first-hand experience. Her reply was: 'India now seems to be in a state which resembles that of USA in the 1960s. But the great advantage here is that once your people recover their balance, they will be able to fall back upon so much that Hindu culture has to offer. Unfortunately, the Americans possess nothing like that for support if and when they feel its need.' The Indian woman celebrity, and the American and Japanese women devotees provide telling comparison from the cultural literacy point of view. This chapter therefore, presents another wide-angled exposure of the raw side of non-education and mis-education India has been suffering since her pyrrhic political independence in 1947. Not a few sensitive yet mute Indian citizens, and understanding foreign observers have been feeling that the intellectual air in this country, blown by its myopic educated elite, is thick with homilies and platitudes. They indicate alienation and hypocrisy. Education here has been caught in the chains of perverse politicization (for nearly six decades), and profane businessization (for nearly two decades). And each trend is tilted at its own angle against the mainstream, sustainable, 'core culture' of Bharatvarsha. Cultural dis-empowerment is the name of the game.

II

Swami Vivekananda's vision of *prabuddha bharat** – how near to or far from this status is India today? For the present, and for the near future at least, India has been and will be receding fast from this destiny. After returning from his first visit to the West, a public address by him in Madras had expressed these forthright thoughts[1].

'A negative education, or any training that is based on negation, is worse than death. The child is taken to school and the first thing he learns is that his father is a fool; the second thing that his grandfather is a lunatic; the third thing that all his teachers are hypocrites; the fourth that all the sacred books are lies. By the time he is sixteen he is a mass of negation, lifeless and boneless.' Few are the educators of today, careerists as most of them tend to be, who can make these strong points and say them strongly too. But then, Vivekananda was a legitimate' educator, an *acharya,* par excellence. Quintessentially, as this author perceives the situation, India is at war today against *Bharat*. It is an 'invasion', a 'siege' of a different character. Vivekananda's quadruple salvo, fired at colonized India, more than a century ago, is now being aimed at a much wider front in independent India. The country was not then studded with IITs and IIMs, nor loaded with caricatures of Universities in almost every town, nor with International (?) schools in nearly every street. hour, 100-channel TV programmes were nowhere on the horizon, waiting to prey upon the nation's consciousness. The institutions of home, sacramental marriage, joint family, etc., were still the rule. Mothers and grandparents were still around the child. This source of sound education has dried-up now. Hence, Vivekananda's indictment remains as valid now as then.

The year 1950 appears to mark a watershed in the history of this land. That year its people were gifted with a written Constitution

---

* Prabuddha Bharat, *means 'awakened India'. A journal by this name was launched by him in 1896, and it is still alive. Also, etymologically, Bharat means* bha = jnan, *wisdom, understanding, and* ratah = *devotedly engaged in.*

which started off by saying, 'India, that is Bharat...'. Sacred *Bharat* was thus officially made secondary. Secular India was accorded primary position. The destiny-makers and educators of post-1950 India have been, apparently at least, ignorant both about the genesis of secularism in Europe, and the English dictionary meaning of the word secular[2]. The *Bhagavad Gita* counsel, *swadharme nidhanam shreya, paradharma bhayavaha* (III.35), was given a short shrift. In a hurry to prove allegiance to the secular model, the sacred recommendations of the 1949 Radhakrishnan Committee Report on Education were discarded, e.g., that, in keeping with the tradition of the country, the working day in all educational institutions should commence with meditation. Of course, now that yoga, meditation, etc., have become a sort of fashion, bearing the approval stamp of the West, they are gradually re-entering our outfits. As only to be expected, the original purpose of these sacred processes is lost in such superficial utilitarian, money-making attempts.

III

A few additional recent cross-country experiences of the author are being offered now. They should reinforce the factual basis for the **India Vs. Bharat** thesis of this chapter. Subverting the 'national mind' (as Sister Nivedita had put it[4]) towards a *nirbuddha bharat,* instead of uplifting it towards *prabuddha bharat*, seems to have been the cumulative achievement of post-1950 education in this country. Invited to deliver the opening address at the Annual Meet (1995 perhaps) of an all-India Women's organization, the author had commenced thus: 'Respected mothers and sisters ...'. The audience comprised women only, including the author's wife. The very first point of order thundered by a lady office-bearer of the organization, at the end of the lecture, was: 'Why did you address us a mothers and sisters? Are we not individuals? Would you address a male audience by saying "dear fathers and brothers"?' The speaker stood speechless for some moments. The sincere intent behind the above mode of greeting was then gently explained by the author. But it was difficult to judge if it satisfied her. Let the reader try to imagine the kind and source of educational inputs which would have prompted the above questions and their tone? Their cumulative consequences for the unique culture-type that Bharat is may be contemplated. Fie to Vivekananda's dream of education to nurture Gargis, Maitreyees *et. al.*, Some time in 2006 the author had read an article in the weekly women's page of a popular daily newspaper. Its woman writer argued at one stage: 'Why do we have to be always a daughter, or a sister, or a wife, or a mother, or an aunt and so on? Why can't we be just individuals in our own right?' Is this really what empowering education is about? How would it sound if this author were to ask: 'Why should I be called the eldest son, the eldest brother, a father, a husband, a grandfather?' Does *Bharat* need this brand of education for a progressive society? Duty-centric, affectionate 'net-working' in the home, and caring in the neighbourhood are regressive?

It was February 2008. The author was requested to speak on 'Change Management' at the Annual Conference of a management school. During the mid-morning tea-break one student came up to the author and greeted him with a 'good morning, Sir'. We reciprocated by saying *'namaskar'*, holding up our joined palms. After a few minutes of general conversation the author asked the student: 'Why didn't you greet me with a *namaste* or its equivalent in any of our languages?' The instant reply was: 'Sir, how does it matter? After all we are now living in a globalized environment, in a global village.' We persisted : 'Do you know, young man, that in no other non-English-speaking country, West or East, local people use English words to exchange mutual greetings or farewells?' Though the boy kept quiet, he did not seem to get the point: Loyalty to indigenous, local idioms and manners has not prevented Japan, China or Malaysia to outperform India in most respects. This peculiar Indian malaise afflicts the whole fabric of society – from janitors to CEOs, from VCs to Secretaries, males to females, teachers to students. Sometime in 2006 the author's nephew, then an MA student of Ancient Indian History and Culture, narrated to him this incident: 'The two Indian epics, the *Ramayana* and the *Mahabharata,* constituted 50 marks in one of our papers. In the first lecture-hour for this portion the concerned teacher came only to tell the class: "Look, I have little time to waste on teaching such rotten garbage." This was followed by about fifteen minutes of vilification of the two masterpieces. And that was all that we saw of him during the entire 30-hour duration for the course.' Visualize reader, if you can, a Western Professor abusing *Iliad* or *Odyssey* in a university classroom, and getting away with it, never to return a second time. The author recalled to the nephew the following razor-sharp rebuke of Rabindranath Tagore, figuring in his Foreword to Dinesh Chandra Sen's Bengali book on the *Ramayana*.[5] 'We must ponder with rapt reverence over the manner in which the whole of Bharatvarsha has so fervently embraced these two epics across millennia. However weighty a critic I might be, if my head does not bow before the consistent verdict of a whole ancient civilization, stretching through aeons, then such arrogance is reprehensible indeed.' This then is the characteristic on-going India Vs. Bharat battle.

It was 2003 perhaps. The author was delivering the Foundation Day Lecture at one of the IIMs. The theme was something like this: 'The Relevance of Indian Ethos for Holistic Development'. The lecture had referred, for instance, to the 1906 motto of the National Council of Education: 'Know India, and Love India'. This had been coined by its founding father, Satish Chandra Mukherji – a classmate of Vivekananda and a friend till his Baranagar days. Gandhiji had nearly repeated the same empowering emotion sometime in the 1920s, 'I pray, O' Lord, that I can know my country more; and so can love her more.' These last lines of a prayer-poem are inscribed on a marble plaque in the verandah of Gandhiji's all-purpose room at Sabarmati Ashram.

Needless to mention, by India both of them had meant Bharatvarsha only. Then at question hour one smart boy stood up to ask: 'I don't know in which country I was born in my previous birth. Nor do I know where I might be born in my next. Therefore, what is the point in loving India merely because I am born here this time?' After a while an even smarter girl student queried: 'Why should we call India as "Mother-land" or "Bharat Mata"? Are you not thus trying to create a sort of emotional intoxication – *madakata?*' The author experienced *Gita dhyanam* in reverse: *vachalam karoti mookam*. Let it also be mentioned that not one sincere, positive question or comment came from the 200-strong audience comprising both students and teachers. Readers may contemplate the scene for a while with eyes closed and breath held.

It was the third or fourth annual convocation of an impressively named (in Sanskrit) Centre for management education. A 2-day conference on various academic, business and social topics was also strung around it. Several high profile personalities had been mobilized. The event took place in early April 2008. This author had been asked to make a 30-minute (which was slightly exceeded and for which he sincerely apologized) presentation on 'Leadership – Its Cultural Mainsprings'. A number of illustrations from the annals of pre-1950 industrial and political history of India were shared to amplify the key ideals. The central refrain was to communicate the *rajarshi netritwa* (king-sage leadership) model from Bharatvarsha's 'core' culture. The 400-strong audience of students, teachers, dignitaries and guardians was informed, for example, about Gandhiji's 1925 confession[6].... 'it is an unbroken torture to me that I am still so far from Him, Who, as I fully know, governs every breath, of my life. And whose offspring I am.' He was fifty six years old when Gandhiji had written these words. His mentality as a boy and young man was not any different. Ten years earlier (1915), at a much younger age of 18, Subhas Chandra Bose, in a letter to a friend, had defined his mission of human development as follows[7]:

(i) To be an embodiment of the past

(ii) To be a product of the present

(iii) To be a prophet of the future.

What quality of education must Subhas have received to be able to compose the above triplet? This could very well serve as a benchmark to judge the end-products delivered at the end of today's programmed educational conveyor belts like IIMs, IITs, etc. Did Subhas write off the past? Or, was it not in honour and love of the 'past' that he had utterly sacrificed himself? From industry, Acharya P.C. Ray was recalled. Though a D.Sc. in Chemistry from Edinburgh and Head of the same department at Presidency College, Kolkata, yet he was the pioneering founder of India's chemical and pharmaceutical industry. Such a marriage between academics and industry in one person has been unique in India, and perhaps in the world. In his 1932 autobiography he had written[8]: 'All through my varied activities I had felt the force of the saying, *tvaya Hrishikesha hridisthitena, yatha niyuktohsmi tatha karomi.* I commit myself to Thee O Lord ! 'Make me Thy agent.' A more recent example from the world of business was also touched upon. This was R. K. Talwar who had been the youngest Indian Chairman of State Bank of India, and later on CMD of the Industrial Development Bank of India. He was living the life of a *vanaprasthi* in Pondicherry where the author had interviewed him in 1997. Among the many things he told was this example of true self education: 'Early on I had started reading a Hindi Gita by stealing it from my mother. I was only 13 or 14 then. Nothing used to seep into me. But I persisted. Then it began to grow into me. Ever since, verse II.47 has been the sheet anchor of my life.' An anti-climax was, however, awaiting the speaker. Late in the afternoon one student approached him for some discussion. He began thus: 'Sir, I have two questions. First, why do you lay emphasis on Indian ethos? Second, is not Indian culture a composite one, enriched by other cultures?' We took him aside for a quieter space and briefly responded thus:

(i) Japanese or American students do not question their teacher when he/she gives priority or exclusive attention to the indigenous ethos. But this issue is raised frequently in India. Education in other countries naturally accepts the intrinsic enduring genius oftheir respective cultures, e.g., Confucianism in China, Buddhism in Thailand, Islam in Malaysia. Why not Hinduism in India?

(ii) More practically, a sitar must be played in accordance with the rules and techniques relevant to it. Then only it can give its best. Superimposing the sarod or violin style will not work. This exactly is the argument for Indian ethos (including Buddhism, Jainism and Sikhism) in the Indian context.

(iii) Other cultures from beyond India have indeed contributed to the mosaic of Indian culture. But such contributions are almost wholly extrinsic. And here too much of it is either imitation or imposition. The one honourable exception is the Parsee community.'

The truth that is evaded is this: No culture had ever entered India with love and peace in the heart. Enrichment of India was surely not their objective. Destruction and impoverishment have been the main storyline[10]. Information about such plain facts should be the basis for authentic education in our society which possesses a 'core culture' of its own, with several tributaries flowing into the mainstream. And these flows had not been augmentation alone, as you are hinting. Much has been and is being drained off too. Let us return again to April 2008. The clock strikes 6.30 p.m. in the large banquet hall of a 5-star hotel. The hall is packed with the expectant graduates of a business college waiting to receive certificates and prizes at the convocation ceremony. The event is being presided over by the President of the college. He is an ace retired bureaucrat of the central government. At one time he was iconized as the nation's conscience-keeper. The Chief guest, the guest of Honour, two other Board members, the Director and this author were also seated on the dais. After the Chief guest and guest of Honour had addressed the audience, the certificate and awards disribution ceremony started. And for the next ninety minutes it was a sight for the Gods (or devils?) to watch and hear. The entire student-body (about 350, of which 175 or so were passing out, and the rest the current batch), comprising girls and boys equally, simply let themselves go. Non-stop shouting, whistling, screaming, gesticulating accompanied every awardee being called up to the dais. All this went on in the name of congratulating the successful colleagues.

Such wild behaviour was mutely witnessed by the dignitaries on the dais facing the students. The Director was watching the display with apparent indulgence. Astonishingly, the formidable President of the institution too maintained stony silence amidst the bedlam. Perhaps he had attained the *nirdwandwic* state for a time.

Only the guest of Honour and this author muttered resentment among themselves about this 'new India'. But does old Bharat preserve still a tradition called *samavartan utsav* for such occasions? Is it the hour of taking solemn life-time vows like: *acharya devo bhavah, matri devo bhavah, pitri devo bhavah* etc. Should such a sacred occasion to commit oneself to responsible citizenship have been reduced to such frivolity? Should the President or Director not have reminded them that the convocation ceremony is not a students' fete?

The sample of personal experiences recounted above should have demonstrated the corrosion caused by a 'modernising India' against the deep-structure foundations of Bharatvarsha? It will be fruitful now to glean some insights from the international crosscurrents swirling around Bharat. They will indicate the nature of alien forces conspiring with domestic dis-orientation to dis-empower this nation.

IV

A 1972 UNESCO report on education had thus advised the developing countries[11]: 'Unquestionably, development... implies *a scientific frame of mind.* Developing countries can only achieve their *renewal*... by *integrating science* into their *traditional* cultures, and by integrating *universal thought* into their own life. A culture can only survive by being able to *change* (emphasis added).' Now, every key word or phrase in this patronizing formulation conveys those notions which a few rich nations hold to be sacrosanct. These impositions do not reflect the democratic spirit the report proclaims at length[2]. Elsewhere in the document the reader encounters several other pretentious assertions[13], e.g., 'education as liberation'; 'life-long education'; 'scientific humanism'; 'complete man'; 'biologically unfinished man'; 'learning society'; 'functional literacy'; 'conscious and unconscious sources of behaviour'; and so on. The report also asserts that 'possibilities of *improving* one's mind and acquiring knowledge and culture are increasing[14]'.

Let this be juxtaposed with this tour-de-force a few pages later[15]: '... it is real humanism in the sense that scientific humanism rejects any *preconceived, subjective* or *abstract* idea of man... He depends on *objective* knowledge...'.

For Swami Vivekananda all this would have only meant 'childish prattle'. But this author cannot go as far as that. Yet, the contempt evinced by such a pronouncement about the dispensability of education about the subjective, the metaphysical[16] implies ruling out altogether the lessons from the longest-living, peaceful culture like Bharat – this much we can say. This stance of the report, backed up by insistence upon the use of 'educational technology', gives the lie to its democratic pretensions. The 1972 report was followed up by another UNESCO report in 1996, its title bearing close resemblance to that of the predecessor[17]. Both the titles had, in fact, raised false hopes initially, and so had attracted the author towards them. Fifteen years ago from today this second report had taken for granted that the future would be 'dominated by globalization'. Accordingly, everything it said was, directly or indirectly, in defence of globalization, conceived in Western terms and executed in its favour. To put it bluntly, this 'favour' boils down to an obsession with underwriting the soaring consumption standards of their own people – at deadly cost to the world. 'I need your greed for my greed' is the philosophy that underpins most of the aid strategies for developing countries – especially those related to communication technologies. The following quote from the report substantiates this inference.[18]

> 'Developing countries [should not] disregard the *classic forces* driving growth, in particular as regards their need to enter the world of *science and technology*, with all this implies in terms of *cultural adaptation* and the *modernization of mentalities*.'

Every legitimate educator for Bharatvarsha ought to possess or acquire the clarity and confidence to ask the authors this fundamental question: 'With all the sci-tech forces, classic and modern, at work for the last three centuries, directed by the dominating nations, why is it that Mother Earth today groans under the weight of overdevelopment?' Yet, a few paras later, the report gratuitously advises 'learning to live together in the global village', and then declares that 'culture is steadily being globalized'.[19] Yes–but what is its template?

Who is calling the shots? All this is indeed the ever-tightening 'bear-hug'. Both these UNESCO reports thus seem to be a continuation of the same uprooting, hypnotizing educational strategy which was launched so efficiently by Macaulay in 1835[20]. Even the apparently friendly Max Muller has not been above board in this respect. Both Bharti[21] and Danino[22] have quoted at different times the following words from one of Max Muller's letters to his wife:

'...the translation of the (Rig) Veda will hereafter tell to a great extent on the *fate of India* ...It is the root of their religion, and to show them what the root is, I feel sure, is the *only way of uprooting all* that has sprung from it during the last three thousand years.' Yet, for such a noble motive to 'educate' India towards her death, post-1950 India rewarded the 'scholar extraordinary' by re-naming all the Goethe Bhavans in the country as Max Muller Bhavans! Myopic educators and other such policy-makers seem to be only too glad to accept and accentuate the 'white man's burden', the 'bearhug' syndrome.

The rootlessness of such professionals was faultlessly detected by Richard Gombrich, a Cambridge University professor. He had bluntly told a large audience of intellectuals at the National Library in 1986[23]: 'Most educated Indians know next to nothing about their culture.' However, a culturally-empowered, legitimate educator should be able to refute or demolish the sophistries gleaned above from the two reports by an organization that professes to educate the world, especially countries like India. Some indications are given below:

(1) Economic 'development' is necessary but at the lower endof the ladder for human society. Pursuit of this rung, through 'classic forces', as the highest and the whole for more than three centuries has left a dismal trail of world-wide colonial exploitation, two world wars, apartheid, nazi and communist pogroms, 11th September, Vietnam and Iraq wars, nuclear brinkmanship and double speak, galloping extinction of living species, swelling seas, monetary and sexual license, shattered homes, existential

misery, drugs trafficking and arms trade, juvenile violence, high-tech terrorism, AIDS, etc..[24] The list is long indeed; it could be longer. Have the 'developing' countries been responsible for any of these? So, why lose one's sleep over educating them? 'Hands off ' – as Vivekananda had once roared at Josephine Mcleod for a jeering remark by her about a disciple.

(2) 'Universal thought' sounds hollow in the light of the above milestones achieved by the much-touted 'scientific frame of mind'. And sermonising about it to Bharatvarsha, which had millennia ago declared and since been practising '*vishwam bhavati eka nidam'* (the whole world is one, single nest) sounds almost blasphemous.*

(3) 'Renewal' of developing countries' – what is meant by renewal? Why is not 'renewal' of developed or rich nations even more important? Since it is the latter's world-view and global agenda which have been hastening chaos and catastrophe, why not they undergo 'renewal' by relinquishing their own hubris? Bharat, if not India, has enough to educate them for 'renewal' towards sustainability and sanity.

(4) The 'bear hug' of sensuous materialism is closing its grip by the hour, and enslaving humans with the chain of unbridled consumerism. Needs not dreamt of yesterday are becoming compulsive wants today. Yet the brains behind the reports expatiate on 'education for liberation'! The world does not need such false prophets.

(5) Speaking of 'complete man', yet rejecting outright the metaphysical, the super-conscious, the spiritual, the subjective culmination of man! This shows that the reports hardly know what they are talking about. Yet 'learning' is the first word in the titles of both. The hidden message for Bharatvarsha is: "You 'un-learn' what you have 'realized' for over seven millennia." This is the disempowerment game that is being played out. Legitimate educators have a duty to see through this ruse.

---

* *The spirit of this pronouncement is quite the opposite to that of socalled 'globlisation' of today. It is out to obliternate all cultural variety to anforce ;one market'*

(6) Some of the cumulative, aggregate consequences of 'scientific humanism' have already been cited above. Hence the case for pursuing 'life-long learning' by the people of this land is a nonstarter. Rather, it is the protagonists of such jargons who should go humbly for the 'life-long learning' that man is *not* a 'biologically unfinished' entity. In the scale of physical evolution he is Nature's finished product. He is, instead, a 'spiritually unfinished' entity. They better learn from Bharatvarsha that it is 'spiritual humanism' which alone can justify the privilege of human birth.[25] The sci-tech-driven man is destined to remain an 'incomplete man'. But the reverse is not true. The 'spirit-centred' man, even without sci-tech, has been, is and can be a 'complete man'.

(7) The edicts of 'cultural adaptation' and 'modernization of mentalities', if they are aimed at cultures like Indian, they are misdirected.

To the extent these trends, unleashed by hedonistic cultures, have already penetrated into this country, one should have a clear idea about some of their net practical consequences:

(i) Sacramental marriage gradually giving way to physical companionship.

(ii) Obscene, lewd advertisements.

(iii) Pre-marital sex relationships. (In the garb of 'life-skill education')

(iv) TV, PC and drugs addiction.

(v) Fast and junk food.

(vi) Depression, boredom, violence among teenagers.

(vii) Neglect, maltreatment of aged parents.

(viii) Proliferating old-age homes and baby creches.

(ix) Vanishing habit of reading wholesome literature.

(x) Beauty parades and parlours.

(xi) Inflated egos and fragile or calculative relationships.

(xii) Money, money–sweeter than honey–brighter than sunshine – nothing like money.

(xiii) Desecration of hoary pilgrim centres for commercial tourism. Cultural tourism is an euphemism.

(xiv) Divorce becoming common, often a sign of prestige, etc.

Many more could be added. Legitimate education should be able to recall 'what is honey for someone could be poison for another'. *Sanyam* has been the building block for character education in Bharatiya culture. This means 'freedom from', not 'freedom of ', lower order propensities, *shadaripus*. It is this bastion which is being stormed. The carnal is displacing the transcendental – on the pretext of liberal education.

(8) As for 'global village', there has hardly been a more treacherous oxymoron. By definition a village is 'local'. It has always been a socio-economically decentralized, self-sufficient and selfgoverning social unit. Its members live and die in intimate contact with the earth and sky, and with themselves. Within their boundaries villagers have largely lived truly 'scientifically' because they were free from the 'bear-hug' of 'classic forces driving growth'. So, they did not ravish Nature. Instead, they always managed to weave the subtle and the sacred into the gross and the secular.

V

The purpose of section IV was to capture the *zeitgist* behind the incidents narrated in section II. Fortunately, and hopefully, there are some honest, beyond-the orbit minds in the West too who have been appraising such forces with sane detachment. Many of them have 'educated' themselves about the truth of the world and of Bharat to an extent that should put most learneds of India to shame. They have been conscientiously warning us against the ruinous moves of the powerful nations – both against themselves and against countries like India. Let us get in touch with a few such minds, beginning with the latest (emphasis added).

(1) Ramsey Clark, 2007[26]: A former US Attorney General has remarked, 'I think those who work towards greater globalization and *domination* want the world *psychologically* to think of itself as a community. It makes their *operations easier*:'

(2) J. R. Saul, 2005[27]: Regarding the 'inevitability' premise of globalization and its complementary educational rhetoric, 'there has *never* been a serious thinker in history in any continent who has suggested that *commerce alone could lead civilization*, and once given such prominence, commerce would therefore be capable of leading itself.'

(3) Barbara Hudson, 2003[28] '... the *modernist optimistic idea* that science and rational government can deliver security, prosperity and general well-being has been replaced by a *pessimistic awareness of the ills* brought about by the scientific-rationalist endeavour.'

(4) J. Carroll, 1993[29]: 'Humanism... of Western culture... attempted to replace God by man...Its ambition was to found a human order on earth ...*without any transcendental* or supernatural supports ...man ...is creator and creature in one.'

(5) Stafford Beer, 1974[30]: A British cybernetician who had worked in India during the 2nd world war, 'The *devastation* wrought in the quality of life in the advanced industrial countries by ... the use of *science and technology* is plain to see. Do *developing* countries really wish to follow the same route?' (Compare with the 1972 and 1996 UNESCO reports).

(6) E.F Schumacher, 1973[31]: 'The *problems of education* are merely reflections of the deepest problems of our age. They cannot be solved by organization, administration or expenditure of money... We are suffering from a *metaphysical disease*, and the cure must therefore be metaphysical.' (Compare again with the 1972 and 1996 UNESCO reports).

(7) Arnold Toynbee, 1969[32]: 'It is already becoming clear that a chapter which had a Western beginning will have to have an *Indian ending*... The primary reason is that (its) *teaching is right* – and is right because it flows from a *true vision of reality*.'

(8) Andre Malraux, 1967[33]: 'To the West...the fundamental obvious fact is the *death* ...; whereas India's fundamental obvious fact is the infinity of life in the *infinity of time*. Who could kill *immortality?*'

(9) Aldous Huxley, 1946[34]: 'A viable society is one in which those who have qualified themselves to *see* indicate the goals...., while those who rule respect...the *advice of the seers.*'

(10) Laura Glenn (Sister Devmata), 1927[35]: Education in India 'has not been mere idle subjective theory. There can be no doubt of its *practical validity*, for centuries before the Christian era we find these *wise masters* teaching virtually all the *axiomatic truths* of modern science.'

(11) Margaret Noble (Sister Nivedita), pre-1911[36]: 'Unless we train the feelings and the choice, our man is not educated. He is only decked out in certain intellectual tricks... By these tricks he can earn his bread. He cannot appeal to the heart or give life...Therefore in every piece of information that is imparted to a child we must convey an *appeal to the heart.*'

The above snap-shots from a century-long procession of deepthinking minds of the West should inspire positively all legitimate educators who aspire to re-empower India back to Bharatvarsha. All these supra-orbital, mentally independent observers have been refuting nearly everything that committed establishmentarian outfits like the UNESCO, their forerunners as well as followers, have been thrusting upon us. The 'bear-hug' has not been able to choke these voices of the West.

VI

Over the same century as above we have heard as many voices of warning and caution from within this country too. And they were all 'knowers' and 'lovers' of Bharat. Let them also speak to our legitimate educators.

(1) **Bankim Chandra Chatterjee.** 1894[37]: 'Do not lose your *reverence for the past*; it is on the past that you must plant your foot firmly if you were to mount high in the future. You are not a race of savages who have no past to remember... I have to make my warning so emphatic because the general tendency of European scholars, who have so great an influence over you, is to *decry our past history*, to call for its erasure from your memory and to lead you in the *opposite direction.*' How amazingly accurate, word for word, was this a forecast made one hundred sixteen years ago, about the educational atmosphere today.

(2) **Swami Vivekananda** 1894-1901: The best definition of education this author knows comes from him, 'Education is the manifestation of perfection already in man'[38]. Kidi, an early disciple, was blessed with this gem in a letter to him from America. For Swamiji, 'perfection' had surely meant emancipation from the thraldom of unquenchable sensuous cravings by an abiding realization of the noncontingent and self-fulfilled *atman* as the centre within. Where does education stand today judged against this benchmark? Education(?) about sex and share markets is now being introduced in progressive schools. Why? Because the 'backward' Indian mind has to 'modernize' itself to receive 'liberating' education and become 'complete'. But Vivekananda's verdicts were contrary:

(a) 'Do you not find in history that the first death-sign of a nation has been unchastity? When that has entered the end of the race is in sight'

(b) 'Isn't it man that makes money? Where did you ever hear of money making man[40]?' But he was primitive, not modern. So, sci-tech, secular wisdom declares that the sooner and quicker after birth the child can be ushered into *kamini-kanchana,* the more perfect it shall become. Hence most of our liberated educators and government policy-makers seem to be heart-and-soul behind this redeeming project!

(3) **M.K. Gandhi,** 1908: Comments on the practical implications of western-inspired formal primary and higher education – 'It is not our *kamadhuk* (milch cow for all desires)... it has its place when we have brought our senses under subjection and put our ethics on a firm foundation ... Our ancient school system is enough. Character-building has the first place in it – and that is primary education.' [41]Close hereafter he adds, 'by receiving English education we have enslaved the nation... It is we, the *English-knowing Indians that enslaved India?'*[42] (And now it is being driven to the peak by Am-lish-knowing Indians). Vivekananda and Gandhi had spoken remarkably alike. But progressive saviours know better. They have, by reversing the old order, begun enlightening the younger generation through the *mantra*: 'If character is lost, nothing is lost; if wealth is lost everything is lost'. For, this seems to be the underlying theme song of 'global village'.

(4) **Ananda Coomaraswamy** (early 20th century)[43] : 'It is hard to realize how completely the *continuity of Indian life* has been severed. A single generation of English education suffices to break the threads of tradition, and to create a *nondescript and superficial being* deprived of all roots,... of all Indian problems the educational is the most difficult and most tragic.' Coomaraswamy's crystal-clear assessment begs no gloss from this author. The events cited in section II fully attest to Coomaraswamy's grave forebodings.

(5) **Rabindranath Tagore,** 1919[44]: 'India has proved that it has its *own mind*, which has deeply thought and felt and tried to solve according to its own light the problems of existence. The education of India is to enable this *mind of India to* find out truth,...and to give expression to it in such a manner as only it can do.' Alas for Tagore ! Were he to live now, he might have revised the key sentences as follows: '*Bharat* had proved that it had its own mind... The education of *Bharat* was to enable this mind of *Bharat*...' He, for sure, was meaning 'Bharat' while mentioning 'India'. India today is crippling this mind of *Bharat* in every detail.

(6) **Sri Aurobindo,** 1919: (a) '...if there is a subordination and servitude, the inactive and weaker culture perishes; it is *swallowed up* by the invading leviathan';[45] (b) If we '... "take over" anything, the good and the bad in it will come in together pell-mell. If we take over for instance that terrible, monstrous and compelling thing...*European industrialism*...we may under more favourable conditions develop by it our wealth and economic resources, but assuredly we shall get too its *social discords and moral plagues and cruel problems?*'[46]

Sri Aurobindo's categorical warning about social discords, etc., has now begun to materialize through the imitative propagation of rights-orientation in homes and educational outfits.* This mentality is rupturing the cohesiveness underlying our society through the age-long practice of duty-orientation.[47] The much-criticised caste system never really militated against such cohesion and cooperation, until it began to be politicized during British rule. Our own rulers have now given it full play for votes.

And then alien, modernistic intellectualism has been adding its share of fuel to the fire. Justice Rama Jois, as we have just discovered, had strongly supported our duty-based design of social functioning. Here are some of his forthright views: 'This basic value, which establishes or national identity and distinction, has been overlooked since independence. This, in fact, has been, over the years, the root cause of our several national problems because it replaced the sense of duty by mere consciousness of the right.' In other words, flouting of the wisdom of the *rishis* that 'duties are the cause, rights the effect' has been a major cause of India's disempowerment on many fronts. Section III has already marshalled some insights into the current manoeuvres of the 'leviathan' Sri Aurobindo had anticipated long ago. Urban Indian elite has surrendered to this 'leviathan' its 'human right' of cultural identity. Section II and portions of section III have offered some glimpses into the 'social discords', 'moral plagues' and 'cruel problems', as forewarned by Sri Aurobindo, that are already deluging us. However, due to its depth, spread, and past momentum, our cultural identity continues to live in the vastnesses of rural India. But the recent *mantras* of 'rurbanization', 'rural marketing', and all they imply, sound ominous. Electronic, audio-visual mass media have already begun to storm these hinterlands of relatively greater contentment, peace, happiness and morality.

Thus, in course of his convocation address at an IIM (March, 2009), a respected figure in Indian IT industry, and in sci-tech generally, was exultant about VISION 2010 of achieving 500 million mobile phone connections, coverage of 85 percent of the country by mobile networks, a mobile penetration rate of 90 percent, exciting developments awaiting the rural telephony market etc. All this, he declared, promised to bridge the 'digital divide'. So-called rurbanization, as evidenced by farmers' cooperatives selling their lands to set up their own industries, may spare no oasis for scorched humanity. And perhaps soon enough not even adequate food for the urban belly. The reader might choose to listen again to the words of Clark, Saul, Hudson, Beer and Schumacher in section V above.

VII

This chapter winds up on the following notes from Swami Vivekananda who had expressed these thoughts sometime towards the end of the 19th century.[49]

(a) 'Social life in the West is like a peal of laughter. But underneath it is a wail, it ends in a sob... Now, here it is sad and gloomy on the outside, but underneath it are carelessness and merriment.' Taking the cue from Swamiji, it may not be impertinent for a legitimate educator from India to ask: Despite the proud claims about stupendous amounts of psychological research in the West (e.g., UNESCO Report, 1972, pp. 109,117-8), can Vivekananda's verdict be challenged today for even a single word?

(b) 'Shall India (meaning Bharat) die? Then from the world all spirituality will be extinct, all moral perfection will be extinct, ..., all ideality will be extinct, and in their place will reign the duality of lust and luxury as the male and female deities, with money as its priest, fraud, force and competition its ceremonies and the human soul its sacrifice[50].'

The serious reader may update these forecasts of both Aurobindo and Vivekananda from 'Sleeping on the job' - (*Times of India* - 12.3.2006) and 'Miserable? Bored? You Must be Rich' (*The Daily Telegraph* - 13.11.2007).

Word for word, metaphor for metaphor, these prognostications of our modern seers have been proving to be flawless diagnoses about the present ills. It is a challenge for legitimate educators to be able to perceive that, tragically, today's fake India is becoming the death-dealer to yesterday's true Bharat.

The majority of our high-powered literates who formulate and execute educational policies belong to two groups: (a) the noneducated, (b) the mis-educated. They are ignorant about the transorbital, supra-scientific facts and truths of our national culture and other world cultures. There is also a third category (c) the educated ones who opt for opportunistic silence or advocacy to promote their career objectives. They are probably the most harmful. For they, knowingly and willingly, tend to become accomplices in a global scheme to dis-empower Bharat from the roots. They welcome the 'bear-hug'.

---

* *The country has recently launched an 'Indian Institute of Human Rights'. Shall we ever have a 'Bharatiya Institute of Human Duties'?*

The hour for a fourth category has therefore arrived — those who understand this mischievous game, and possess the courage to stand up for Bharat. They should be prepared to pay some personal price for it. They ought to be convinced that such loss, if any, will be more than offset by the true blessings of all the great souls of the recent past, if not those of the *rishis* of the yore. Shall the latter be let down by their descendants (recall our *gotras*)?

For the commencement of such re-empowerment from our own roots little hope lies in the organized manufactories of degree holders. Pump-priming must begin in our homes and apartments. Each such social unit should aim at becoming a mini-*gurukula*, a *grihastha-ashrama*. Bharatvarsha has been an *ashramic* culture and civilization.

Its root principles have to be revitalized. Parents will need to become the gardeners, the *acharyas* of such *ashrams*. *Naanya pantha vidyate ayanayah*. For such responsibility shouldered conscientiously, the Divine guarantee of *yoga kshema vahamyaham* should be the unfailing conviction. Let them feel inspired. And inspire, in turn, their children. The country is in dire need of a lofty sense of cause, of a high cultural mission pervading our educational outfits. It must transcend the selfish, money-making ego buzzing around the *rajaso-tamasic shadaripus* (e.g., greed, lust, vanity, envy, etc.)

The goals and hopes just highlighted are of course still a far cry. For, the 'bear-hug' seems to be getting tighter than ever before through the new 'genetically modified' breed of International Baccalaureate Schools. The February 2010 in- flight magazine of a private sector airline informs that 65 such 'gm' schools exist now, charging annual fees upto ` 1.2m. per student. Most of them belong to business houses. That 77 per cent of the population lives on less than ` 20/- per day (Arjun Sengupta Committee Report, 2008) matters not. Piano lab, horse riding, rifle shooting, 24/7 WIFI, swiming pool, AC class rooms, interactive white board, amphitheatre, observatory etc. are some of their facilities. 'International' perspective is what parents want for their children, and are willing to pay for it. Sitar or sarod, flute or shehnai, bharat natyam or odissi, meditation room or prayer sanctuary–all such stuff is excluded. They must be too 'national' to figure in the ' gm'. IBS's. Nalanda was not international[51], nor was Tagore's Vishwabharati *

Sister Christine, a German–American disciple of Vivekananda, and Sister Nivedita's self-effacing co-worker, must have been out of her wits to have expressed these emotions a century ago.[52] 'Our love for India came to birth ...when we first heard Sw. Vivekananda say the word India. ...Ever after, India became the land of heart's desire. Everything concerning her became of interest – became living. ... And so began a new life, a life of study, of meditation. The centre of interest was shifted.' Heaven may know what character elite India will acquire after the 'gm' IBS's have done their job. Will the likes of Sister Christine feel anymore the impulse to shift their 'centre of interest'?

References

1. Vivekananda Swami; *Complete Works*, Advaita Ashrama, Kolkata, 1982, Vol. 3, pp. 301-2.
2. Chakraborty S.K. and Chakraborty, D; *Spirituality in Management*, Oxford University Press, New Delhi, 2008, pp. 3-4.
3. Quoted in *Philosophy and Practice of Education For India*, ed. S.K. Chakraborty: Sri Aurobindo Samiti, Kolkata, 2006, p. 30.
4. Nivedita Sister; *Hints on National Education in India*, Udbodhan, Kolkata, 2005, pp. 29-30.
5. Quoted in *Philosophy and Practice of Education for India*, op. cit., p. 16.
6. Gandhi M. K.; *My Experiments with Truth*, Navjivan, Ahmedabad, 1972, p. xii.
7. Bose Subhas Chandra; *Collected Works*, Netaji Research Bureau, Kolkata, 1967, vol-III, 201.

---

* *Blows to the nationalistic sentiments of the silent majority await them just round the corner. Thus, in February 2011 we noticed four long banners hanging from the ceiling of the revamped D-1 terminal check in hall of the 'International' airport in New Delhi. Three of them displayed quotations from T.S. Eliot and one from Henry Miller. Imagine, if you can, a similar scenario at Beijing or Narita or Bangkok airports! How tragic! Kalidasas, Tagores, Bharatis et. al., get no chance or pride of place in their own motherland (Mind you, plenty of English translations of their works are available). Again, it is the Thai Airways hostesses who welcome you aboard with a folded palms 'namaskar', but not their counterparts in secular India.*

8. Quoted in *Culture, Society and Leadership*. eds. SK Chakraborty and D. Chakraborty, ICFAI University Press, Hyderabad, 2006, p. 6.
9. *Ibid, p. 285.*
10. See Dutt, RC, *The Economic History of India*, vols.-I and II, 1987, Publications Division, Govt. of India; Will Durant, *The Story of Civilization*, Simon and Schuster, New York, Part I, 1954, p. 463.
11. UNESCO, *Learning To be*, Paris, 1972, p. 91.
12. *Ibid., pp. 70-80.*
13. *Ibid., p. 141, p.142,p. 146, p. 155 and 158, p. 157, p. 160, p. 154, p. 141.*
14. *Ibid., p. 137*
15. *Ibid, pp. 146-147.*
16. *Ibid, p. 147.*
17. *UNESCO, Learning : The Treasure Within, Paris, 1998, p. 14.*
18. *Ibid, p. 15*
19. *Ibid, p. 16.*
20. Quoted in 'National Education : Problems and Prospects' in*Philosophy and Practice of Education for India*, op. cit., pp. 102-3.
21. Bharti B. D; *Max Muller- A Lifelong Masquerade*, Era Books, New Delhi, 1992, pp. 163-4.
22. Danino M and Nahar, S; *The Invasion That Never Was*, Delhi; The Mother's Institute of Research, 2001, p. 24.
23. Gombrich R; *The Telegraph*, April 4, 1986.
24. Chakraborty S. K. *Against The Tide*, New Delhi, Oxford University Press, 2003, chapter 7.
25. Aurobindo Sri; *The Synthesis of Yoga*, Pondicherry, Sri Aurobindo Asharam, 1988, pp. 5, 7-8, 11-2.
26. *The Hindu*; November 17, 2008.
27. Saul J. R. *The Collapse of Globalism*, New Delhi, Penguin, 2005, p. 18.
28. Hudson B; *Justice in The Risk Society*, London, Sage, 2003, p. 43.
29. Carroll J; *Humanism: The Wreck of Western Culture*, London, Fontana, 1993, pp. 2-3.
30. Beer S. J; *How Many Grapes Went Into The Wine,* England, Wiley, 1994, p. 321.
31. Schumacher E. F; *Small is Beautiful*, New Delhi, Radhakrishna, 1977, p. 92.
32. Toynbee A. J; Foreword to *Sri Ramakrishna and His Unique Message*, Swami Ghanananda, Kolkata, Advaita Ashrama, 1969, pp. viii-ix.

33. Malraux Andre; quoted in *Indian Mind- Then and Now* by Michel Danino, Auroville Press International, Auroville, 2000, pp. 73-4.
34. Huxley A; *The Perennial Philosophy*, London, Flamingo, 1994, p. 260.
35. Devmata Sister; *Days in An Indian Monastery*, Chennai, RK Math, 1975, pp. 108-9.
36. Nivedita Sister; *Hints on National Education in India*, Kolkata, Advaita Ashrama, 2005, p. 24.
37. Quoted in Danino's *The Invasion That Never Was*, op. cit. pp. 143-4.
38. Vivekananda Swami; *Complete Works*, Kolkata, Advaita Ashrama; vol-4, p. 358.
39. *Ibid., p. 101.*
40. *Ibid., p. 455.*
41. Gandhi M. K; Selected Works, Ahmedabad, Navjivan 1968, vol. 4, p. 184.
42. *Ibid., p. 185.*
43. Quoted in Danino's *Indian Mind- Then and Now*, op.cit., p. 62.
44. Tagore Rabindranth; *The Centre of Indian Culture*, Kolkata, Viswabharati, 1988, p. 1.
45. Aurobindo Sri; *The Foundations of Indian Culture*, Pondicherry, Sri Aurobindo Asharam, 1998, p. 439.
46. *Ibid., p. 438.*
47. Chakraborty S. K. and Chakraborty, D; *Human Values and Ethics*, Hyderabad : ICFAI University Press, 2006, pp. 84-91.
48. Jois M. R; *Human Rights and Indian Values*, New Delhi: National Council for Teacher Education, 1997, p. 14.
49. Vivekananda Swami; *Complete Works*, Vol. 8, 2006, pp. 261-2.
50. *Ibid., Vol. IV, 2005, p. 348.*
51. Garten J. E; 'Really Old School', *New York Times,* December 9, 2006.
52. Extracted from a quotation of hers in the backcover of *My India, Eternal India* by Sw. Vivekananda, RKM Institute of Culture, Kolkata, 2008.

CHAPTER 5

SCIENTIFIC TEMPER: A Clinical Probe

ऋतं वदन्नश्द्युम्न
वदन्त् सत्यकर्मन् ।
(ऋ:-९/११३/४)

Declaring the Law,
Splendid by Law
Declaring Truth,
Truthful in Act.
(*Rig Veda* 9/113/4)
(*Ibid.*, p. 293)

I

This chapter engages in a rigorous scrutiny of India's educational scenario from a different angle. It argues for the fostering of 'right temper' (RT) first*. RT is the abiding willingness to prioritize the sacred and the subtle, and then to judge the value or dis-value of all thoughts, things and acts in the secular, material sphere in the light of the former. 'Scientific temper' (ST), so far as popular usage goes, may then be cultivated as an adjunct, an ally to RT. If ST undermines RT, then brakes should be applied to ST. This ST should be distinguished from 'scientific methodology'. The latter has for ever been a universal process as much for the ***mantra-drashta rishis*** in ashrams, as for the physicists, etc., in laboratories. Swami Vivekananda, a perfect model of RT, had thundered thus in London (1896)[1]. "Take the world as it is; sit down calmly and as comfortably as you can and be

* In the text RT will mean 'right temper' or 'right-tempered', and ST 'scientific temper' or 'scientific tempered'.

contented with all these *miseries*. When you are driven around like *slaves*, say you are free. Day and night tell lies to others and to your own soul...."

'This is what is called *practical wisdom*, and never was it more prevalent in the world than in this *nineteenth century*. ....We cannot hide a carrion with roses ; it is impossible.' (emphasis added) 'Miseries' above primarily mean man's internal, existential afflictions. 'Practical wisdom' is what science and technology, business and politics (STBP) thrust upon us. The metaphor 'roses over carrion' conveys the shiny deception that hides the dark side of present social and educational strategies. The visionary warning of Swamiji has palpably failed to make any dent on the educational policies and institutions of 21st century India. Below therefore, follows, a quick stock-taking of world-thought from several courageous and incisive minds of the East and the West across a century.

A few personal experiences of the author have also been included. The teacher will thus realize that several no-nonsense thinkers have been consistently smelling the stinking 'carrion', and signalling us about it. They have, in effect, been challenging the increasingly brazen call for wanton living by STBP. This call is now a hundred-fold more strident than it was in 1896.

As a starter we may get a little foretaste of the rapidly swellingmass of 'carrion' from a June 2008 report in the *New York Times*[2]. 'The *loosening of financial inhibitions* has meant more options for the well-educated, but more *temptation and chaos* for the most vulnerable. ... They have been less socially conscious about *money* and *debt*. The *agents of* destruction are many... Fifty-six per cent of students in their final year of college carry *four or more credit cards*.' Similarly, the advent of television in India in the mid-seventies marks a watershed in informal education.

Its explosion to date, powered by STBP, has been a confirmation of Swamiji's fears about 'lies' and 'enslavement'. A letter to the editor of *National Geographic* (July 2008) goes like this: 'What a sad commentary: The violence and misogyny of American gang culture has been successfully marketed, presumably through TV and internet, to the youth of Bhutan, one of the most isolated nations'. Imagine then the vulnerability of the English-knowing youth of India.

Sometime in September 2000 we had seen on display a book titled somewhat like this: 'Education in India – The Disputed Territory'. The contents page showed chapters on the educational projects of Rabindranath Tagore, Mahatma Gandhi and others. Intriguingly, however, those of Swami Vivekananda and Sri Aurobindo were omitted. Looking carefully at the jacket it was discovered that the author was a professor at a high-browed Central University. Probably for this erudite scholar the two latter personalities were too spiritual to be considered as 'scientific-tempered'. Coincidentally, while revising the draft of this chapter we came across another recent instance of such secularist allergy. This time it was a Nobel winner[3]. Possibly for such emancipated souls (if they have a soul!) even to utter the latter names could be a sin. Pradip Bhattacharya, a redoubtable bureaucrat and *Mahabharata* scholar, was recently dealing with the genesis of *Vande Mataram*.

He had referred to an address by Sri Aurobindo wherein the hidden message of the song was captured in a most profound and unique way. Bhattacharya had concluded his piece with this ardent appeal:* 'Can we pledge on the 15th August to *immerse* ourselves in India's heritage that spans body, mind and spirit – the entire gamut of human existence, and thus lift our Mother out of the maelstrom of imitative life that is sucking her in?'

This indeed should be the highest prayer, the deepest yearning of all *legitimate* educators in India. But just the opposite has been happening through the mis-directed, secularized, self-serving scientific temper of the powers-that-be. Recall the agonizing fiasco over the celebration of the centenary of Vande Mataram just two years later in 2006.

Whatever little has just been sampled constitutes a blue-print of the contextual milieu of education brewing from *within* the country. Another critical contextual dimension is impacting from *without*, in a uni-polar world. From behind the facade of world-organizations like the UNESCO, UNDP, United Nations Universities, etc., the few rich and powerful countries are craftily imposing 'new improved' philosophies, methods, models and technologies of education on the rest.

---

* 'The Need of the Hour', *Shraddha*, August, 2004, p. 9

Non-thinking educators and policy makers in India are avidly supporting their implementation, often perhaps by selling their conscience. In pre-independence days many bright and enterprising Indians used to go chiefly to Great Britain for higher studies and returned to India with re-doubled love, respect and self-sacrificing idealism for their country and culture. Gandhiji, Sri Aurobindo, Netaji Subhas are just a few names in this class.

But in the post-1950 era the flow has diverted itself towards North America, USA chiefly. While learning was the earlier principal motive when students went to Europe, today money is often the prime motive for crossing the Atlantic. And coming back after completing one's studies, etc., has become an exception. Such is the lure of lucre among most new generation careerists. Of course defensive rationalizations to hide such desertion are aplenty.* Another dubious feature of the educational context in India is the prevalence of English as the medium of instruction at all levels. This factor does not act as opium in other Asian countries like China or Japan. The English language in India has no doubt been a stimulus in many ways. But beneath the veneer, as many sensible people are now realizing, this legacy is turning out to be a real bane than a true boon. The English-educated Indian mind is probably the easiest entrydoor for all sorts of untested, harmful 'practical wisdom's storming in from clever cultures. The population of 'Indian Body, Western Mind' people may be growing at a rate faster than that of the population as a whole. Compared to such softness and vulnerability if the Indian mind, the Japanese and Chinese minds have been much more self-assured and circumspect. They have not allowed their deepstructure cultural temper to be fiddled with at will by the so-called ST mind of the English-speaking world. It is important to bear this fact in mind. There must be a vital clue in this reasoning if the performances of China and India in the 2008 Olympics are compared – the glorious versus the dismal .

These are but a few broad signs, constituting a kind of initial sketch of the pattern of education in post-1950 India. Given this

---

* We have to recall Sri Aurobindo's advice to the students of Bengal National College on the eve of his resignation in 1907: 'You will go abroad...sothat you may bring back knowledge to do service to her.

backdrop, the dominant focus below will be on a critical examination of the issue of 'scientific temper'(ST). The many-sided explorations will revolve around two main sources: A recent 'international bestseller' by two Western scientists, one of them being a Nobel physicist of 1977; and an even more recent paper by an Indian scientist of international repute. The purpose is to appraise whether their key ideas embody 'right temper' (RT), over and above merely 'scientific temper' (ST).

II

The first work is a book which promises *Order Out of Chaos* (1984), authored by Ilya Prigogine and Isabelle Stengers.[4] (Hereafter it will be cited as the P-S book). Because of our non-scientific (not un-scientific) background, we have tried to sift the major ideas of the book by concentrating on Alvin Toffler's Foreword and the authors' Preface, Introduction and Conclusions. An efficient way to acquaint the readers with the essential features of ST presented in these portions of the book could be to highlight a series of formulations which have appeared as striking to this author[5] (emphasis added).

1. *Dissection* is one of the most highly honed *skills* of Western science. But the task of putting the pieces together again is *forgotten*.
2. Accelerated social change is characterized by *disorder, instability,diversity, disequilibrium, temporality, time-obsession,* etc.
3. The P-S book claims that the next revolution in science will be a *new dialogue* with nature and society.
4. The universe gets *better* organized as it ages.
5. *Irreversible* processes are the source of Order.
6. *Chance* and *necessity* are partners in destiny.
7. Science and technology are *getting closer* than ever.
8. Bio-technology and information technology promise to change our lives in a *radical way*.
9. Vision of nature will change *radically* towards the *multiple, temporal* and *complex*.
10. Is not science a communication with nature? Nature responds to *experimental interrogation*.

11. *Surprising success* of modern science has led to an *irreversible* transformation of our *relations with nature*.
12. Science initiated a *successful dialogue* with nature.
13. *New* science will give *objective* meaning to Life, Destiny, Freedom, Spontaneity, etc.
14. An automaton needs an *external* God.
15. *Meta-physical* view of nature is *anti-scientific*.
16. *New* view of matter– not passive, but associated with spontaneous activity.
17. A *new* type of order has appeared (bio-systems).
18. *Chance* and *necessity* both essential to describe non-linear, far-from-equilibrium systems.
19. *Man* is altering his natural environment on an *unprecedented* scale – creating a '*new nature*'.
20. Leitmotiv of this book– the question of the relation between *being* and *becoming*, between *permanence* and *change*.
21. *Irreversibility* is the mechanism that brings *order* out of chaos.
22. The most irreversible process accessible to the human mind – the *progressive increase* of knowledge.
23. Society has a wide spectrum of *Cognitive Techniques* – so science can do *poetical interrogation* of nature – active, manipulating, etc.
24. Now we are bringing *earth to heaven – by transiting towards the* temporal *and the multiple*.
25. *Classical psychology* dealt with conscious, transparent activity. *Modern psychology* engages in the opaque functioning of the unconscious.
26. Due to profound change in the scientific concept of nature, need for *new relations* between man and nature, and man and man.
27. We are living in a *dangerous* and *uncertain* world that inspires no blind confidence.

It is hoped that the reader would have been able to study with patience the above snippets from the P-S book. So we may now offer some point-by-point, non-scientific or even supra-scientific reflections on the claims implied by them from a commoner's perspective.

- If 'dissection' has been the forte, the *swadharma* of four centuries of 'old' science, unleashing social 'disorder', 'instability', 'dis-equilibrium' etc., then what is the assurance that 'new' science will create Order? Besides, it would have been more honest not to say 'forgotten', but to admit that science is 'incapable' of joining up the pieces. Significantly, Bohm (a Nobel physicist) and Peat (henceforth called the B-P book) had conceded in 1987 the essentially 'fragmenting temper' of science. This innate tendency had caused scientists to miss out the unforeseen *negative* consequences from fragmentary modes of thought.
- Points 3, 9, 10, 11, 16, 17, 22 and 26 contain repeated allusions to 'new', 'irreversible', 'radical', 'revolutionary' (a marked fascination for such words in the book) relations between science-nature, man-nature, and man-man. Of them at least two striking observations of P-S appear to be:

(a) Nature responds to 'experimental' interrogation;

(b) 'Surprising success' of modern science in initiating irreversible transformation of man's relations with nature.

Such narcissistic claims prompt one to ask: What about 'experiential communion' and 'adoring reciprocity' between Nature and man then? We need to approach a Valmiki, a Kalidasa, a Wordsworth, a Tagore to be educated about these processes. A person sunk in sorrow or dejection has turned, and will continue to turn, to these RT personalities. Tagore's *Gitanjali*, not Einstein's *Relativity*, will provide him/her with existential succour, even though both deal with Nature. The botanist *analyzes* the rose objectively. The poet *realises* the rose subjectively. The former need not tresspass into the realm of the latter. Point 23 proclaims the capacity of science to do 'poetical interrogation' of nature through 'cognitive techniques'. Tagore, on the other hand, tells us: 'A flower is nothing when we analyze it, but it is positively a flower when we enjoy it. This joy is real because it is *personal*.'[7] If ST were to suggest us to treat Tagore's words as sentimental froth, then it would reveal their bankruptcy of 'right temper' (RT). (Incidentally, P-S have a few approving words for Tagore in the book [8]).

- Points 5, 7, 11, 12, 19 and 21 may now be clubbed together. *First,* it is hard to fathom what PS mean by science having initiated a 'successful dialogue' with Nature. It is said that the proof of pudding lies in its eating. Leave alone the *rishis* and *yogis* of the days of yore. Numerous Western thinkers, even top notch scientists, who are able to view things from beyond the orbit as it were, are heard now to voice strong reservations about this claim. As we see it, there has really never been a 'dialogue' in the first place. Science has been 'interrogating' alright (not decently often). And interrogation is not 'dialogue'. This is not quite a mark of 'success'-ful relationships.

Second, 'man's' alteration of natural environment is not a correct statement. It is the sci-tech and business politics (STBP) nexus which has been committing this aggression. The rest of common humanity is a helpless victim of such assaults. *Third,* 'creation of new nature', obviously by sci-tech coming closer together (points 7 and 19), has not been explained in the PS book. Such an assertion only causes greater apprehension, even fear, in the common man. For, he is already aware of the several irreversible disturbances and damages which have been afflicting this earth e.g., from ozone layer holes in the Antarctica (2 million square miles in area vide a Nasa news report in September, 2000) to global warming, from extermination of species to dwindling of genetic diversity, from nuclear waste to electronic waste, etc., etc. The simple-minded man-on-the-street, not yet drugged into amnesia by propaganda, fails to see any order or success in all this. Another anguished letter had appeared in the *National Geographic* July 2008. 'Something is missing regarding the construction of the Large Hadron Collider: benefit? ... the LHC does not appear to offer one practical benefit for mankind. Oddly, it took an army of curious scientists years and undisclosed millions of dollars to think up an experiment they are totally in the fog about. ...'

- Daniel Quinn voices truth in his bitingly satirical novel *Ishmael*. This book had appeared nearly ten years after the P-S book. Ishmael, the Gorrila-guru in the novel, is the hero. He says[9]. 'In Taker* mythology the world needed a ruler because the gods

---

* The novel dwells at length on the duel between the Takers-ethos of 10,000 years, and the Leavers-ethos preceding it by a few million years (pp. 41-2).

had made a mess of it. What they had created was a jungle, a howling chaos, an anarchy. Was it that in fact?' 'No, everything was in good order. It was the Takers who introduced disorders into the world... Mankind was not needed to bring order to the world.'

- Science, classical or modern or post-modern, is not conscious of the perennial principle and fact: When, out of pride, man's fractional, objectivising intellect and rationality try to be too smart with the Universe, irreversible damages are inevitable. 'Human mind is an inveterate divider of the Indivisible' – as Sri Aurobindo had put it aphoristically.[10] Sri Ramakrishna had made this very point through his characteristic home-spun simile: Can a one-litre bottle hold ten litres of milk? Whether science accepts this truth or not, the Universe and beyond is the projection of a Transcendental Integral will with operates with Infallible Intelligence. It is not a causeless accident.

The *rishis* and true prophets had realized this Truth by resolutely purifying themselves of their separative ego. The result was true dialogue and communion, and also respectful co-existence with Nature. Creating 'new nature' was not on the agenda of these suprascientific, RT personalities. They were not automatons in need of external god (point 14). *They were Consciousness-personified who had realized Godhead in full measure within and without. Their *ashrams* and *tapovans* were never meant to 'interrogate' Nature, and to misread it. They had educated humanity to live and learn in harmony with 'given Nature'. Of late a few honest scientists like John Wheeler (a physicist) have begun to admit: 'One has the feeling that the thinkers of the East *knew it all,* and if we could only translate their answers into our language, we would have the answers to all our questions.' The basic spirit in this testimony is well-taken. But 'translation into our language' is a rather facile suggestion. First; 'thinkers' is not the right word; 'realizers' is correct. There is a world of difference between the two groups. *All realizers are thinkers too, but few thinkers are realizers.* Second, the very act of authentic

---

* They had attained supramental perception of God both within and without. The 'statistical terrorism' implicit in objectification (13), and the rejection of the metaphysical (15) constitute infringement of basic human rights.

translation presupposes adequate preparation and attainment of realizational Consciousness. Even the most superlative thinking power cannot accomplish this task – by itself. *Third*, P-S have claimed that matter being spontaneously active is a 'new view of matter' (point 16). This claim goes too far. The suprascientific realizers have repeatedly said that in the ultimate analysis nothing is insentient, passive – even a grain of sand. But leaving this aside for the time being, it should be recalled that JC Bose had, at the beginning of the 20th century, demonstrated 'objectively' that even metals experience fatigue, even plants have emotions. That is to say, such non-human members of Nature are also endowed with consciousness. So, the whole of Nature responds or reacts to whatever man does to her. Such has been the RT informing the rhythm of daily living in Bharatvarsha.

- It may be in order to mention here an experience of ours at a Tokyo conference in 1998. A certain UN body had sponsored it. We were explaining the above point in a small group of participants. The moment we finished, a British participant snubbed us rather insolently saying that our reasoning was an exercise in solipsism. We had another opportunity to present the idea before a larger plenary audience in the afternoon. Here too, even before halfway through the allotted time, the Canadian coordinator suddenly snatched away the handmike from our light grip. We were left stunned. The international audience of sixty or so kept mum. So, this is the general character of ST. Wheelers are exceptions.

Fourth, the P-S book speaks about other profound themes also like being and becoming, permanence and change, necessity and chance etc. (points 18 to 20). Poor as we might be in our capacity to comprehend, we have failed to extract anything meaningful about these notions from the book. Bewilderment goes high when the book ends with a 'dangerous and uncertain world' which 'inspires no blind confidence' (point 27). Following the long train of brave, new ideas quoted earlier, these closing words sound anti-climactic. It is possible to link such a denouement to a couple of ideas already extracted from the P-S book – point 13. 'New science' is expected to give 'objective' meaning to Life, Destiny, Freedom, etc. This is a staggering speculation of ST crossing all sane limits. It implies that human existence in the scientific world will be stripped of its 'subjective' characteristics altogether. No wonder then that it has to be a 'dangerous world', inhabited by 'automatons' only. On the other hand, in point 24 we are told that the earth is being brought to heaven through the highway of the 'temporal' and the 'multiple'. Once more the authors deny us the RT education of the ancient *ashrams* that 'Heaven' partakes of the Eternal and the One. But for ST Change is all, no Constant at all. Phenomenon is all, no Noumenon at all. The movie film is all, no stable white screen at all. The RT'd Swamiji offers invaluable education on this issue.

(a) 'We cannot conceive change without there being something *unchangeable*;'

(b) 'We are bound to admit that there must be something which *never changes* at all;'

(c) 'The *noumenon* is not something different from the *phenomena*, but it is the very noumenon which has become the phenomena;'

(d) 'The *whole* must be *unchangeable*, because there is no other thing besides it in relation to which change would be possible.' Thus, the ST'd learning implied by the P-S book, that 'Heaven' should also incorporate earthly 'temporality' and 'multiplicity' as its keynotes, is seriously flawed. No wonder then that the 'dangerousness' and 'uncertainties' of the earth shall invade Heaven also. The existentially miserable man will thus be denied his last solace and refuge.

A 'heaven' built on *apara vidyas*, scientific-empirical education, will end up as a 'hell'. RT education, on the other hand, will begin with *para vidya*, Transcendental learning, and thereafter incorporate *apara vidyas* in measured doses. Such education shall assuredly know when and where to stop.

Fifth, in the light of the flawful theoretical paradigm of the P-S book, the intention to 'change our lives in a radical way' sounds ominous (point 8). Shall such radical (technological) ways amend man's alienation from his Eternal Beingness, from his pedestal of the Infinite? RT'd education should prompt this crucial question: Why should man allow himself to be continuously manipulated as 'object' in the mindless sci-tech game? As we shall see below, there is hardly any evidence over the last four centuries or so to show that man has become inwardly more peaceful and happy through sci-tech advances, compared to the pre-scientific era. Therefore, why should he trust
116 the so many 'new' states and conditions postulated in the above

book? Readers may be informed that quite a few people of our age group have shared with us this secret aspiration of theirs : 'Enough is enough. All we want is— return to us the Kolkata of the 1950s.' Yet, 'radical changes' have been abundant during this timespan e.g., TV since the 1970s, cell phones since the 1990s etc. etc. Why are they already tired of them?

For the time being, the last idea that merits comment is this P-S thesis: The need for 'new relations' between man and nature, and between man and man (point 26). The reader is again left in a quandary. In the past, successive advances in sci-tech have been associated with utilitarian exploitation of Nature for human comfort and indulgence, and with world-wide colonization by powerful nations. Thus, the record of sci-tech-driven man-Nature and man-man relationships has been shameful. Without any clarification about the adjective 'new', it is difficult therefore to take this exhortation from P-S on its face value. Since they repose sole faith in 'cognitive techniques' and subconscious psychology, and deny the supra-cognitive, super-sensuous level of integral understanding, their thoughts do not qualify for RT education.

- This rather lengthy probe into the P-S book has been warranted by the fact that it has come to be regarded as an influential work. Much research in economics, education,,etc., is said to have sprung from it. The English-educated Indian mind, generally gullible and imitative as it is, might very well leap into converting its alluring but dubious pronouncements into educational policies and practices in India. With no prior grounding in RT and *para vidya*, the seduction of ST jargons could be irresistible. Indeed, it is already at work.

III

By this time some progressives might have construed our thoughts as regressive or obscurantist. It should be useful therefore to present now some appraisals from RT men of sci-tech in the West itself.

- Weizenbaum, a leading MIT computer scientist, had remarked (in a 1986 conference in Mumbai, two years after the P-S book) as follows[14] (emphasis added): 'Perhaps modern science's most *devastating* effect is that it leads its believers to think it to be the *only legitimate* source of knowledge of the world. This must sound very strange here in India. 'Of course as many other speakers have remarked, the whole human race is in an extremely *dangerous* situation. '...when one accepts that God is intelligence, *not love*,...then the extinction of the human race becomes an acceptable end. 'As perhaps the most highly developed intelligence in the universe, we have now succeeded in creating our truly worthy successors: *computers*. They will be able to *reproduce themselves*. We have the tools of destruction in our hands, but we have sent computers into timeless, endless space. And thus having fulfilled our destiny, we have no reason to grieve over the *probable death* of our species.' This then is a scientist's estimate of the sci-tech-dictated, *apara vidya*\based milieu of human existence. In the light of this backdrop, the P-S proclamation, 'From Earth to Heaven – The Re-enchantment of Nature', rings as a hollow hyperbole[15]. It is a wonder why the word 'Heaven' was used at all. Moreover, unintelligible comments on or about God lie scattered at several places in the book[16].

- Almost fifty years earlier to the two contending perspectives cited above (that of P-S on one side and that of B-P, Quinn and Weizenbaum on the other), a Nobel laureate in medicine and surgery, Alexis Carrel, had aimed primarily at those who are responsible for rearing and educating children i.e., school teachers, hygienists, physicians, social workers, judges and politicians. (Curiously, the list does not include parents). The Preface of his book had launched a frontal assault on the material and machine sciences. It alerted the readers that they 'have not understood that our body and *consciousness* are subject to *natural laws*, more obscure than, but as inexorable as the laws of the sidereal world. Neither have they understood that they *cannot transgress* these laws without being punished.'[17]

What a contrast between the tall claims in the P-S book, and the candour in Carrel's Preface.

The concluding para of this Preface goes on to urge upon the readers 'to understand the *necessity*... of the *overthrow* of *industrial civilization* and the advent of another conception of human progress[18].' Later in the book Carrel cautions scientists about the *whims* of scientific discoveries, about the flaw that 'science follows *no plan*', about its dependence on '*fortuitous* conditions', about its being '*not* at all actuated by the desire to improve the state of the human being.'[19]

These charges against science are followed up by indictment of *technology* too: it produces *unexpected*, strikingly *different* results compared to the *hoped* for effects. With but a few exceptions, seventy five years later, the Carrelian criticisms are generally and universally irrefutable. It is remarkable too that the index at the end of Carrel's book (1935) contains as many as thirteen entries for 'consciousness', while that of the P-S book (1984) contains not a single. This fact itself raises suspicion about the relevance of such recent books for education about RT. Rather, it comes close to Swamiji's intuition about 'hiding carrion with roses'.

- We should return again to Ishmael-the-Gorrila. Here is a pungent dose: 'The world was made for man to *conquer and rule*, and under human rule it was meant to become a *paradise*. This clearly has to be followed by a "but.".... This is because the *Takers* have always perceived that the world was far short of the paradise it was meant to be... They wanted to turn the world into a *paradise*, but being human, they were bound to *screw it up*.... by *stupidity, greed, destructiveness* and *shortsightedness.*' With due respect to P-S, will the large package of 'new's in their book be able to regain the paradise lost by Takers through sci-tech etc.?* Incidentally, while doing all this blunt-speaking, Gorrila-the- guru was taking his student through an 'educational journey'[22].
- This phase of critical probe could profit by listening to Tagore again, a RT personality in the fullest sense of the phrase. After all, his long life was a saga of ceaseless loving communion with Nature, and of passionate love for humankind. His 'successful dialogue' with them required no experimental or even poetical 'interrogation'. No wonder, therefore, that he could bestow 'deep comfort', and also shed light upon even some of the baffling scientific dilemmas of Werner Heisenberg. This Nobel scientist was the poet's guest at Shantiniketan in 1929.[23] Much earlier, during 1916-7, Tagore had expressed these views before an American audience[24]. 'Our scientific world is our world of *reasoning*... We are ready to pay homage due to it. But when it

* One might recall here John Milton's satan in 'Paradise Lost' who had characterized hell as 'in the lowest deep a lower deep'.

claims to have discovered the *real* world for us and laughs at the worlds of all simple-minded men then we must say it is like a *General grown intoxicated* with power, and usurping the throne of his king. For, the reality of the world belongs to the *personality of man*, and not to reasoning which, useful and great though it be, is not the man himself. Not only the world but God Himself is divested of reality by Science, which subjects Him to *analysis* in the aboratory of *reason*, outside our *personal relationship*, and then describes the result as unknown and unknowable.'

It is doubtful whether the P-S book, which has frequently alluded to 'relationships', approaches anywhere near the exalting sentiment conveyed by Tagore's pregnant adjective 'personal'. This only highlights that unless one nurtures the emotional capacity to go beyond the orbit of logical theorems and mathematical models, RT shall remain elusive. The authors cited earlier in this section have also been extra-orbital, in their own ways, to speak of existential human concerns earth. So, for educators here is a critical choice: To go for the P-S orientation of post-modern or 'new' Science, or to embrace the pristine Tagorean paradigm anchored in personalization?* Which temper has a better potential to bring out 'the perfection already in man', and to eliminate the 'carrion' that Swamiji had seen through?

- As this chapter has been contending so far, it appears to be well-nigh impossible for most professional sci-tech people to ascend beyond their constricted orbits, and take a detached and 'true' (not 'new') view of the seemingly impressive ideas in the P-S book. Here is one more exceptional instance of detached and true view from a thinker with RT – Aldous Huxley. He too had written a grimly satirical novel (much like Quinn) in 1932, three years before Carrel.[25] After Hiroshima, Huxley had added a Foreword to this book in 1946. Advances of scientific research in biology, physiology and psychology, accompanied by rapid technological changes, would trigger economic and *social confusion*, he wrote. This will be accompanied by *stretchings and amputations* of mankind by applied science – of a far more

---

* When the P-S type of left-brain, noisy 'research' wishes to supercede right-brain, silent 'realization', all-round human misery can only increase.

drastic kind than in the past. Mankind will be educated for '*love of servitude*' by sci-tech maintaining *silence about truth*. Here is a whipping sentence towards the close of the Foreword: 'In a few years no doubt, *marriage licences will be sold like dog licences*, good for a period of twelve months, with no law against changing dogs or keeping more than one animal at a time.' Thus, Swamiji's 'carrion' had become very much a reality, not a mere figure of speech – as early as 1946. Add the two letters of July 2008 in *National Geographic*, quoted a few pages earlier, and a complete update since 1896 is available. Sixty-two years after Huxley had voiced these supra-orbital, hence far-sighted warnings, 'a legitimate' educator aspiring to cultivate RT could go back to the long list of P-S pronouncements of the STvariety, and arrive at his own philosophy.

IV

Quite a number of leading Indian intellectuals and sci-tech personalities feel ashamed and apologetic about the lack of 'enlightened citizenship' (EC) in the country. Several of them are influential members of various committees on education and allied matters. Their weighty ST opinions often find their way into school textbooks, clubbing many indigenous traditions, customs and rituals under an omnibus derogatory term 'superstition'. Brahminism is often the alleged villain of the piece, and is duly flogged. JV Narlikar (JVN), an eminent contemporary Indian scientist, has recently expressed his disappointment about the 'rising trend towards superstitions', despite much effort to spread ST in post-1950 India.[26] Consequently, progress towards EC has been tardy – according to him. He has cited several deplorable superstitious incidents of recent times to support his thesis. Before dealing with some of these incidents, it is necessary to clarify the meaning of the phrase EC. JVN's article implies that elimination of all that he deems as superstition would usher in EC. Surprisingly, the whole ground of ethics, morals, human values, civic virtues, etc., etc., is left out from his purview of EC. The subject is not viewed by him in terms of mounting civic chaos, filthy corruption in all compartments of society, libidinous sports and advertisements, promiscuity in campuses, indulgence to baser instincts in the name of entertainment, hiving off the responsibility for old parents and children to third parties, and so on. It is hard to understand how ST can choose to be tight-lipped about such ruinous and wide-impacting aspects of what we may call *negative citizenship* (NC). Perhaps such silence really means ST can draw only a blank along this flank. RT alone has the wherewithal to pick up the challenge. Education against the alleged superstitions, in the light of RT, might then have a minimal role only. And that too would tend to be of a positive kind. Some details are in order. Among the so-called superstitions which, according to JVN, are deflecting India from the path of EC are horoscopes, astrology, *vaastushastra, sati,* drinking of milk by Ganesha idols and the like. Feeling much upset about such 'un-scientific' stuff, our author goes on to expatiate on the 'miracles of science' which 'benefit all' . The response to this line of ST reasoning can commence with some of the RT thoughts Swamiji had expressed in New York in 1895:[27]

(a) 'You ought to remember that there is a worse *popery* coming than ever existed in the church — the so-called *scientific popery* which has become so successful that it *dictates* to us with more authority than religious popery.

(b) 'We are *bound to follow superstitions* all the time – old, hoary superstitions, either national or belonging to humanity in general– superstitions belonging to family, friends, to country, to fashion, to books, to sex and to what not.

(c) 'It is *very hard* to believe in reason and to follow truth. This whols world is full either of the *superstitious,* or of *half-hearted hypocrites.* I would rather *side with* the superstitious and ignorant, than stand with these half-hearted hypocrites. *They are no good.'*

The first retort by Swamiji (popery) recalls Tagore's metaphor (intoxicated General) cited earlier. His second point correctly affirms that to be 'superstitious' (belief in the mysterious or the super-natural) is a constitutional element in the human design. Is it *also not a superstitious* belief among ST people that increasing doses of sci-tech will make for peace and *happiness* — even though all cumulative evidence is to the contrary? Swamiji's third quote states emphatically his values-based choice: to side with the ignorant believer than with the hypocritical skeptic. The 'technoxicated'[28] ST person forgets to apply his 'reason' in tracing the evolution and intent behind what he calls un-enlightened superstitions. The chief difficulty for the majority of Indian intellectuals and sci-tech leaders appears to be the lack of 'understanding' (not surface knowledge) about 'Hinduism as a way of life'. Take, for instance, the 'Ganesha idol drinking milk' episode of about two decades ago. Its epicentre was a temple in the heart of Mumbai – India's most modern metropolis. The entire English press had unleashed a torrent of ridicule, even abuse, against the widespread public response to this phenomenon. A few days after this journalistic tirade had subsided, *The Statesman* had reprinted a longish article from the London *Times* contributed by one of its past editors, William Rees Mogg.* He had these lines: It has demonstrated the spontaneous capacity, the live sensitivity of a whole people to such extraordinary events. A feel for the super-natural, the cosmic, the inscrutable, the non-rational is very much an active ingredient in the natural Indian or Hindu mind An older metaphor from Sri Ramakrishna may be recalled as a parallel to Mogg's evaluation : the Hindu mind (regarding the super-natural) is like a 'dry match box' – ignitable at first strike. The relevant RT question is this: Did this un-enlightened, superstitious behaviour of so many people cause any harm or damage to any aspect of the environment (e.g., emission of carbon dioxide), or to any non-participating segment or member of the society? Are the selfish corrupters of the social fabric, from mercenary doctors to manipulative financiers, not to speak of politicians and so on, more 'enlightened' than these believing masses? Let us note again point (c) of Swamiji. Even if the allegation that some mischievous priests might have been playing tricks on the people were granted, why focus only on the trick and the trickster? Why not, instead, leave the chaff and collect the grain: The innocent and simple collective mind of the Hindu which can still quickly soar beyond the mundane tangle of desultory daily existence into the realm of the sacred. At any rate, let us not forget that we the ST citizens do often pay handsomely for a magic show of pure deception by the professional magician .

Similarly again, the alleged abominable tradition of *sati* (*sati-daha* to be correct). The original name for this tradition is *saha-marana*. This means voluntary self-immolation by a chaste wife coinciding with the demise of her husband. Forced burning of unwilling widows is diabolical and unacceptable. *Sati-daha* implies this cruelty. But *saha-marana* is charged with a sublimity which the contemporary mentality misses. We have read several mythological, historical or biographical accounts which reveal the true spirit of this tradition. The eminent historian Radha Kumud Mukherjee, for instance, informs

---

* It is regretted that the exact date could not be given.

us about the intent of Harshavardhan's sister Rajyasri to perform self-immolation which he did not allow. Earlier, his mother Yasovati had done so, against strong resistance by her son, by saying, 'Not to die, but live at such a time would be unfeeling ...'[29] Similarly, we learn about Ahalya Bai's resolve for self-immolation at the death of her unworthy husband. But her father-in-law persuaded her to desist from this act. And she went on to become a legendary queen.[30] In the *Mahabharata* too we see queen Madri doing *saha-marana,* following the demise of Pandu. In the Ramayana too we have the example of the widow Shabari. She had waited in penance in the forest for years to have a *darshan* of Shri Ram. When at last her *tapasya* was rewarded with Sri Ram's appearance during his exile, she expressed her resolve for self-immolation. Lakshman was asked by Ram to prepare the pyre to honour her wish. Sometime in the 1980's a young widow (Roop Kanwar) had performed voluntary self-immolation in Rajasthan. This event had evoked a flood of criticism from the English press and great commotion in the Indian Parliament.

A few weeks after the great outburst *The Statesman*, had again published a two-part article by an American research scholar on the whole issue.* He was Patrick Harrigan, then working in Sri Lanka and India. His analysis of the ntire drama was a vivid illustration of Swamiji's charge against the 'new popery' and the 'half-hearted hypocrisy' of the leaders of politics and ST in India. Their sole objective was, according to Harrigan, getting a little back-patting from the patronizing West. This colonized Hindu mind has not yet recouped its freedom even after thirty years of the Rajasthan saga. As against the extremely rare occurrence of such an event, the frequency of diabolically executed female murders in high society today is alarming. Do these incidents go well with EC? Idealistic *saha- marana,* once in a while, is therefore not a matter of shame. Foul murders, regularly at

---

* November 5-6, 1987. In a follow-up article in the Statesman on January 5, 1988 Harrigan had hit out again at the 'alienated' and 'privileged elite' of urban India, asserting that they had no right to 'judge' village India. 'The greatest aberration of all that Indian civilization has ever had to face is the invading mentality that covertly subverts traditional values at the same time that it ridicules them. Why should it need a foreigner to remind you of this?' – was Harrigan's wrenching cry, passionate query. Indian intelligentsia and educators may care to listen.

that, are. ST has to set right its appraisal of traditions which it chooses to frown upon in a huff.

The reader may be interested to know that Swamiji, in his ninevolume *Complete Works,* seems to have made but one short critical comment on *sati.*[31] Scanning of the indices has indicated this.

Moreover, our continuous study of the many writings of abindranath,* Gandhi and Aurobindo has not detected any evidence of their being haunted by this tradition – RT as they were. Teachers have a duty to educate pupils about the supreme ideals underlying such traditions, and open their eyes to the deadly sores in modern life. JVN also assails the tradition of consulting horoscopes to decide about the compatibility of would-be marriage partners. The practice of considering the positions of stars and planets at the moment of birth, death, etc., is also debunked. In support of his rejection of such alleged superstitions, a 40-year old American statistical study has been quoted. This is irrelevant evidence. What eludes the ST of our enlightened thought-leaders is the following capital insight: It is the theory and philosophy of Cosmic-human inter-relationships, a corner-stone of the planning and organization of Hindu society, which is concretized by these methods, and thus integrated into all aspects and phases of secular life. (Recall the claims of P-S about 'new' man-nature relationships!

Sanatan Hindu culture did not disabuse itself of the inscrutable yet unbreakable reciprocity between Cosmic Nature and human nature. This supra-scientific integral view of total existence has been immaculately captured in verses 3.11-14 of the *Bhagwad Gita.* The central note here is that of *saha-yajna* – a mutual process of loving, sacred benedictions from the supra-human, Divine or Cosmic powers, and the grateful acknowledgement and reciprocation of such bounties

---

* In fact a 42-year-old Tagore, in 1902, had offered obseisance to those grandmothers of yesteryears who had partnered their way all through, even to the moment of death of their husbands. They ascended voluntarily (though not everyone) the funeral mount as a newly wedded ride. They could transmute the pyre into the nuptial bed.
Thus was eath made beautiful, benign and blessed by them (Rabindra Rachanavali, Bengali, Vishwabharati, 1986, vol. 3, pp. 675–6. Rendered into English by the author).

by human beings. This is indispensable education for RT. Only then the aggressive and exploitative proclivities of ST and sci-tech could be abated. It is a unique duty and privilege of only the human species to receive and practise such saving education.EC would flourish naturally thereafter.

On the practical side, we recall our college days in the early 1950s. During these years our octogenarian grandmother used to insist, much to our annoyance for curtailing our 'free will', on consulting the almanac for auspicious dates and times before starting off for any out-station journey. Much of this choice would also depend on the direction of the destination from the starting point. Today we can appreciate how these injunctions did not allow human movements to be cut off from Cosmic movements. Moreover, her insistence contained as much of concern for our safety and security, as may be for her authority. They also gave us some subtle training in restraint about undue hurry and instant gratification. Similar is the enlightened logic underpinning the observance of various *vrats* and *upavasas,* both on a regular basis e.g., (*ekadashi, amavasya, poornima*), and on special occasions e.g. (*shiv ratri, janmashtami, ramnavami, vijaya dashami, pongal, onam,* etc.). One of the unique *vrats* is that of *chandrayan.* Here the individual gradually increases the quantity of food consumed during the bright lunar fortnight, and then slowly reduces it as the dark lunar fortnight advances. This is enlightened 'man-Nature' relationship at its practical best. But unfortunately it is 'old'.

Swami Brahmeshananda's recent article is a useful delineation of the deep, enlightening import of the various *samskaras* spanning all phases of the life of a Hindu man or woman.[32] JVN's essay attributes to *vastushastra* too a superstitious character. One of the widespread rituals in Bharatvarsha is the performance of *bhoomi pooja,* earth worship, before starting any building construction. This may be taken as one simple lesson from *vaastushastra.* It is laden with profuse meaning for exalted 'man-Nature' relationships. But ST is too impatient to understand or appreciate the worth of these concrete processes. Not a hint of such practical aids is available in the P-S book. It has only empty words for this aspect. Although not mentioned in the above JVN essay, observances during eclipses and *shraddh* ceremonies are also ridiculed by modern ST.

A full solar eclipse was experienced in India in 1995. Around 9.00 hours, when the eclipse had just ended, we had stepped out of home towards the main road for the workplace. The entire residential locality was steeped in serene silence. Vehicles were yet to begin to ply. The shop shutters were down. Not even the birds did chirp or fly. The atmosphere was like that of an early dawn twilight. Even more gripping was the stillness when we reached the main road— a busy state highway. No buses or trucks were roaring along the road. Scores of vehicles were parked on both sides of the highway. No vendors had come out yet, hawking their wares. Pedestrian traffic was scarce and quiet. Back at home, the fireplace was not lit up, nothing was eaten, leftovers of the previous night's dinner were given away to stray cows or dogs or birds. The inmates hardly spoke for the whole duration. Those who could, went to a nearby river to take a holy dip. What does all this convey? The transcendental insight and creativity of the RT social architects of ancient times had seized upon such a rare Cosmic phenomenon, and ensured that its mysterious grandeur received the reverential attention of people lost always in the sterile routine of daily living. The Cosmo- Human nexus was nourished through a Cosmo-centric set of regulated behaviours (derisively spoken of as empty rituals). As usual, English newspapers were pouring scorn on these traditional practices for days together. The ST people and institutions seemed to turn the event into a kind of big scientific jamboree, a carnival. Painfully watching all this shortlived scientific euphoria, accompanied by denigration of the enduring sacred tradition, this author had written an editorial protesting about all this in an internal newsletter published by his institution. Within a few days about forty left-leaning academic colleagues of the author shot out a signed complaint letter to the Director about this editorial. They sought chastisement of the editor, proscription of the newsletter, and shutting down of the newly inaugurated Centre for Human Values.* This much then for open-minded, liberal ST ! We realized that secular, leftist fundamentalism and persecution could be as nasty as any other.

---

* This Centre, financed entirely by donations, was born out of the courage and vision of Dr. Subir Chowdhury, the – then Director of IMC, supported by Dr. S, Ganguly, Chairman BOG. Shri L. N. Jhunjhunwala, Chairman Bhilwara Group, was the first donor and had continued to be a mentor in many ways. The most munificent support came from the House of Tatas, piloted by Shri Ratan Tata,with great spontaneity in the spirit of nishkama karma. The author is indebted to them, and to all the other donors as well.

The Director asked us to give a written reply to the grievances in the complaint letter. A point-by-point response was supplied. The Director then copied it to all the signatories. The latter had to swallow their own venom. But the undercurrent of hostility and ostracism continued in many ways till the author retired. This seems to be ST at its unscientific nadir.

As for the *shraddh* rituals, this author being the eldest of the five brothers, has had the privilege of performing them for many years. Given the right attitude and feeling, we can vouch for the amazing power of sacred, practical creativity of our *shastrakars*. The comprehensive and profound symbolism inhering in the various steps and acts (for about three hours) serve to renew one's awareness about the unbroken relationship between the physically departed and the physically living. Existence is not mere physical body. Not only for one's own parents and ancestors, but for other deceased relatives or friends who have left no progeny, even for the deceased pets and domestic animals *pindas* (boiled rice morsels) are offered. The essence of the entire process is three-fold: expressing *gratitude*, seeking *forgiveness*, and wishing *well-being* to the subtle entities of the physically deceased. What more enlightened or new man-man relationships, founded on concretely emotional processes, can books of the P-S kind or essays of the JVN-kind offer?

It is RT education to listen to Swamiji once more at this stage (San Francisco, 1900)[33]. 'We believe in *all the superstitions* that ever existed. But there is no superstition in the world that does not have some *basis of truth*. If I cover my face and only the tip of my nose is showing, still it is a bit of my face. So with superstition– *the little bits are true*.' The following is an illustration of Swamiji's truth. The *Times of India* (June 6, 2005, Ahmedabad) had reported on the details of a Saurashtra village performing *shuddhikaran yajna* (purifying sacrifices). For five decades this 2500-strong village had been in the throes of 'unrest, discord and lack of socio-economic development'. The villagers *believed* that the land on which it was built was 'impure' as they had recently discovered human skeletons while setting-up the village. Perhaps a battle had been fought here at some point of time in the past, making the land 'impure'. Hence, all the intractable problems. So the entire village was evacuated, and a four-day *yajna* was undertaken under the supervision of eleven *shastris* or priests. The youth and the village leaders had organized round-the-clock vigil for the empty village on all the four days. For re-entry a new *pravesh dwar* (entry gate) was built according the *vaastushstra* rules. The first sentence of the report read: 'Saurashtra and Superstition are Synonymous'. The 'halfhearted' reporter is entitled to his sneering tone about the process. By the same token, the author too is entitled to his respectful opinion: The episode vividly demonstrates how a whole village community had put into action the sacred law of 'Cosmic-human interdependency'. No one was harmed in any way. Only some good came out of it – gradual return of amity and solidarity among the households. The urbanized modern ST mentality has no substitute for such constructive RT mentality. Were the villagers enlightened citizens or not?

The essay being alluded above has also rebuked the UGC for recognizing astrology as a subject of study. Sri Aurobindo had turned the argument the other way round* : 'As a matter of fact astrology has never been scientifically disproved' any more than 'constant failure of doctors to heal diseases proves anything essential'. Rejecting the a-priori arguments against astrology, Sri Aurobindo had recounted quite a few crucial events in his own career wherein the astrological forecasts had proved precisely accurate. He had noticed 'the great mass of un-inquiring prejudice which now exists against it'. This, prejudice, he declared, is 'itself based on the 'superstition' of the all-sufficiency of the new method which really applies only to a limited field'. About the empirical, factual veracity of astrological predictions, this author too has had a few personal experiences. Concern with astrological data and inferences has been a component of the '*sanatan* way of life' for ages e.g., Kautilya's daily time table for the King includes time for astrological consultations by Chandragupta I.**

Sri Aurobindo lifts the whole purport of *shastras* to a level of superb clarity (emphasis added). 'Shastra does not mean a mass of customs, some good, some bad, unintelligently followed by the customary routine mind of the *tamasic* man. Shastra is the knowledge and teaching laid down by *intuition*, *experience* and *wisdom*.... the *best standards* available to the race. The *half-awakened man* who leaves the observance of its rule to follow the guidance of *his instincts*

---

* Culled from SABCL, 1972, vol. 17, pp. 285–9 and vol. 22, pp. 467–8

** Detailed in Spirituality in Management, by S.K. Chakraborty and D. Chakraborty, OUP, 2008, pp. 184–5.

and desires, can get pleasure, not happiness. For, the *inner happiness* can only come by *right living*.' The following key lessons emerge from the above extract:

(1) Shastras have sprung from pure intuition cultivated by selfless well-wishers of society (*sarva bhuta hite ratah*);

(2) The mistaken assumption that every one knows what is good or right for one's own well-being, the refusal to admit that one is 'half-awakened';

(3) The perverse modern temper that higher consumption and greater wantonness, not 'right living', bring happiness.

Thus, between them Swamiji and Sri Aurobindo effectively refute that philosophy of enlightenment which JVN's essay tries to advocate. His type of ST will be a poor substitute for RT in our laudable quest for functional citizenship. Civic sense and discipline, and public morality are never in question however.

V

Exultation about the 'miracles of Science' which 'benefit all' is another feature of the JVN-article. In part, upto a point, this is alright. But how such miracles 'benefit all' is not clear. For instance, how have man-landings on moon (since 1969), etc., benefitted us? Satellite communication has enhanced the ease, volume and speed of human interaction. But has all this been beneficial for all? Are we not becoming the victims of dissipative and dangerous over-communication? What about the pollution of space by the increasing quantity of debris from defunct satellites? These are the irreversible harmful effects: the debris emerging with varying time-lags, out of almost all sci-tech miracles.

At any rate, the dig at the miracles by *yogis* is uncharitable. The correct way to assess their feats is to understand them from the existential standpoint. Help in the vast domain of existential miseries cannot come on a mass scale. It must be individualised here. This author, like many others, bears personal testimony to the unlimited range of physical, psychological and spiritual benefits people (including the most literate and enlightened ones) have been deriving from yogic miracles. Back to 'miracles of science'. A sort of sample score-card about the debris that come trailing behind these miracles may be offered (emphasis added):

1. A. Carrel (a Nobel Scientist-1935)[35]:

'The sciences of *inert matter* have led us to a country which is not ours. We have *blindly* accepted all their gifts. 'We *must break* the frame of the *school*.... and *reject* the very principles of technological civilization. 'We must *liberate* ourselves from *blind technology*.'

2. P. Sorokin and W. Lunden (1969)[36]

'*Sensate culture*...intensely cultivates scientific knowledge of *sensory reality*. ...It is also quite successful in making a legion of *technological inventions* aiming at increasing the *bodily comforts* of sensory life.'

3. AJ Toynbee (1976)[37]

'....elementary science sufficed to secure the survival of our species. The enormous subsequent advance has been *superfluous*.... and it may actually end in the *self-destruction* of man. 'The *poorness of ethical performance* is made ... *humiliating* by its contrast with the brilliance of our technological performance. '*Human dignity* cannot be achieved in the field of *technology*... It can be achieved only in the field of *ethics*.'

4. B. Griffiths (1976)[38]

'The more we explore the physical universe and the further we extend our control over it, the further we move from the Centre in which .... truth is known,... Science and technology... when they *forget their source* (centre), they lose their meaning and lead to *disaster*.'

5. J. Rifkin (1980)[39]

'Each attempt at *forcing order* with highenergy *technology* will only *speed up the chaos*. Genes will be manipulated to create new forms of renewable energy or to cure disease or to raise IQ; but in the process, the *evolutionary wisdom* of billions of years will be irreversibly *destroyed*. 'Completely divorced from nature, our *urbanized intellectuals* have really *no insight* into our true relationship to our *environment*. (In) our high-energy culture... we have *no* real chance to become *enlightened*.'

6. M. Wilkins (Nobel scientist) (1986)[40]

'The world view engendered by science is in many ways a *very undesirable* one because it focuses attention on the material aspects of life and on *technological solutions* to human problems. I think this is *very bad* for human attitudes.'

7. D. Peat (1987)[41]

'It seems to me that the more science and technology develop, the *more dangerous* the whole situation is becoming.'

8. R.R. Ernst (Nobel scientist) (2000)[42]

Ernst quoted these declarations from the address of a former US secretary of State,.... "the first settlements *beyond our galaxy* will have occurred by 2500, we will have left the *solar system* by 2200, we will have permanent colonies on moon, mars, etc., by 2100." Thereafter Ernst sighed: 'If such a vision is representative of the American majority, *then good gracious.* '

Some readers may recall a September 2000 NASA report that the ozone layer canopy above the Antarctica had developed a hole about 2m. square miles in area. This is four times the geographical area of the USA. An article of February 2007 (in *National Geographic*) had reported that in less than one hour rainforests covering an area as much as four football grounds were being felled along the Amazon basin in Brazil. This was connected with growing soyabean for cattle feed to yield more milk in Europe.[43] In June 2008 a newspaper report informed the Indian public that the GOI had launched a large research project to verify the harmful radiation effects upon the users of cell phones. Such instances of sci-tech debris could be cited almost endlessly. They constitute pathetic examples of 'marry in haste, repent at leisure'. Of course, great noise and publicity accompanies subsequent shows of ST by mounting so-called 'research' projects which only confirm the earlier warnings of RT people.

The renowned cosmologist, Carl Sagan, had headed a group of thirty leading scientists (no Indian) in 1990. They had appealed to the religious leaders to commit themselves (with scientists) to stop 'the self-inflicted, swiftly moving environmental alterations', which 'represent a trap for the human species, amounting to *crimes against Creation*'.[44] It is a baffling mystery how the leading lights of ST in India continue to simply ignore these issues.* Our religious-spiritual

---

* Some years ago a good Danish Professor-friend had suggested us to appeal to the Templeton Foundation for some financial help to our entre for Human Values. Back came a condescending reply asking for 'data' and 'proof '! The matter was dropped there, for, the culprit had turned plaintiff.

leaders also prefer to stay mute about such life-and-death matters. Some of them often speak or write, going overboard with glee if a Western institution or writer happens to refer to Om or Consciousness. The day for Indian philosophy and spirituality is won — so they think — succumbing often to deceptive lip-service. Perhaps the reader's patience has been taxed a little too much.

But there seemed to be no better way to make him or her aware of the grave fears many RT, extra-orbital thinkers of the West itself have been fearlessly voicing over a pretty long time. We could have gone back even earlier to listen to such honest scepticism from the horse's mouth as it were. Each and every inference or interpretation of this author in the previous pages could be checked against the above set of quotes. The portions in italics could also be understood as categorical denials of the tall claims about 're-enchantment' and 'enlightenment' made in the P-S book and the JVN-essay.*

- It may now be useful to concisely recount here a couple of personal encounters with leading figures in the world of Indian sci-tech. During our presentation at a Human Values Conference in 1996 at Geneva, the author had said that 'human values' spring more from the soil of feelings and emotions of the heart, not so much from intellect or reason in the head. The session had been chaired by a high profile sci-tech personality who held many top positions in various government ministries and institutions in India. In course of summing up he rebuked the author in the plenary forum declaring that it was 'superstitious' to state that feelings emanate from the heart. The heart is only an internal blood-pumping organ. Emotions are a product of the brain cells in the head. As we were later mulling over this public reprimand, it appeared to carry two 'scientific' lessons for an ignoramus like us: (a) to write off the bulk of world's poetry, music, literature etc. (b) to henceforth say 'a kind-headed woman', or 'a broken-headed lover', or 'they had a head-to-head talk over a heady meal' etc. etc.

Is common humanity so sub-standard compared to our brilliant sci-tech liberators? Or, does Vivekananda's charge of scientific 'popery' stand fully substantiated? The apex national council of one of the.

---

* All the quotations above, when distilled for their essence, remind us of the saying: 'The operation was successful, but the patient died'.

largest and oldest professions of India had constituted an Ethics committee in 2002. It was chaired by a former Director of one of the IIT's. This author was also picked up as a member. In the first meeting practically the entire time was consumed by the Chairman in explaining his grave concern about how to save the professionals in this field from the possibility of 'double jeopardy'. In the next meeting some initial time was spent in deciding about those foreign countries whose corresponding ethical codes could be procured quickly. We sensed that, as usual, the efforts of the Committee would boil down to cutting-and-pasting borrowed stuff. Then suddenly the Chairman decreed: 'No references to any ideas from religious sources would be allowed during our deliberations on ethics.' Members were left stunned by this abrupt ordinance. After the meeting was over, the author could recall the following words of Einstein spoken in 1951: '... a *positive aspiration* and effort for an *ethical-moral configuration* of our common life is of over-riding importance. Here *no science can save us...* The cultivation of this most important spring of moral action is that which *is left to religion*'; and '... the independent and fundamental definitions of goals and values remain *beyond science*.'

Incidentally, this second meeting was the last one we had attended. Mahendralal Sarkar might well be regarded as the doyen of institutionalised science in India. He had launched the Indian Association for the Cultivation of Science in 1876. It has, however, been a great surprise to recently discover his condemnation of the Hindus and their belief systems. This denigration is matched by his fulsome praise for the physical sciences. In his view they have helped to raise man to 'the sublime rank of master of nature', and to achieve his 'conquests over her vast domain'.[46] In this sense, Mahendralal would seem to have been a forerunner of the present-day myopic scientists. Presumably the former had expressed such euphoria about ST before he had come into intimate touch with Sri Ramakrishna during 1885-6 as his chief personal physician. Acharya (Sir) P C Ray, a D.Sc., in Chemistry, a professor, and the founder of the Indian Chemical and Pharmaceutical Industry, however, is one bright example of RT in the midst of the ST people just cited. Here is one of his remarkable testimonies (1932)[47] 'Whatever field I have ploughed I have ploughed as an *humble instrument* in the hands of Providence. My *failures* are my own... But my *successes*, if any, are to be attributed to the *guidance* of the All-knowing who chose me to be his humble instrument.'

Also, unlike his worthy predecessor, Mahendralal, Ray was not sycophantic towards the-then rulers of India. Be this as it may, today, one hundred and forty years or so after Mahendralal's simplistic eulogy of science, the 'spirit of inquiry' is being directed towards sci-tech itself. The debris are too dangerous to be ignored. But such 'inquiry' in India often tends to be dubbed as 'panic reaction' or 'techno-phobia', and is followed up with the retort: 'Should advances in sci-tech stop then?' The essay cited above is an apt example of this common defence mechanism. But abundant thoughts have been marshalled in this section, and in the earlier pages, which empowers an RT person to firmly declare: *'Yes, all so-called "advances" in sci-tech ought to stop.'* Many RT people of our age-group often ruefully express, their existential despair about modern sci-tech driven living. Modern culture is obscene and un-peaceful, they sigh.

Here is a recent frank confession about the existential aftermath of sci-tech 'miracles', which 'benefit all', from the most advanced ountry in the world (1995)[48]: 'Americans are *fried* by work, *frazzled* by lack of time. Technology has *not* made their life better. No wonder that a quarter of them say they are *exhausted*. They need to chill out before they hit the *breaking point*.'* The RT person should be able to grasp the underlying lesson from this honest confession. Such an unbearable state is the culmination of the pursuit of the 'objective' philosophy of enlightening sci-tech which treats, on the whole, man as a means, as a resource, as a dumping ground.

Still more recently (2006) an American woman scholar has drawn public attention, based on her research findings, towards another sinister phenomenon triggered with the help of sci-tech: High-tech, high-price commodification of procreation in fertility clinics for childless couples. She has called this 'Baby Business'.[49] In early April 2008 a Pune newspaper had carried a feature article with the title: 'Need for De-addiction Among Women'. On August 2, 2007 a Bangalore newspaper had published a field report on 'The Rising Divorce Rate in The IT Sector'. Among other points, this report informed that neither financial security, nor financial independence among spouses was able to stem this rot. And all these *dramatis personae*, Indian or American, belong to locales which are considered to be the most enlightened ones in their respective countries.

---

* Shreyah and Preyah from Katha Upanishad.

What should be held to account: Superstitious, traditional, restraining norms; or the sci-tech-fuelled, commercialized, degenerate baser instincts. Because the superficial ST does not recognize the inherent downward gradient of the human mind, it glibly advises people to choose between the good and the bad. Why then did the 'enlightened citizens' involved above not choose between the wholesome and the pleasurable?* They could not.

VI

One hears frequent self-castigation in business and sci-tech circles about poor innovative capabilities among Indians. At its own level, compared to, say, Japan or China, this lament seems to be justified. But judged from a higher level, and from a different angle, this apparent deficiency conceals a wise orientation of Bharat's *sanatan* culture. Careerist educators, however, lack clear, strong conviction about the enormous saving worth of this outlook. Let us therefore seek this impetus from some understanding about the mind of our *rishis* who did all the basic creativity and innovation for our timetested culture. Sri Aurobindo offers us good education about the *rishi:*[50] '... the ancient Indian idea of the *Rishi* is one who has lived fully the life of man, and found the word of the supra-intellectual , supra-mental spiritual truth ... He has the *complete inner knowledge* and the *highest surpassing knowledge*. Therefore he can guide the world.'

The common stock of ST people will tend to brush aside the ascriptions of 'complete' and 'highest' to the knowledge of the *rishis*. Hence, their role as 'guides' is automatically ruled out. It is instructive therefore to hear a testimony for the *rishi* from Toynbee: 'I believe that the Hindu dictum *Tat Tvam Asi* meaning that the individual is the universal, expresses the truth about the relation between an individual living being and ultimate Reality.'[51] Such *apta vakyas* or supreme guidelines had been followed through in the entire spectrum of life and living in society. The apparent paucity of inventive ability needs

---

* A British journalist, covering America in the Presidential election year of 1992, had discovered that 'swamped by a homogenized blanket of junk learning', living 'better than any other people on the globe', the Americans were wondering why they felt 'so depressed, so sad'. The answer, it seems, is that 'Americans are not getting enough happiness for their money'. [The Statesman Miscellany, November 22, 1992].

to be judged against this panoramic canvas. Sister Devmata (Laura Glenn) of the Ramakrishna Order had been able to do so as early as in 1927.[52] 'They did not spend their time in inventing lifeless instruments... They asked: "Why not tame the mind, unfold all its inherent possibilities and through it apprehend *Truth directly?* "(Thus) they were able to arrive at a *subjective knowledge* of the Universe no less precise than that which modern science has reached by more objective processes.'

The long-term aggregate result of this priority to 'subjective education' over 'objective knowledge' should be obvious to RT people who can discern and see. Three decades after Devmata, Sorokin had echoed much the same conclusion.[53] 'Ideational Culture cares little about scientific study of sensory phenomena and technology... such activities are but a waste of time and energy... For this reason ideational culture is uncreative in the field of science-technology... here science functions as the handmaid of religion.'

Incidentally, educators may note that Toynbees, Devmatas, Sorokins *et.al.,* have not cared to say a word about superstitions in Ideational Cultures like Bharatvarsha's.

The author has been an admirer of APJ Abdul Kalam, and has quoted him many times in earlier writings.[54] He has perhaps been the most sensible Indian in important ways in recent decades.

That is why a re-reading of one of his books, while writing this chapter, was disappointing. His vision of 'new, developed' India is sketched in terms of 'bio-technology, bio-sciences, agricultural sciences and industrial development'. The chapter on 'Knowledge Society' goes to great lengths in visualizing a transformed India through 'information technology' for 'knowledge production and utilization'.[55] Following Devmata, it is clearly 'objective' knowledge which comprises Dr. Kalam's eulogy of 'knowledge society'. But this policy is accelerating Sorokin's 'sensate culture' by wiping out the last remnants of 'ideational culture'? Will the mass of 'carrion', as warned by Swamiji, or the 'debris' highlighted by so many RT people of the West, be reduced by such 'development' as Kalam's book seems to hope? To the alleged low-key inventive temper of our culture there is another allied source of inferiority feeling: So few Nobel winners from such a large country! But an alert teacher should take a hard look at this source of remorse. Since the Nobel award had been launched in 1900 (and very recently the Abel award in Mathematics), around one thousand scientists would have received it till date. Without intending to berate their sterling achievements in themselves, one may ask: What has been the cumulative aggregate trail left behind by such feats? A happier humanity? A more peaceful world? A more sustainable and richer environment? As the previous sections have amply shown, these questions have to be answered in the negative only. Let it also be noted that it is only after 1900 that two world wars have been fought, localized wars have multiplied, arms trade has galloped, drug trafficking has become a menace, and high-tech terrorism has grown savage. These are but a few correlations. RT people who have been able to lift their heads up from under the sand, have all along been warning, much like Vivekananda and Toynbee, that a lot of modern science has been superfluous and dangerous.

Therefore Kalam's concluding 'Song of Youth' in the book mentioned above sounds insipid.[56] Here are the first three lines. "As a young citizen of India, armed with technology, knowledge and love for my nation, I realize, small aim is a crime." Perhaps Nachiketa's or Satyakam's 'aim' to be 'armed' with the 'knowledge' of the *atman* was 'small' and hence.... These 'young citizens' of ancient Bharatvarsha were perhaps 'un-creative', 'under-developed' souls, spurning all objective seductions with all their might. Such backward souls have been the cause why India has been a shackled and poor country till to-day. (It is a wonder, then, as to what the likes of Nadir Shah and Robert Clive had come to plunder from this land!

No. The genuine lamentation ought to be this: With the outlook education is now adopting, India may never again give birth to towering figures like Tagores and Gandhis, Ramanas and Ramakrishnas, Vivekanandas and Aurobindos and their ilk.

VII

It may be assumed that the above charge of non-inventiveness was nonetheless deemed true, and so the ST Constitution of India has prescribed the cultivation of the 'spirit of inquiry' as a duty for all citizens. But did Nachiketa approach Yama with a 'spirit of inquiry'?

Did Narendranath Dutta dash to Sri Ramakrishna driven by a 'spirit of inquiry'? As Devamata had pointed out, 'subjective inquiry' had been the keynote of education in Bharat's culture. So, one suspects that the Constitutional 'spirit of inquiry' is only 'objective inquiry'.

Such a slant strikes at the root of the *sanatan* (or mainstream Hindu) ethos. A searching scrutiny of the many persistent trends since 1950 is required to perceive this as a major problem of education for RT in India. Let Swami Ramakrishnananda (a brother-disciple of Swami Vivekananda) speak to us.[57]

> 'It (India) begins by questioning the man himself. Why should it be assumed that the whole universe is for man's enjoyment? ...What is he made up of?... What is the difference between man and the dull universe around him? By any manipulation of matter can intelligent life be produced?... The inquiry was made subjective not objective as in the West. Is it not a *folly to try to understand the subjective through the objective?*' (emphasis added).

It is exactly such a 'folly' that ST has been committing, and this lies at the root of the self-inflicted perils and traps the Sagan Committee had acknowledged in 1990. And as it desired, a man of religion from India had done his anticipatory bit a century ago to forecast such 'folly' with the force of silent realization, not noisy research.

Besides the ones articulated by Ramakrishnananda, the other common 'subjective inquiries', constituting the warp and weft of our *sanatan* cultural temper, have been: Why are we born as a human being, not as an animal or a tree? Do birth and death of this physical body comprise the alpha and omega of human existence? What is the distinction and relationship between the One Reality and multiple realities, the Infinite and finites, the Eternal and the transients? Does abiding Bliss issue from the growing aggregate of externals which feeds on the deficit-driven self or *vyavaharik vayktitwa*? Or, does it inhere in the autonomous, self-fulfilled (*poorna*) Self or *paramarthik vyaktitwa*?[58] RT education had flourished from such 'inquiries' in the days of yore. They are the perennial stuff of saving education. Teachers and educators need to clearly appreciate that as opposed to what the run-of-the-mill votaries of ST want them to endorse, the current environmental and other crises of the world are not due to overpopulation. At a 1995 conference among theologians and scientists at Boston the general consensus about the 'real issue' was 'over consumption in the developed countries', lately being forced upon and adopted increasingly by developing countries. *Over-production* and *over-consumption* were acknowledged as the real culprits by a high US government official also. He was RT, which includes honesty. Swami Budhananda had brilliantly summed up the distinction between the *sanatan* subjective line of inquiries, and that of the scientific objective line[60]: 'At one pole of existence is the awareness of the fact, at another is the fact of Awareness. The former is the subject matter of science, and the latter of religion... *Science will inform, religion will transform.*' This indeed is the irrefutable justification of RT scientists above looking for help and hope from true religion.

Yet another imperative for RT teachers is to pierce the glittering veil of globalization rhetoric, and see its real face. The following recent personal encounters of the author should help:

- When the WTO was on the anvil, a senior Danish professor had made this sad remark: 'Little do the developing countries realize what a terrible thing the WTO would be for them.'
- A New Zealand professor had narrated the backstage manipulations done by the WTO representatives from developed countries at the time of its launching. In the first round of voting the Thai representative was elected as the Chairman of WTO. This was unacceptable to the rich nations. So they manouevred to get the first round vote rescinded, and made sure that a Western representative became the first Chairman.
- A Swiss-French professor of business, and a director on the boards of a few European pharmaceutical giants, had confided to us: ' These MNCs are sharks and crooks.'
- A Libyan student at a German university (in 2001) had just attended an economics lecture where the professor had spoken on globalization for an hour or so. The student voluntarily told us later that during the entire lecture the professor elaborated only on the advantages that would be accruing to the developed countries from globalization; not a word was said about its effects on developing countries.

Our teachers, it is hoped, after learning about just a few such back-stage goings on, will attend future conferences espousing change, progress, development, transformation, knowledge, etc., with greater alertness and circumspection. For, in every Indian forum on such matters they are likely to hear from every speaker — business executive or bureaucrat, politician or academic — the following chant:

'Globalization is here to stay. It is the best thing that could have happened to India'. China, by contrast, has refused to be so gullible and naïve. Why this difference? Let us think deeply. To help them do so, the point about English being the medium of education in India, as mentioned in section I above, may be recalled.

China has remained fairly insulated, by contrast. So, their policy makers would have been much less prone to being driven around by each and every catchy but deceptive slogan dinned into Indian ears from the English-speaking world. Teachers and educators should take a hard, long look at, for example, two UNESCO Reports. *Learning To Be* (1972) and *Learning – The Treasure Within* (1998).* Both concentrate on science, technology and modernization of mentality as the saviours of developing nations. They must be de-culturized from their proven traditions to be eligible members in the 'global village'. This is colonization by the backdoor. Such UN outfits are sponsoring seminars in colleges and other educational institutions in India to push down their own notions of progress etc. into our young minds. We have had a couple of invitations to such events in the last few years. One invitation was declined. In the other our critical comments were presented openly.

The 'spirit of inquiry' was applied to unravel the garbed agenda of globalizers. Swami Satprakashananda, a scholarly senior monk had formulated a profound principle.[61] 'A balanced life does not rest on equal regard for all the aspects of life... they have to be adjusted to the spiritual life.' We may, however, put it a little more emphatically: *Sanatan* Indian temper had never recoiled from the principle of *prioritization*, not just adjustment e.g., *shreya* over *preya, para* over *apara, nivritti* over *pravritti, tyaga* over *bhoga, brahmacharya* before *garhasthya, antarmukhita* before *bahirmukhita*, and so on. All this had emerged from a 'spirit of inquiry' belonging to the province of RT, not ST. Will Durant, the celebrated author of the eight–volume *The Story of Civilization* had once reflected thus (may be with India in mind)[62]. 'It is dangerously fatal to break sharply with the past, to court the *discontinuity* that brings madness, the social amnesia that comes from the shock of sudden blows or mutilations. The *sanity* of the individual lies in the *continuity of his memory*; the *sanity of its traditions*; in either case a break in the chain involves a *neurotic reaction* and a *disturbance dangerous* to life.' (emphasis added).

---

* See chapter 4 for earlier mention.

India to-day is a perfect picture of these grim forebodings of Durant – a RT thinker. Our educators have a great moral duty to fathom the implications of these words. UNESCO reports on 'Learning' and other similar gratuitous advice must be appraised in the light of true counsel. Sri Aurobindo, a few decades before Durant, had warned us about the same threat[63]: that 'Asia must become culturally a province of Europe' And so the great peril for India is close, 'forcing her to choose'. What is this imperative choice before her? To, live or to perish? If this choice was 'close' in Sri Aurobindo's time, then India today seems to have surrendered altogether her 'right to choose'. This is the context in which our teachers are supposed to be educating the youth for India's resurgence. Hence they should be fully alive to this fundamental problem at the heart of education. Should ST be allowed to drag us into the void of identity-destruction? Long ago an English poet had sung: 'With all thy faults, I love thee, England'. The US President Kennedy had also said this : 'Ask not what the country can do for you; ask instead what you can do for it?' And here is Bharatvarsha, relatively the least faulty of all nations, where we do not care to educate our children students with this first and paramount inspiration.

The absence of such commitment does not escape even some Westerners who come to India with RT, backed up by a constructive spirit of inquiry. Here is an instance from Ramsey Clark (2007), a former US Attorney General.[64] 'The difference between the old imperialism and the new globalization process* is illustrated well in India. The country suffered the brutalities of foreign domination, the impoverishment that resulted from it. But until globalization, if you look at the Indian movie industry for instance, its facial aspects remained Indian. Now, with the intensity of globalization reaching into every corner of life, even the comedians, the jokes, the rhythm of the music have started changing. This really makes *consumerism and materialism deadlier than armed occupation*.' (emphasis added). Sri Aurobindo's diagnosis above thus stands fully vindicated almost

* Frankly, 'globalization' is factually 'westernization' which, in turn, is 'Americanization'. Look at the writings on T–shirts for example. From American universities to cities, from playboy to rebel spirit – this is the character of the subtle indoctrination going on.

ninety years later. Michel Danino, a French scholar of Indian culture and history, now settled in India, complements the above picture from the other end of the spectrum, as it were. He had conducted an all-India survey among 11,000 school students (9-12 classes) in 2005. From his extensive Report submitted to the NCERT, a sample of replies by students is noteworthy[65]:

- 'We students get to learn only about other countries, and nothing of India.'
- 'We imbibe only selfishness, money-mindedness.'
- 'Nothing other than a materialistic approach to life.'
- 'How to get good marks, how to throw off competitors.'
- 'Lies and dishonesty', etc., etc.

These then are the bitter fruits of an educational system which is severed from its roots. This has been happening, ironically enough, much more concertedly in the post-1950 independent, democratic republic of India. Many powers and forces, internal as well as external, labeled as modern and scientific, seem to be conducting a campaign of *mahatih vinashti* (grand destruction). Swamiji's clarion call for man-making education has been stilled. Money-making education holds sway instead. And we are acquiescing in the preaching of this un-characteristic feature of education in Bharatvarsh, almost like children plunging into the sea, dancing to the mesmeric music of the vengeful pied piper.

VIII

How do we recover the roots? A few snapshots from Tagore's autobiography should now be apt[66]:

- 'Luxury was a thing almost unknown in the days of my infancy. The standard of living was then, as a whole, much more simple than it is now. Apart from that, the children of our household were entirely free from the fuss of being too much looked after. Our food had nothing to do with delicacies. A list of our articles of clothing would only invite the modern boy's scorn. On no pretext did we wear socks or shoes till we had passed our tenth year... It never entered our heads to consider ourselves ill-off for that reason.'

- 'Elders have become cheap to modern children; they are too easily accessible, and so are all objects of desire. Nothing ever came so easily to us... The result was that what little we did get we enjoyed to the utmost... The modern child of a well-to-do family nibbles at only half of the things he gets; the greater part of his world is wasted on him.'

Tagore was writing all this in 1912 during his voyage to the West. He was then fifty-two years-old just a year before he won the Nobel award. The two extracts above provide a graphic account of the child-rearing and values–forming ingredients of those days in one of the most wealthy and cultured families of Bengal. (As the eldest son in a teacher's large family, this author had experienced almost identical conditions in the late 1940s and early 1950s).

With all the denials, privations and strictness around, the flowering of a complete personality did not stop. No mental depressions or frustrations, followed by professional counselling. Educators and students alike should intensely meditate today on these benchmark extracts. This will foster that RT which should precede *before* the much-fancied ST can be of some good use. For, ST has been associated with robbing humanity of the perennial ideal of 'simple living, high thinking'. It is a sacred truism that subjective heights cannot be scaled unless the objective entanglements are minimal. If this principle is flouted, all the 'miracles' and 're-enchantments' proclaimed by sci-tech will not be able to stem the deadly cyclone of 'complex living, low thinking'. Incontrovertible evidence of this abounds around us. This is not progress – at least existentially speaking. Swamiji, in his times, had no doubt wanted Western science for India, but along with Vedanta. He had also exhorted India to be more *rajasic*, not at the cost of *sattwa*, but at the expense of *tamas*. What has been happening now, however, is: Vedanta is out of sight, *sattwa* is gone. The net result: Only sci-tech, coupled with rising *rajaso-tamas* or *tamaso-rajas*. Chapter 16 of the Bhagwad Gita had forecasted the *asuric* (demoniac) consequences of such a combination. For instance[67]:

Verse 10 – 'Filled with insatiable desires, full of hypocrisy, pride, and arrogance, holding evil ideas through delusion, they work with impure resolve.'

Verse 11– 'Beset with immense cares ending only with death, regarding gratification of lust as the highest, and feeling sure that that is all.'

Verse 12 – 'Bound by a hundred ties of hope, given over to just and wrath, they strive to secure by unjust means hoards of wealth for sensual enjoyment.'

Verse 13 – 'This today has been gained by me; this desire I shall obtain; this is mine, and this wealth shall also be mine in future.' This picture of the human condition was drawn at least three millennia ago. It exposes the 'carrion' of our present educationalsocial milieu with surgical precision. However, aggressive propaganda by STBP ceases not from spreading an alluring cover of 'roses' over this 'carrion'. This is the consequence of *rajo guna* domination, freed from the bridle of *sattwa guna*. *Rajas* is indispensable, but it is dangerous too. Sri Aurobindo had depicted this destructive scourge aptly and forcefully[68] :

> '...if the *rajasic* qualities are given the upper hand, cultured to *the diminution of sattwa*, then the trend of Karma and its results necessarily culminate... in the *highest exaggeration of the perversities of the lower nature*... because of the very immensity of the misused divine power...' (emphasis added).

In other words, RT gets eliminated altogether. This elimination has been hastened by the rapidly expanding amplitude of STBP since the second world war. Sister Devmata had identified the great difficulty posed for India by the above phenomenon. She had identified a crucial cultural divide between the East and the West[69]:

'The special task of Western nations seems to have been to *apply* rather than to *discover* Truth. While the East joins the ideas of Truth and *Being*, the West more often connects Truth with *doing*.' In other words, India's pristine educational priority of *sattwa*– based 'Being' is being ruled out by the Western priority of *rajas*-dominated 'doing'. This is good neither for India, nor for the rest of the world. For, Devmata had added that this RT emphasis in India had nurtured 'the most *complete* and *comprehensive* system of education known.

These last words from Devmata should be more inspiring than any others to set India's educators on the RT path to re-claim and regain the solid ground of true education in tune with her original genius. Cautious incorporation of time-related changes is a subordinate, incidental task. Without the compass, we cannot negotiate stormy waves. In its absence we are well on the way to run aground.

Here are a few compelling words from Francis Dore of the University of Paris (1986), as if to lend his support to what Devmata had averred sixty years ago[70]:

> 'It (Hinduism) offers the way to an indispensable... *spiritualising of materialism* itself... Science can take its inspiration from Hinduism forits greater enrichment and finality.'

The thrust of Dore's views is that the imperative is not so much for *sanatan* Indian RT to abandon its traditions, as it is for modern ST to shed its pretensions. One may fittingly refer here to these observations of Swamiji[71]:

'The sage is often ignorant of physical science, because he reads the wrong book – the book within; and the scientist is too often ignorant of religion because he too reads the wrong book – the book without.' This is why *the religion of sanatan Hinduism* had never tried to impose itself on science e.g., no inquisitions, no imprisonments, no burnings etc. But ST today is often cussed enough to pass judgements on God, religion, heaven, enlightenment, etc., or to redefine them with little comprehension of the 'book within'. Educational principles in India should therefore preserve their original and proven sanctity – priority to the sacred, the holy, the cosmic. *Abhyudaya* in the material sphere will then follow with due moderation. Ever-new teaching pedagogies and technologies, rushing in from *rajasic, bahirmukhi*, 'doing' cultures, are only outer forms and passing fads. Our educators should not be carried away by them. Instead, they should redeem the content, the substance. The following set of seven books is suggested as 'good substance' for continuous selfeducation for all teachers and students working in the Indian context. They are the fruit of RT:

1. *Reminiscences* – Rabindranath Tagore
2. *Lectures from Colombo To Almora* – Swami Vivekananda
3. *Hints on National Education* – Sister Nivedita
4. *Autobiography* – Mahatma Gandhi
5. *The Foundations of Indian Culture* – Sri Aurobindo
6. *The Indian Pilgrim* – Subhas Chandra Bose
7. *Our Heritage* – S. Radhakrishnan

They all stood tall on the twin foundations of devotion to the Divine and love for their Mother culture. Secular India frowns on both. Consequently, the typical, bright, educated youth of 21st century India often resembles a drifting cloudlet – without identity, without purpose. Bankrupt of RT, they tend to weaken the nation at the roots. This invites lethal blows from all quarters, to which India meekly 'reacts' with childish verbal protests. In other parts of the world (like the USA) all undergraduate students, irrespective of their nationality and religion, have to study Socrates, Plato, the Iliad and Odyssey, etc. Our teachers too have a duty to develop a wider and deeper mental framework beyond the compulsions of their syllabus-driven special subjects — irrespective of the community to which they belong. The same task is valid for all students too.

Impertinent though its repetition may sound (see Section VII above), our teachers and students alike must practise adequate detachment to ask this all-important question: 'For more than a century nearly a thousand famous Nobel Scientists have contributed immensely to foster and broadcast "scientific temper". Yet, is the condition of man and earth any better? Has higher speed, greater greed, longer life, more arms, more sex— has any of them given more peace, security and sustainability to mankind and other species?' India has the richest store of experiential and metaphysical insights and theories to force open these issues. But our sci-tech and other intellectual stalwarts appear to have abdicated their world-responsibility. They probably will not, they probably cannot speak up. So, we are compelled to listen to those Western critics who have seized the problem by the scruff and dissected it on the operation table. Ten years ago Postman, a New York University teacher had written an incisive critique on technology.[72] He asked: 'Is it a Blessing or Burden?' His article ended with a list of six questions which, he stressed, must be asked of any technology proposed to man: What is the problem? Whose problem is it? What new problems will be created?, Who will be seriously harmed? etc. Postman's article came our way only in May 2009. And lo. How mazing (and delightful ! – can you blame this author?) was the fidelity of this list with two similar lists furnished in a book published jointly by this author in 2006?73 Even men-not-sogreat can also think alike – across continents! But no resonance within India — as yet.

References

1. Vivekananda S. W; *Complete Works*, Kolkata: Advaita Ashrama, 2005, Vol. 2, p. 122.
2. 'Seduced By Money', reprinted in *Times of India*, June 12, 2008.
3. Bhavaharananda S. W: 'East-West Dialectic and Swami Vivekananda', *Prabuddha Bharata*, June 2008, p. 355.
4. Prigogine I. And Stengers I; *Order Out of Chaos*; Toronto: Bantam Books, 1984.
5. *Ibid.; pp. xi, xix, xv, xx, xxi, xxiii, 1, 2, 4, 5, 5, 6, 6, 7, 7, 9, 13, 14, 22, 291, 292, 301, 306, 312, 312, 313.*
6. Bohm D and Peat D; *Science, Order and Creativity*, Toronto: Bantam Books, 1987, pp. 12-13.
7. Tagore, Rabindranath: *Personality*, New Delhi: Rupa 2002, p. 68.
8. *Prigogine and Stengers*, op. cit., p. 292.
9. Quinn D; *Ishmael*, New York: Bantam, 1993, p. 145.
10. Aurobindo Sri; *The Synthesis of Yoga*, Pondicherry: Sri Aurobindo Ashram, 1970, p. 281.
11. Chakraborty S. K. and Bhattacharya, P; *Human Values – The Tagorean Panorama*, New Delhi: New Age International, pp. 256-83.
12. Quoted in Capra, F; *Uncommon Wisdom*, Toronto: Bantam, 1989, p. 40.
13. Vivekananda S. W.; op.cit., vol. 2, pp. 273, 344, 345.
14. Weizenbaum, J; 'The Computer as Idol', in *Synthesis of Science and Religion*, ed. T.D. Singh, Bombay: The Bhaktivedanta Institute 1988, pp. 281, 283-4, 284.
15. Prigogine and Stengers, op. cit. 291.
16. *Ibid, p. 50, p. 86.*
17. Carrel, A; Man — The Unknown, London: Hamish Hamilton, 1936, p. 13.
18. *Ibid.; p. 14.*
19. *Ibid.; 34.*
20. *Ibid.; pp 34, 258, 259, 260, 274, 298.*
21. *Quinn; op. cit., pp. 82-3.*
22. *Ibid.; p. 37.*
23. Capra; op. cit., p. 43.
24. Tagore; op. cit., p. 56.
25. Huxley A; *Brave New World*; Harmondsworth: Penguin, 1962, pp. 9-13.
26. Narlikar J. V; 'The Scientific Temper — Indispensable To Enlightened Citizenship', *Prabuddha Bharata*, January 2006, p. 25.

27. Vivekananda S. W.; op.cit., 2006, vol. 9 pp. 212, 215, 216.
28. Chakraborty S. K; *Against The Tide*, New Delhi: Oxford University Press, 2003, pp. 186-91.
29. Mookerji Radha Kumud; *Harsha*, London: Oxford University Press, 1926, pp. 177-8
30. Madhavananda S. W. and Majumdar, RC (eds.); *Great Women of India*, Kolkata: Advaita Ashrama, 1977, pp. 358-9.
31. Vivekananda S. W.; op. cit. 2005, vol. 4, p. 491.
32. Brahmeshananda S. W.; 'The Spiritual Family', *Prabuddha Bharata*, June 2008, pp. 331-5.
33. Vivekananda S. W.; op. cit., 2005, vol. I, p. 490.
34. Aurobindo Sri; *The Message of the Gita, Pondicherry*: Sri Aurobindo Ashram, 1977, pp. 229-30. 154.
35. Carrel; op. cit., p. 256, pp. 292-3, p. 298.
36. Sorokin P. A and Lunden, W; *Power and Morality*, Boston: Porter Sargent, 1959, p. 118.
37. Toynbee A. J; *Choose Life*, New Delhi: Oxford University Press, 1987, p. 35, p. 342.
38. Griffiths B.; *Return To The Centre*, London: Collins-Fount, 1987, p. 68.
39. Rifkin J. and Howard, T; *Entropy*, Toronto: Bantam, 1980, p. 244-47.
40. Wilkins M.; 'Science and Social Concerns', *Synthesis of Science and Religion*, op. cit., p. 36.
41. Bohm and Peat, op. cit., p. 13.
42. Ernst R. R; 'Science in Third Millennium: Expectations Between Hope and Fear', in *Thoughts on Synthesis of Science and Religion*, Kolkata: Bhaktivedanta Institute, 2001, p. 544.
43. Wallace S.; 'The Last of The Amazon', *National Geographic*, February, 2007, p. 49.
44. Quoted by M. Cremo in 'Vedic Ethical Principles', *Thoughts on Synthesis of Science and Religion*, op. cit. p. 83.
45. Einstein A; *Ideas and Opinions*; New Delhi: Rupa, 2003, p. 50, pp. 53-4.
46. Sarkar J; *Dr. Mahendralal Sarkar*; Kolkata: Advaita Ashrama, pp. 128-31, p. 145.
47. Ray P. C; *Autobiography*, London: Kegan Paul, 1932, pp. 443-4.
48. Quoted in *Human Values and Ethics*, S.K. Chakraborty and D. Chakraborty, Hyderabad: ICFAI University Press, 2006, p. 234.
49. Spar D. L.; *The Baby Business*, Harvard Business School Press, 2006, pp. XI-XIII.

50. Aurobindo, Sri, *The Human Cycle*, Pondicherry: Sri Aurobindo Ashram, 1985, p. 169.
51. *Choose Life*, op. cit., p. 25.
52. Devmata Sister, *Days in An Indian Monastery*, Chennai: Sri Ramakrishna Math, 2003, p. 318.
53. *Power and Morality*, op. cit. pp. 119-120.
54. Chakraborty S. K., and Chakraborty, D., *Spirituality in Management*, New Delhi: Oxford University Press, 2008, pp. 97-98.
55. Abdul Kalam APJ, *Ignited Minds*, New Delhi: Viking, 2002, p. 116
56. *Ibid, p. 196.*
57. Ramakrishnananda S. W., *For Thinkers On Education*, Madras: Ramakrishna Math, 1972, p. 49.
58. *Human Values and Ethics*, op. cit, p. 213.
59. *Synthesis of Science and Religion*, op. cit., p. 290.
60. Budhananda Swami, *The Saving Challenge of Religion*, Madras: Ramakrishna Math, 1980, pp. 144-145.
61. Satprakashananda Swami, *The Goal and The Way*, Madras: Ramakrishna Math, 1981, p. 254.
62. Quoted in the 'Introduction' of *For Thinkers on Education*, op. cit, p. ix.
63. Aurobindo Sri, *The Foundations of Indian Culture*, Pondicherry: Sri Aurobindo Ashram, 1988, pp. 8-9.
64. *The Hindu*, December, 2007.
65. Danino M., 'Indian Students Speak on Education' *(mimeo)*, pp. 5-6.
66. Tagore Rabindranath, *Reminiscences*, New Delhi: Macmillan, 1987, pp. 8-10.
67. Swarupananda Swami, *Srimad Bhagwad Gita*, Kolkata: Advaita Ashram, 1998, p. 243.
68. *The Message of the Gita*, op. cit., p. 228.
69. Devmata, Sister, op. cit., p. 321.
70. Dore F., 'Impressions on Hinduism and the Scientific Approach' in *Synthesis of Science and Religion*, op. cit., p. 161.
71. Vivekananda S. W., *Complete Works*, op. cit., Vol. 6, 2006, p. 81.
72. Postman N., *Resurgence*, May 1999.
73. *Human Values and Ethics*, op. cit., Chapter 12.

CHAPTER 6

LEARNING FOR MODERNITY: What Does It Mean?

द्यौ: शान्तिरन्तरिक्षं शान्ति:
पशथिवी शान्तिराप: शान्ति रोधय: शान्ति ।
वनस्पतय: शान्तिर्विश्वे देवा: शान्ति व्रंह्य शान्ति
सर्व शान्ति: शान्तिरेव शान्ति: सा मा शान्तिरेधि ।।

(य:-३६/१७)

Peace of sky, peace of mid-region,
Peace of earth, peace of waters,
Peace of plants.
Peace of trees, peace of All Gods,
Peace of Brahman, peace of
the Universe, peace of peace,
May that peace come to me.

(*Yajur Veda* 36/37)

(*Ibid.*, p. 287)

I

- A Dutch academic had once declared (perhaps during 1999-end) that India had failed to modernize herself. We kept silent. He seemed too cocksure for a response.
- A noted Indian film-maker of the post-Satyajit era had concluded an annual lecture at an IIM (in 2004) with a dramatic flourish: 'India has leap-frogged into "post-modernism", while bypassing modernism'. An elitist audience applauded the pronouncement enthusistically. Yet, neither phrase had been explained by the speaker.

- Early in 2010 an Indian doctor, settled in the USA for forty years, had come for a short stint of social service at the RK Mission Sevashram in Vrindaban. During conversation one morning he told us that he was happy that he could convince and help two of his brothers also to emigrate to the USA. But he lamented that the other two brothers refused his help, preferring to live in their own mother land. These fellows are backward, failing to move along with a dynamic world — he said.
- The elder son (now settled in the West) of a former student of ours had recently advised his father to 'modernize' himself. 'What did he mean?'— rued the puzzled father.

Much like this father or brothers, the author has also frequently wondered about jargons like modern, dynamic, modernism, modernization, modernity, etc. It has often seemed to many alert and sensitive minds all over the world, and to a few rare Indian minds too, that this family of words focuses on 'recentness'. Even antiques should be recent!

The later any idea or object is, the more modern it is — so it seems. The corollary is: The more recent or later anything is, the better it must be. Newness and betterness automatically go together. But the subjective condition of the human being and society has to be the final yardstick for assessing the end-result of all proclaimed structural, technological and ideological change or modernizing strategies. How well or ill modernity (i.e., Westernity) fares on this ground? The latest 'world happiness' survey (http:// www.le.ac.uk/pc/aw57/world/sample.html), including the CIA too as a partner in the study team, and using a revised methodology for 2006-09, shows Denmark at rank 1, while Bangladesh and India at 67 and 125 (mean scores 4.24, 1.00 and 0.85 respectively on a 5- point scale). USA is ranked 16, while Britain 21. Three factors of happiness measurement have been used : health, wealth and education. Assuming that our memory is right, the first happiness survey of 1995, done by the London School of Economics, had however shown Bangladesh at the top, India at 5 and USA at 45 or thereabout. (We cannot recall the factors used in the 1995 survey). Three possibilities may be suggested for this intriguing snake-and-ladder game of ranking in course of fifteen years:

(a) Liberalization, globalization, privatization, information technology, nine percent growth, etc., have made India essentially a far unhappier nation than before. Even China and Japan, 82nd and 90th respectively, are apparently much happier today than India. JRD Tata (1904 – 93), after receiving the Bharat Ratna award (1992), had told a Western correspondent that he cared little if India might shortly become an economic super-power; he wanted his India to be a 'land of happy people'. What a shock would he have felt, if he were alive today, to know this lowly latest world happiness ranking of India.

(b) The latest methodology may have been ingeniously so devised that richer nations would tend to float up and the poorer ones slip down in the rank order. The self-esteem of the former may have been finding it hard to accept their relatively low ranking in the initial surveys. If they rank high in material affluence, technology, economic power, etc., they must so rank in subjective terms like happiness, etc., too. The sacred, the spiritual traditional cultures *have* to be unhappy.* This surmise is not as far-fetched as it may seem. It could well be one of the latest manifestations of the same occidental mentality which has for long fabricated the myth of 'Aryan invasion theory' as the origin and foundation of Indian culture. The message seems to be: The occident has to be on top in everything — from culture and happiness to ethicality and spirituality too. Who knows, world spirituality surveys in the near-future may put India at the bottom.

Reviews on the back cover of Sw. Tathagatananda's book *Relief of Tension, Depression and Anxiety* (Advaita Ashrama, 2009) contain these words of a Los Angeles College professor: 'If affluence could bring happiness, we in the West would have been very happy... instead the "misery index" is higher than ever.'

(c) The general question in this survey was: 'All things considered, how satisfied are you with your life these days?' It has to be borne in mind that the common (not elite) Indian mind still

---

*The following wisdom statement, attributed to Einstein, was recently read on the wall of a well-known college in Kolkata; 'Not everything that can be counted counts; and not everything that counts can be counted'. How true!

largely retains the impress of the world's most sustainable culture. Therefore it is rational to hypothesize that Indian responses would have implicitly judged the present-day chaotic disruptions against a more profound and deeply internalized standard of happiness. Hence their dejection and apparent helplessness manifested in such a low happiness score. This may be an answer to the researchers' 'surprise' with the score.

It is high time for the educated Indian apostles of modernity, post-modernism, de-constructionism, liberalism and all that to see through the dense fog of such verbiage which only misleads rather than leads. They should know that the *Time, Newsweek, Fortune* and other Western magazines and top newspapers have been frequently publishing (1980s and 1990s) exhaustive research articles on the epidemic of stress and other mental disorders in the 'healthy-wealthyeducated' Western societies. It is said that hospital beds for mental patients exceed those for any other group in some of these countries.

Moreover, a few reliable sources say that in some of these societies 50 percent of the population is attached to personal psychiatrists on a regular basis. Will our modernist educators pause and ponder: How can happiness and mental stress coexist? Buddhism is now said to be on the ascendant in the West. Educators of the world should learn then this Buddhist maxim. 'A desire conquered gives more happiness than a desire satisfied'. Education and wealth are almost always associated with mounting greed and crooked selfishness. Yet, they are claimed to be the sources of happiness and sustainability. Wisdom is now in exile. For, wisdom always thrives in persons and places which stand upon centripetal consciousness.

When centrifugal endeavours spring from this centripetal baseline, only then they can restore sanity and happiness. It is well worth holding firmly to this inviolable law: That era and society which lean heavily towards matter and money i.e., the acquisitive end, they cannot be happier than the ones which tend towards God, Divine, Spirit i.e., the ascetic end of the continuum. Sustainability also inheres in this law. Similarly, of late 'learning' seems to be more in fashion than 'education'. Recoil from 'education' was already evident in India a few decades ago when the GOI had renamed the Education Ministry as 'Human Resource Development Ministry' (HRD Ministry in short).

The GOI may have unthinkingly 'learnt' this glamorous gospel from some Western management gurus. Of course, in industry also management development or training centres and colleges are being frequently re-labelled as 'learning centres'. With this shift is also associated fashionable usage of phrases like 'strategic HRD', 'knowledge economy', 'life skills', 'emotional intelligence', 'intellectual capital' and so on. The cumulative after-effects of all such posturings of restless modernity are, however, culminating in individual and global demise of psychological peace and material sustainability. Human character also seems to be touching its nadir. The central issue in happiness and sustainability is not 'production — consumption'. It is 'distribution'. But so far, 'learning for modernity' has been, on the whole, 'anti-frugality' and 'pro-promiscuity'. Hence it is seriously questionable. Outside the parochial orbit of modernistic intelligentsia and policy gurus, the common man keeps helplessly watching how he is being seduced to learn to live on credit card and debt, on mortgages and speculation. They may be good for business, but not for happiness.

II

'Learning' was probably first formally circulated by the UNESCO Report of 1972, *Learning To Be*. Briefer references to this and the subsequent report have occurred elsewhere in this book. True to the inferiority complex of a conquered race, this document has apparently been held as a gospel of true learning by India's policy masters. With all their critical acumen reserved only for indigenous ideas and ideals, they seem to have uncritically accepted most of what this Paris Report had sought to expound. The blurb on the back cover of the Report had declared, inter alia: 'If it be our hope at once to fulfill the promises of democracy and to establish man firmly in the scientific and technical revolution,..., it cannot be reduced to a mere matter of state grants and family traditions,...(but) offer to everyone the opportunities of the learning society. This age...of the finite world can but be the age of complete man.' These Delphic oracles were pronounced by a Commission which did not visit a single Asian country (except Singapore).[1] Yet, the entire corpus of 'metaphysical' learning garnered over several millennia, primarily in Asia (India), was simply swept aside in a couple of lines in the text and in a footnote.[2] By some ordained coincidence, however, we discovered that in the very same year, 1972, the renowned Catholic theologian, scholar and author, Thomas Merton, had written thus while alluding to the *Bhagwad Gita*[3]

: 'The *Gita* can be seen as the main literary support for the great religious civilization of India, the oldest surviving culture in the world...(It) brings to the West salutary reminder that our highly activistic and one-sided culture...lacks the inner depth of an authentic metaphysical consciousness. Without such depth our moral and political protestations are just so much verbiage.'

Merton's alleged 'verbiage' is indeed exemplified by pompous intellectual terms like existentialism, post-modernism, beyond postmodernism, deconstructionism, learning etc. Yet, such glitzkreig has given succour to none. The reader may note that the UNESCO Report visualizes the 'complete man' by clipping one of his two wings — the supra-sensory, the infinite, the metaphysical. The allegation of 'one-sideness' leveled by Merton is fully corroborated by the absolute dictatorship conferred on 'scientific' and 'technological revolution' in the said Report. This is 'technoxication' at its zenith[4]. Going by Gita psychology, such a phenomenon is rooted in the unbridled indulgence given to *rajo guna* (blind activism), setting afire the *asuric sampats* (demoniac energies) in man and society[5]. So, it is now more of a 'burning' society than a 'learning' society that is looming large on the horizon. The Report ensures the spread of the former by dismissing the roles of the state and the family in 'learning to be'. More about this later.

Nearly twenty-five years later (1996) the UNESCO presented a follow-up Report to the world. Its essential message could be gleaned from the back cover blurb[6] : '...building on the four pillars that are the foundations of education– learning to be, learning to know, learning to do and learning to live together – all societies aim to move towards a necessary Utopia in which none of the talents hidden like buried treasure in every person are left untapped.'

Like its predecessor, the 1996 Report too assigns globalization and technology the highest importance in the implementation strategy for the above heroic goals. In such a design for the 'necessary Utopia', the so-called developing countries, including India, are seemingly treated as lands peopled all along by brutish primitives. For, they have been advised to adapt culturally and to modernize their mentalities.[7] For this the West, via UNESCO *et. al.*, imposes its own template as the model for change by such below-par cultures. Modernity is Westernity, Modernization is Westernization. Take it or leave it!

Merton's words on this issue as quoted above may be recalled again. Once more, by Providential convergence as it were, the following views were aired by an eminent engineer-scientist, Willis Harman, in 1996 (in his Foreword to a book by us)[8] : '...the materialism and amorality of the Western scientific worldview, and the strong emphasis on rights over obligations (especially *vis-à-vis* the natural environment) have contributed to systemic dysfunctions...which raise serious questions regarding the long-term viability of modern society.' yet, the twin Reports above try to foist just this sort of dysfunctional sci–tech Utopia by harping on the alleged 'backward' mentalities of cultures like India's which have epitomized viability for over five thousand years.

Unfortunately, such a forthright challenge to the sci-tech utopia never comes from eminent Indian sci-tech personalities. We have heard or read from some of them. Most of them sing the glories of modern scientism, accompanied by ample doses of shameful regret for their own superstitious culture. The few who have been able to escape this syndrome, treat the problem at the superfine border line of Unified Field Theory and Consciousness, or *Chit-Achit* and measurability. The former stance is taken by Mani Bhaumik[9], the latter by Raja Ramanna.[10] While such writings constitute impressive excursions into the realm of theory, their muteness about the concrete irreversible damages caused to human society and its environs (as listed by Harman) is amazing. Our sci-tech stalwarts appear to have put their social conscience to sleep. Reasons for this may be known to them. But their aloofness runs contrary to the head-on, unequivocal critiques of sci-tech by a growing number of Nobel laureate scientists from the West itself. A lot from their writings has been culled by us earlier (chapter 5) for quick familiarization, to be followed by a courageous and responsible stand by our sci-tech leaders in this matter of life and death.[11]

At any rate, the four learning pillars are pretty vague in their import. For instance, what is the meaning of 'learning to be'? If anything, over the four decades or so after 1972, people all over the world seem to have 'learnt to be' more greedy, more aggressive, more manipulative, more selfish, and so on. It is no wonder that these trends should accompany an ethos, an era which reposes sole trust in the 'modern' materialistic, sensory consciousness, while rejecting outright the 'primitive' metaphysical or transcendental consciousness.

Learned report writers of august world bodies may themselves wish to learn that 'backward' cultures like India had seized upon the eternal verity that greed is bad, and her *rishis* had designed comprehensive structures and processes for society where greed could not be rationalized, let alone deified. The family had been the social unit where containment of greed used to be one of the cornerstones. We have witnessed and grown with this in our lifetime.

III

Pitrim Sorokin of Harvard, a pioneering and outspoken figure in sociology, had offered wide-ranging factual accounts of the degenerative consequences of the type of 'learning' as propagated by what he called 'sensate culture', 'sensate science', and 'sensate values', updated till the 1950s.[12] Chapter 8 of his book under reference is titled 'What is Pathological in the Main Compartments of our Culture?' By 'our', Western culture is implied. We were on the verge of completing our college and university education during the decade when Sorokin's book was published. In India, certainly as a whole, none of the pathologies detected by Sorokin were noticeable during that period. Here are a few of those pathologies:

- The major premise of sensate culture — true reality-value is sensory, all cognition is sensory knowledge, non-sensory metaphysics as unscientific.[13]
- Moral and social irresponsibility of sci-tech has grown – sci-tech must undergo a radical change.[14]
- All the degrading theories in the socio-cultural sphere, pressed in the name of sci-tech, have contributed to the barbarization of man.[15]
- The very roots of the tree of sensate culture are hopelessly unsound — the longer the rotting roots of sensate culture persist, the more withered becomes the entire tree.[16]

Almost five decades after Sorokin had exposed deep sores beneath the shiny skin of modern (Western) culture, these scourges have now widely surfaced externally. And the contagion is penetrating into sober and sound cultures at an alarming pace. For, the plethora of sci-tech means of mass-communication was unavailable in Sorokin's days. In any case, the Reports cited above show scant understanding about what 'learning to be' signifies. Their authors might as well learn that a rapid-action, 24×7×365 hours society, with call centres and credit cards and much worse, rules out every factor that is indispensable for learning to become the 'being' in me, in one continuum with the 'Being'. Swami Vivekananda had spoken these words to a Los Angeles audience in 1900:[17]

> 'The bee came to sip the honey, but its feet stuck to the honey- ot and it could not get away. Again and again we are finding ourselves in that state. ...why are we here? We came here to sip the honey and we find our hands and feet sticking to it. We are caught, though we came to catch.'

Modernising gurus from developing countries may note that through the above poignant imagery of 'bee-and-honey-pot' it is metaphysics which is addressing them. Even a hundred 'learning' Reports are unlikely to match the realism and pathos captured in this single image.s

One hundred and twelve years on since Swamiji had uttered this tragic truth, the situation is decidedly more grave today. The technoxicated mentality of the learned Commission assumes absurd proportions in the fourth learning pillar of its 'necessary Utopia' i.e., 'learning to live together'. Given the record of history, it is hard to swallow such a sermon from quarters which had colonized and exploited large parts of the world for over three centuries. Sci-tech was their chief ally in this adventure of political and military subjugation of peaceful cultures. The same process is now unfolding through cultural colonisation for the sake of a so-called 'global village' (read, occidental colony or global casino).

The writing off of family traditions (1972 Report) represents the other end of the string. The honourable Commission members seem to be ignorant about the truth that cultures like Indian and Chinese, where living together within large joint families had been perfected through millennia, have also been living peacefully with other cultures as a whole.* But taking the modernistic cue, in recent years some of our liberated women have also begun to question: 'Why should we be labeled as sisters or mothers, as daughters or aunts, as wives or grandmas? Why can't we be left alone simply as individuals?' Thus, living together, through a refined and varied network of bonding relationships, is being sabotaged right inside our homes. Conflict and

---

* Unfortunately, the 'yellow peril' is now becoming a fact – for India and Tibet at least.

much else is becoming pervasive. Sacred marriages of responsibility, restraint and selflessness are being replaced by calculating, rights-based, secular companionship. Contracts of convenience are sweeping aside covenants of trust. Meanwhile, the legal profession is having a field day — almost like Nero fiddling while Rome is burning.

On the other hand, if peaceful living together among neighbouring developing countries is meant, then this is pure doubletalk bordering on hypocrisy. For, it is the developed countries which have been selling arms and ammunitions on a massive scale for decades to the developing countries round the world.

Fifty years ago Sorokin had accused, primarily the West, about the crisis that had overtaken sensate culture through the overthrow of the family. Even at that time he had detected the onset of 'companionship' resting on 'egoistic contractual association' in the interest of 'pleasure and utility'. Such unholy hedonism prevented the blending of egos into a 'single' collective 'we'. Freudianism and unrestrained sexual freedom had become the driver of modern-style sensate marriage.[18] The UNESCO Reports seem to be, on the one hand, provoking our cultures to 'learn' these poisonous 'modern' ideas, and on the other preaching that each and all societies should live together. Funny indeed.

What was Sorokin's prescription for the malady he had diagnosed in the 'modern' family?[19]: 'Its (family) basic function, that of inculcating deep sympathy, compassion, love and loyalty in its members, not only in relation to one another but towards humanity at large *must be restored and fully developed*.'

So, here we are: Sorokin vs. UNESCO experts. Indian education faces a life-and-death choice at this juncture. Almost at the same time as Sorokin was doing his research and writing, Lizelle Reymond, a French woman, had been living, learning and writing in Bharatvarsha (1947-1953). Her method was novel and daring: She lived for close to a year within an orthodox Brahmin family comprising four generations under one expansive roof. A book emerged out of this extraordinary experiment and experience — first in French in 1957, followed by an English translation in 1958, and reprinted again in 1972.[20] (Yet another curious coincidence: The 1972 'Learning' Report dismissing family traditions, while the 1972 Reymond book paying homage to the same— and both from France.

She had participated whole-heartedly in every detail of family life with reverence and patience. 'Learning' indeed was her aim e.g., 'I loved those hours spent in rice-sorting'.[21] She was told[22]: 'The penetration (of Western progress) has so shattered the economic structure of our family that no one can imagine the outcome. We used to live under an *ideal form of communism*, supported by our traditions. That has now been destroyed. The rules laying down the *duties* of each member of the family were stern, but they *protected the freedom* of the individual and defended the weak against the strong.' She also learnt from her anchor-person in the family[23]:

'The family presents the environment through which the Divine Power best finds its way. There it can penetrate gradually into our minds, hearts, bodies and blood, 'until the dead centre is reached'.' That she had imbibed such sacred learnings in full measure is proved by her warning to Republican India that unless the clash between the *diametrically opposite trends* of Western materialistic modernity, and that of Indian idealistic traditionality, is maturely handled, the nation could dis-integrate.[24] Five decades afterwards, her warning stands largely vindicated. (Also, Kathleen Raine's thoughts in this book may be recalled here.

Preceding Reymond by nearly five decades again, another Western woman, Margaret Noble (Sister Nivedita of the Ramakrishna Order), had also lived long in the heart of poor, ordinary families in North Calcutta. She has given us this valuable insight born of profound empathetic learning[25]:

> 'Among the luxuries of the West I have sometimes thought that the deepening of human tie was proportionate to *simplicity of surroundings*. A people to whom all *complexity of externals* is impossible, must live by thought and feeling, or perish in the wilderness.'

It is no wonder then that Sorokin too, an exceptionally mature and wise social scientist that he was, had the courage to recommend the rejuvenation and reinstatement of the family as the primary social unit where education for altruism could flourish. And this is the lifeblood of 'learning to live together'. From experience we say: This is very much true. Gratuitous advice for 'living together' is redundant for India. Selfish exploitative cultures, sermonising about 'living together are hypocritical. But Niveditas, Reymonds and Sorokins are nonentities in India's educational milieu. Gusty winds of blinding modernity have now begun storming our schools too. So we cannot resist paying attention to Sorokin once more [26]:

- 'Virtually the only devices for moulding character, various sports ... are based on an explicitly competitive principle, animated by the ethos of rivalry... There is little competition in humility, sacrifice, social service, and so forth.'
- 'The ideals inculcated by our school system are those of becoming a wealthy businessman, a powerful politician, a successful professional man, and the like. Thus our sensate schools breed egoists rather than altruists, fighters rather than peacemakers.'

So, the UNESCO Reports, forty years or so after Sorokin, fail to convince some of us how they intend to ground the fourth pillar of 'learning to live together' on something more solid than 'mere verbiage' (vide Merton). For, events like 'sit-and-draw', 'quiz', 'beauty', 'modelling' competitions etc. are a regular fare for our children — from nursery schools onwards. The same spirit of one-up-manship assumes more blatant forms and techniques in IITs. IIMs etc., embracing both students and teachers. From the annual pay-package for an MBA to the price tag of a car for the Director – that is the range. What are we 'learning to be'? And, on such a basis, what can 'living together' mean?

IV

Sometime in early March, 2009, some British newspapers had reported that a robot had been fabricated in Japan which could substitute for a teacher in the school classroom. It could show anger, make faces and perform many other functions. Families are gone. Intimate human relationships are being disowned. And now the teacher is on the way out. Could this be the summit of 'technoxication'? The two Reports above appear to swear by sci-tech as the wellspring of the 'necessary Utopia'. Is the robot-teacher meant to be the key symbol of such a weird Utopia? Pierre Thuillier, a noted historian of science, had observed as follows (1995)[27]:

> 'Christian theology defined a conception of nature perfectly adapted to technicist ambitions...a radical transformation had taken place, earth, air, water and fire, now theologically stripped of all "Soul", were no more than

objects which *Homotechnicus* was free to manipulate as he wished....Through its doctrine, the Judeo-Christian tradition somehow legitimized officially the most daring technical enterprises.'

Now, the robot-teacher is indeed a 'most daring technical enterprise', as Thuillier might have foreseen just about fifteen years ago. What a stupendous contrast to the philosophy and practice of *gurukula* education in Bharatvarsha in bygone ages!

Yet, sci-tech determinism and dictatorship in the territory of education has been accelerating. After reading a summary of the 'Education for All' global monitoring report of 2005, Manoj Das reaches this conclusion[28]: 'The Report gives a call to the governments concerned (including India, China) to undo the situation (of child and adult literacy)... but (all) have looked at education as technology-intensive training.' Thus, to the discerning eye the original paradigm shift enforced by the Judeo-Christian belief- system has now snow-balled into a concerted campaign of globalised hypnosis in favour of sci-tech. Global markets are indispensable. So, tickling the inferiority complex of the economically less developed countries, and a show of commiseration for the poor or illiterate in these populous places, is the subtle stratagem to expand the demand for sci-tech products. *Invention has now become the mother of necessity* for the sake of 'necessary Utopia'. And, as correctly pointed out by Das, India's careerist academics, bureaucrats and journalists are mostly quite eager to be duped by such deceptive manoeuvres. One is pretty sure, for instance, that not one among the three groups of learneds just mentioned would have read, leave aside assimilated, the following categorical words of Jacob Needleman[29]:

'Throughout the Western world the realization is dawning that contemporary science, including psychology, provides nothing for man that takes the place of the struggle for self-knowledge... human life within cosmic schemes (is) more purposeful than the universe of modern science.'*

---

* For instance, take the rather common prayer mantras before starting our daily chores: The hymn to the 'navagrahas' (nine planets), '*surya arghya daan*', '*surya gayatri*'. These chants humbly seek cosmic wisdom and express gratitude to these major cosmic agents.

These are some of the counter-sci-tech views of Needleman contained in his editorial remarks for the 'Penguin Metaphysical Library' series. Our students are kept systematically insulated from a large body of such honest appraisals.

It is an undeniable phenomenon that with the spread of literacy, the simple-minded, unselfish, honest and frugal Indian learns generally to be more clever, self-centred, spendthrift and dishonest. The higher one climbs the ladder of formal learning in different fields, the higher tends to be one's greed, craftiness and egotism. The galloping dehumanization of learning processes through sci-tech devices like video programmes, internet, power points, and now robots, is turning out 'caricatures of man', instead of 'complete man'. One of the most sacred human relationships is that of an ideal teacher with his/her ardent pupils, is vanishing from modern society. Swami Vivekananda had said this: '*Education is the manifestation of perfection already in man*'[30]. It is because the votaries of ' modern mentality' are uneducated to grasp the truth in the above aphorism, we find that their protestations about 'learning' are precipitating just the opposite: *Aggravation of imperfections already in man.* And this tragedy is taking place in the land of the *gurukula,* of *guru-griha-vasa,* right under our nose. A classic proof indeed of T S Eliot's 1934 characterization of modernity[31]: 'An age which advances progressively backwards'. Four centuries ago William Shakespeare's Hamlet, the tragic scholarly hero, had shot out an interesting statistic[32]: 'Ay sir, to be honest as this world goes, is to be one man pick'd out of two thousand.' What figure could this score card show for today? One in two hundred thousand? One in two million? Do the 'learning' Reports aspire to inspire modern man to achieve an honesty score at least as much as it had been in Hamlet's medieval time? The irreverent might suspect that even the motives behind the Reports could fall short of honesty

Later in the play, Hamlet, the Prince of Denmark, is heard to ask himself.[33] 'To be or not to be, that is the question'. A thinking man that he was, he was assailed by disillusion and futility — a pervasive mood in European society then. So, his dilemma seemed to be whether to be a meek, suffering martyr in the hands of 'outrageous Fortune'; or to be a fighter and victor against these odds and evils? Likewise a disillusioned, thinking reader of these Reports could today ask the same question a little differently: 'Learning to be a meek follower of outrageous technoxication, or to be a valiant fighter against its wild excesses?'

V

A hard look at another pillar, 'learning to know' , also exposes its fragility. What is to be 'known'? – that is the key question. The second Report talks about self-knowledge/self-understanding.[34] But these expressions are bereft of the capital distinction between information and knowledge which help man to make money on the one hand, and those which help him to gain his Soul on the other.* Building up a vision and structure of Utopia only on the first as the foundation shall yield a crumbling chaos only. Knowledge, understanding and progressive realization of the transcendental, unitive, ' kingdom-of-God-within', the SELF or Soul alone can answer to the call of Utopia. But treating the metaphysical being unscientific taboo, these Reports simply deny such a conception of Higher SELF, and the duty to realize it.[35]

From the epistemological angle too, the 'learning to know' recommendation is ineffectual, insofar as the 'complete man' is concerned. The self-imposed secular restriction of conceding only the sensual intellect and reason as the ultimate method of gaining knowledge is self-defeating. Limited intelligence is by nature a dividing tool. The indivisible Whole cannot be comprehended with its help alone. Supramental, pure Intuition is indispensable to grasp the Higher and the Whole. Wise people have always accepted and cultivated this capacity, while the learned have disputed it. It is to the first tribe that the true saviours of mankind have belonged — throughout history down to our times. Brain-stilling, not just brain–storming; silence and solitude, not just speeches and conferences (or commissions) have always been the pre-requisites for 'right knowing'.[37] The subordination of the local to the global, as the 1996 Report recommends, will destroy all possibility of such 'right knowing'. The ghosts of global booms and busts, caused by 'false knowing', will be haunting mankind continually. The much-ridiculed ancient mentality of India, for instance had known and practised a perfect 'global consciousness', while poised completely in the local. *Shrinvantu Vishwe Amritasya Putrah* (listen ye mankind

---

* Vivekananda's Guru had summed up the essence of so-called education as 'paddy and plantain learning'. This he had rejected in his early boyhood and remained nearly illiterate. Yet he had become the greatest personality of 19th century India to whom all the learneds used *to bow.*

all over the world — thou art the progeny of the Immortal), or *Vishwam Bhavati Eka Needam* the whole world is a single nest) were the soulful calls from the *rishis* of Bharatvarsha's ashrams. They were not empty, diplomatic pronouncements. Throughout history India has conducted her relationships with other cultures on the basis of these gospels. Our *rishis* needed no sci-tech gimmicks for such 'knowing'. But the way sci-tech dominated transient knowledge is invading us today, truth is fast getting out of reach for man.

Minus Truth, what else then will or can be 'known'? And what sort of Utopia shall it yield? It has to be taken by heart and head that there can never be anything even near to a Utopia or a 'complete man' by rejecting the 'subjective' core, the very essence, the uncaused cause of all 'objective' creation. If the ancient mind had gained and preserved this 'knowing' for us, modern mentality should bow down and learn about it from the ancient. That is how Krishna Prem could speak about 'The timeless wisdom of the Indian tradition'.[38] *The West-East teacher-learner relationship has to be reversed to that of East-West.* Such an essential reversal is clearly indicated by casual allusions like ' one must first know oneself ', 'discover who they are' etc in the 1996 Report.[39]

> The adorable genius, Helen Keller, who had pioneered methods of learning and teaching of the blind, had approximated, more than a century ago, closely the drift of the above argument about Truth[40]:

'At present the world is undergoing a complete revolution... How can one produce any great literary work at all in such times? This is an age of workers, not of thinkers.... When the rush and heat of achievement relax, we can begin to expect the appearance of grand men.' The *rishis* were the 'grand men' of Bharatvarsha who never wallowed in the 'rush and heat of achievement' of sensate character. So, they had 'seen' Truth in the luminous silence of the supramental. The 'rush and heat' of myopic and chaotic change is still more ominous today than it was in Helen Keller's time. Both the UNESCO Reports are a product of such times. Henry Thoreau had spoken these unpalatable but honest words[41]:

> 'In the morning I bathe my intellect in the stupendous and cosmogonal philosophy of the *Bhagwad Gita,* in comparison with which our modern world and literature seem puny and trivial.'

Therefore, much though the patronizing world bodies might implicitly wish it otherwise, a sensible, viable 'world society' can be founded on timeless oriental insights only (and their occidental equivalents).

VI

As for 'learning to do', the 1996 Report yields little that is worthwhile. This is not surprising because 'learning to know the self ', a condition precedent to doing, itself is beyond its ken. For instance, while it is argued that advances in 'knowledge' have to be transformed into 'innovations' for creating 'new business', it is also added that 'learning to do' cannot mean accomplishing a 'practical task' which will contribute to the 'manufacture' of something[42]. Pray, what then would this 'new business' consist of? Probably machines would do the 'practical task' of manufacturing 'innovated products'. But machines themselves have to be manufactured in the first place. So it is an endless series— machines making machines to make machines.

Now, considering the world as a whole where human population is always increasing, what is the future life process for mankind which such technoxicatron is going to build? Competence, commitment etc., in an abstract 'knowledge' environment will be unsustainable. The human being must have scope for using his hands and feet and heart, not merely his head for concrete things. Only then he may have a chance of being a 'complete' man. If not, he will be reduced to a foolish adjunct to machines, sitting statue-like in an air-conditioned cabin. Let us strive to anticipate, with due diligence, the psycho-social consequences of this possibility for human society. Confusion gets compounded when one reads that in the 'hightech organisation' of the future, especially in 'de-materialized' advanced economies, 'stable and effective relationships between individuals' will need people with greater behavioural, intuitional, judgmental and team-forging capabilities[43]. What will this high-tech organization itself be 'doing'? *It is ironical that while destroying stable relationships at home, one hears about them for organisations?* Are proliferating service (abstract) organisations ends in themselves? Wherefrom will man secure his modern apartments, clothings, automobiles, TVs, cell phones, packaged drinking water, refrigerators, sleeping pills, golf sticks, hard drinks — nay, an infinite number of innovated 'concrete' objects?Moreover, the almost angelic kind of futuristic employees visualised above will also remain a pious hope. The fretful, consumerist culture, inevitably igniting materialistic competitiveness all around, cannot nurture such human beings.

The twin reports have expatiated on ' learning throughout life'. This by no means is an original exhortation. It has been there all along, as a matter of course, in the heart of every society. However, it is now said that continuing education has to keep in step with the 'needs' of modern society.[44] But these needs are not spelled out. Instead, we are told that the 'educational continuum, coextensive with life has to embrace the whole society.[45] The honourable Commission, we dare say, has not considered that the four-stage *ashrama* system of Bharatvarsha had so perfectly conceived and implemented ages ago this apparently new 21st century idea, that hers has been temporally the most sustainable, and globally the most hospitable culture of the world. Accurate metaphysical sense of proportion, translated into a meticulous operational framework, had nurtured a people which, in general, neither impoverished environment nor other lands. Man was not treated as a tool, a resource to be hammered into shape to minister to the needs of 'high-tech organisations' in 'advanced economies'.

A deception seems to be concealed behind the repeated emphasis in the Reports on increasing the freedom of decision-making by the individual. The soaring rate of complexity and cumbrousness in daily life, a relentless drive towards 24-hours society, ugly seductive tactics employed for selling needless needs— how is all this contributing to individual freedom? With flexible employment policy (i.e., hire - and-fira), in a messily entangled global economic regime, some high-tech organizations may have more freedom. But how can the hapless employee, with pay cuts or lay offs or sackings, experience this blight as freedom? Hamlet had it right[46]: 'There are more things in Heaven and Earth, Horatio, Than are dreamt of in our philosophy'. Equally, there are more things in freedom than are dreamt of by the rich economies.

It should be more correct and useful to understand 'learning throughout life' at two levels:

(a) Essential learning: and

(b) Circumstantial learning

On the one hand, 'essential learning' has little to do with the ever-changing world. In fact, it is timeless. And this timeless learning base is indispensable for competent management of a world-influx on the surface. This learning deals with perennial issues like: Is self merely an amalgam of body-mind-senses? Or, is the real Self a portion of the eternal, the infinite, free from the bottomless needs and endless hungers of the physico-mental self? What is the purpose of 'human' birth? What is death? How to prepare for it in life? How to prepare for post-death existence? How does it fit into the ascending ladder of evolution from matter to life to mind to Spirit? What about the universally inherent and powerful negative tendencies in man like anger, greed, vanity, envy, lust etc.? Why and how can they be tamed to allow the more desirable but difficult inclinations (altruism, for instance) to blossom? What meaning will then freedom, responsibility, etc. take on? How can the designing and functioning of society and its institutions first take on these 'essential' issues and learnings before asking man for creativity, imagination, innovation, etc.,? The messiahs of an 'ever-changing world' urge for a 'necessary Utopia'. This is absurd. They cannot dream about its fundamentals (vide Hamlet). Natural change and man-made change are poles apart. It is man-created, artificially excited change, with technoxication as its fountainhead which, triggers the chain of 'circumstantial learning'. As the days go by, it is becoming clear that such frenetic learning is merely time-serving, evanescent by nature. Innovation and obsolescence march hand in hand. No enduring verities or certitudes inform such learning. Immediate, partial, measurable results are its aim. It is now almost forty years since the first Report, and fifteen since the second. All extra-orbital, mindful people agree that human and world conditions have worsened over this period.

These Reports, accompanied by annual Nobel prizes, seem to run parallel to the successive perilous slippages in man's ecological, social and moral states. Each round of Utopia, promised almost every fifty years since the sci-tech era of the last three centuries, has ended in unmanageable fiascos. It would have been prudent if such high-potency, high-density phrases as 'learning to be' 'learning to know' were avoided in such establishment-dictated Reports. For, their contents betray the expectations of readers who have some 'learning' about what such expressions really signify.

VII

Hence, the following 'needs of modern society' suggest themselves from the standpoint of 'essential' learning:

- The need for cooling down
- The need for slowing down

- The need for a working belief in Cosmic Wisdom
- The need for centripetal awareness
- The need for faith in Nature's retributing power
- The need for frugal simplicity in lifestyle and process
- The need for cleansing of the heart
- The need to align with Nature's own 24-hr. rhythm*
- The need to stop production and trade in arms
- The need to cultivate transcendental Consciousness
- The need for inner peace in leaders in all fields.

Such are a few of the 'essential learnings' to combat the bewildering impact of 'circumstantial learnings'. As always in the past, these essential learnings also constitute a whole-life responsibility. The chief mark of difference, however, is this: Perennial essential learnings have been handed down by the great, altruistic lovers and saviours of man and earth; ephemeral circumstantial learnings are being imposed by humans who can scarcely see beyond the nose of their immediate self-interest. Here is a testimony for the kind of essential learning indicated above from another American Transcendentalist, R.W. Emerson.[47]

'I owed a magnificent day to the *Bhagwad Gita*..... it was as if an empire spoke to us, nothing small or unworthy, but large, serene, consistent — the voice of an old intelligence which in another age and climate had pondered and thus disposed the same questions which exercise us today.'

As a foil to Emerson, we might allow John Yale (later Swami Vidyatmananda of the Ramakrishna Order), who had visited and lived in India for sometime in the early 1950s, to speak to the readers[48] :

'In the art of living at peace with oneself it is increasingly evident that now, as in the past, it is the West which must be the learner, with the Oriental the teacher.' Is not the 'peace' of the Swami what the modern man 'essentially' needs to learn about today? Let Thoreau, Raine, Nivedita and Reymond be recalled again.

---

* Call centres in India symbolize the worst of globalized commercial dictatorship and enslavement. It is one instance of 'social plagues' as Sri Aurobindo had forewarned long ago.

But this plain fact eludes the present–day educated Indian. Why? Not long ago an American scholar of Indian and Western philosophy had provided this frank answer.[49] '...among Indians there is a disposition today, to view the glories of Indian philosophy as gracing a bygone epoch; the future is entrusted, if not to science exclusively, at least to Western modes of thought. If Indians themselves succumb to this view, it is not surprising that few Westerners are aware of *how relevant is much in classical Indian thought to the problems that occupy us today,* to say nothing of the problems that do not occupy us but should' (emphasis added). Essentially the same indictment was leveled more recently by an American psychologist who too had studied Eastern thought (Indian and Japanese)[50].

'But the integration that Indians have to make, in contrast to the Japanese, has been contaminated and complicated by two centuries *colonial denigration of everything Indian*: that what is good is Western, and what is inferior is Indian. This has by *no means disappeared with independence*' (emphasis added).

Besides the above consciously prolonged colonial hang-over, two other post-independent corrosive forces have been grievously wounding Indian culture: Communist fundamentalism and semitic religious fanaticism. The modern educated Indian, in the name of scientific temper and polling-booth fixation, remains unconcerned about such destructive forces. Readers should therefore listen attentively to Sri Aurobindo, a 20th century *rishi,* on the issue of modernity as sci-tech would have it v. sanity as spirituality would recommend[51]:

'Whether the future hope of the race lies in a rational and or mechanized, or in a spiritual, intuitive and religious civilization and culture, that, then, is the important issue.' Elsewhere he had spoken more decisively with transcendental foresight that, if the choice by man favours the first route then, 'like the too massive Titan, it [commercial age] will collapse by its own mass *mole ruet sua'*.[52]

Swami Vivekananda too had sounded a far-sighted warning: If India gives up spirituality and adopts the materialistic culture in the same way as the West, it would be an extinct race in three generations.[53]

We get back again to Sri Aurobindo's vision and courage of conviction to thus advise humanity[54]:

'The unity of East and the West is the drift of this era. But if in this endeavour the West is treated as the foundation or principal plank, we shall be committing a capital mistake. The East is the principal plank, the foundation. For, the external world is founded on the internal, not the internal on the external.'

References

1. UNESCO; *Learning To be*, Paris, 1972, p. 271.
2. *Ibid., p. 147.*
3. Bhaktivedanta Swami, A.C. ; *Bhagwad Gita as It is*; Mumbai : Bhaktivedanta Book Trust, 1972, quoted inside the front cover.
4. Chakraborty S. K., *Against The Tide*; New Delhi: Oxford University Press, 2001, pp. 186-91.
5. *Bhagwad Gita*, op. cit. chapter 16.
6. UNESCO, *Learning: The Treasure Within*, Paris, 1996, 1998.
7. Ibid., p 15.
8. Tagore Rabindranath; *Human Values: The Tagorean Panorama*, translation by S.K. Chakraborty and P Bhattacharya, New Delhi: New Age, 2008, p.vi.
9. Bhaumik M.; quoted in *Truth*, Platinum Jubilee Issue, Kolkata: Shastra Dharma Prachar Sabha, 2008, pp. 204-05.
10. Ramanna, Raja; 'Indian Holistic Experience and Analytical Rationality'; *Prabuddha Bharata*, November 1988, pp 438-40.
11. Chakraborty S. K. and Chakaborty D; *Spirituality in Management: Means or End*; New Delhi : Oxford University Press, 2008, chapter 5.
12. Sorokin P. A.; *Reconstruction of Humanity*; Bharatiya Vidya Bhavan: Bombay, 1958, pp. 98-104.
13. *Ibid., p. 105.*
14. *Ibid., p. 106.*
15. *Ibid., p. 106.*
16. *Ibid., p. 118.*
17. Vivekananda, Swami, *Complete Works*, Kolkata: Advaita Ashrama, 2005, Vol. 2, p. 2.
18. Sorokin, op. cit., pp. 133-135.
19. *Ibid.; p. 136.*
20. Reymond L.; *My Life With a Brahmin Family*, Penguin Books: Baltimore, 1972.
21. *Ibid., p. 75.*
22. *Ibid., p. 111.*
23. *Ibid., p. 130.*
24. *Ibid., p. 7.*

25. Nivedita Sister, *The Web of Indian Life*, Kolkata: Advaita Ashrama, 1999, pp. 48-49.
26. Sorokin, op. cit., p. 138.
27. Quoted in *The Indian Mind: Then and* Now by M. Danino, Auroville Press International, 2000, pp. 90-91.
28. Das Manoj, 'The "Business" of Education' in *Philosophy and Practice of Education for India*, ed. S. K. Chakraborty, Kolkata: Sri Aurobindo Samiti, 2006, p. 119.
29. Reymond, op. cit, p. 2.
30. Vivekananda Swami, *Letters*, Kolkata: Advaita Ashrama, 2008, p. 70.
31. Quoted in Bhattacharya, Pradip, 'Education for Character- Building', *Philosophy and Practice of Education for India*, op. cit., p. 147.
32. Shakespeare W., *The Tragedy of Hamlet*, Penguin Books: Harmondsworth, 1950, Act Scene 2, p. 65.
33. *Ibid., Act 3, scene 1, p. 81*
34. op. cit., pp. 18-19
35. Chakraborty S. K., and Chakraborty D., *Human Values and Ethics*, Hyderabad: ICFAI University Press, 2006, pp. 210-218.
36. Krishna Prem (Nixon, Ronald), *Initiation Into Yoga*, BI Publications: Bombay, 1976, p. 67.
37. Aurobindo Sri, *The Ideal of the Karmayogin*, Pondicherry: Sri Aurobindo Ashram, 2007, p. 40.
38. Prem Krishna, op. cit., p. 75.
39. *Learning: The Treasure Within*, op. cit., p. 93
40. Keller Helen, *The Story of My life*; Popular Library: New York, 1902, 1958, pp. 347-348.
41. Bhaktivedanta Swami, AC, op. cit., back cover quotation.
42. *Learning: The Treasure Within*, op. cit., p. 93
43. *Ibid., p. 90-91*
44. *Ibid., p. 99*
45. *Ibid., p. 100*
46. Shakespeare, op. cit, Act 1, Scene 5, p. 54
47. Bhaktivedanta Swami, AC, op. cit., back cover quotation.
48. Vidyatmananda Swami, *The Yankee and The Swamis*, Chennai: Ramakrishna Math, 2001, p. 7.
49. Foreward by Huston Smith to Swami Satpakashananda's book, *Knowledge and Its Methods* – Kolkata: Advaita Ashrama, 1974, p. 12.
50. Foreword by Alan Roland to S. K. Chakraborty's book, *Managerial Effectiveness and Quality of Worklife*, New Delhi: Tata McGraw- Hill, 1987, p. vi.

51. Aurobindo Sri, *The Foundations of Indian Culture*, Pondicherry: Sri Aurobindo Ashram, 1998, p.16.
52. Aurobindo Sri, *The Human Cycle*, Pondicherry: Sri Aurobindo Ashram, 2005, p. 81.
53. Vivekananda Swami, *Call To The Nation*, Kolkata: Advaita Ashrama, 2006, p. 66.
54. Translated by the author from *Sri Aurobindo's Bengali Writings*, Pondicherry: Sri Aurobindo Ashram, 2005, p. 127.

CHAPTER 7

'LEARNING TO DO': The 'Essential' Way of Four CEO's

प्रत्नान मानाद् अध्या ये समस्वर छ
लोकयन्त्रासो रभसस्य मन्तवः ।
अपानक्षासो बधिरा अहासत
ऋतस्य पन्थां न तरन्ति दुष्कृतः ।।
(ऋः. ९/७३/६)

Those that from ancient seats
manifested themselves –
The Guides of song and Counsellors
of movement,
From these the eyeless and the
deaf have turned aside.
The evil-doers do not travel
on the path of Eternal Law.

(*Rig Veda* 9/73/6)

(*Ibid.*, p. 293)

I

The *Bhagwad Gita* has been mentioned at several places above. It so expounds the sacred art and science of 'doing' as probably no other psycho-philosophical text has ever done anywhere. Our efforts to derive anything meaningful about 'doing' in the 1996 UNESCO report were a failure. 'Circumstantially', at the start of the Mahabharata war, Arjuna was shirking responsibility on shallow, sentimental grounds. Sri Krishna put him in the right frame of mind 'to do' – first in chapter 2, and thereafter re-affirmed the one 'essential' learning needed for discharging a major role-specific duty. The following four examples from work-life demonstrate the realisation and advantage of this 'essential' learning in our own times, even in business. These individuals speak to us in their own words, as recorded during interviews done in the years 1997-2003. To the author they emerged as sacred pilgrims amidst secular travails. They had struggled successfully to practise 'timeless', 'essential' sacred learning 'to do' what arrived before them. 'Conviction', not 'calculation', was the driving force within each one of them.

1. The CEO of a Commercial Bank and a Development Bank

'I began to secretly read my mother's Hindi *Gita* at the age of thirteen only. Though I could understand nothing then, I stuck to my habit. And gradually I felt that the *Gita* grew into me. Since then verse II.47 (to do duty alone you have the right, but not to personal fruits therefrom) has been the bedrock of my work-life. I felt no compulsion for advance proof of the practicality of the Education in India: A Tree Without Roots *nishkam karma* principle. It simply went straight into me. Ever since it has shown me the light on the path.

'Once in my years as a probationary officer in the Bank, I happened to get into an argument with my superior who was many years and levels ahead of me. After a few minutes, he told me in a quiet but firm voice: 'Look, young man, discuss "yes", but argue "no"'. This essential learning too had loyally stood by me till my retirement. 'I took pre-mature retirement six years before it was due. I did not allow myself to bend my principles which the powers-that-be found to be uncomfortable. I was advised to meet a powerful person in New Delhi, though he was not a member of the government. I rejected the idea replying, "He is not my Minister." Since retirement I have been living in this small apartment in such a remote little town. All offers of directorships, committee chairmanships and the like have been declined by me. My wife and myself enjoy our spiritual practices, morning and evening walks, and occasional visits by our son with his family.

'Whenever any praise came to me for official work, I used to silently pass it on to the feet of the Divine. I felt that it was the Divine who was managing the bank. Once I told as much to the Finance Minister. From time to time I used to find myself at my wits end in tackling intricate business problems. On such occasions I would suspend all my internal and external telephone calls, and no visitors or meetings would be allowed. Then I would go into one partitioned corner of my office chamber and practise "brainstilling" in order to calm down the excited intellectual storm caused by the particular intractable problem. Since I had full faith in the existence of Higher Intelligence, I tried to allow its access into my thoughtless awareness. My problem would be presented to it as it were. Then I waited for some intimation from it – without being impatient or imposing my preference. This process had hardly failed me.

'I had a couple of credit cards presented to me by some banks. But I never used them. If ever in need of money, I borrowed against my bank deposits. Credit cards are a license to spending. 'Our heritage has all the answers to all our problems.'

2. CEO of an Entertainment-industry Firm

'My grandfather was a painter. In those days this vocation meant a hand-to-mouth existence. So two of his sons were sent to Japan (one was my father), and another to Egypt to fend for themselves. I did my B.Sc. (Honours), followed by an MBA from one of the earlier IIMs (Indian Institute of Management). ... We are Jain; but my father's personal ideal and idol was *maryada purushottama* Sri Ram. And yet our home had no image. Under his direct tutelage, I began to understand that Sri Ram was perhaps an appropriate leadership model for the *satya yuga*, while Sri Krishna was so for the *kali yuga*. Thereafter I got in touch with the thoughts of Ramana Maharshi and Christ. All this seemed to push me towards spirituality.

'I was involved in a turnaround case. Such cases are inherently more complex and demanding than normal ongoing companies. So I began to study more and more spiritual literature. It was becoming clear to me that I have an innermost Being which transcends the hectic turmoil of body-mind-thought. I was getting convinced about the need to access this pure consciousness which is happiness itself. I started meditating twice a day. At the same time, I became a little confused. Often I felt tempted to retire and devote all my time to such pursuits. Somehow, during the last three or four years I had mentally decided to attain *moksha* in this very life. 'At this stage came this new proposal to pilot another turnaround. I had then just got hold of the *Bhagwad Gita*. There I hit upon the right perspective for my immediate dilemma. This perspective I did not get elsewhere. This book held out the full agenda of human life. So I accepted the fresh challenge, and resolved not to get stressed. The *Gita* has helped me to sustain my tempo for corporate life without losing sight of the goal of *moksha*. ...

'The *Gita* helped me to realize that most of my life and workproblems, including stress, were springing from personal ego. With the help of insights from the *Gita*, I am able to dis-identify myself more and more from egocentric tensions arising from any cause.

'... I was also able to realize from this book that one of the biggest causes of unethical behaviour, as well as stress, is fear of failure. Besides, if one is focused all the time on success, the capacity for risk-taking also declines. ... 'Prayer or *prarthana* has been an unfailing prop in managing my personal effectiveness. ... 'To be born in *Bharatavarsha*, India, has been a great good fortune for me.'

3. Executive Director of an Oil-refining and Marketing Company

'Today, the core of my existence is yoked to a kind of deep spiritual Being. All decisions, major or minor, emanate from this core. Sometimes it is a conscious process, but often it is natural. This core sums up my life and its purpose. All decisions are taken there for me. The individual 'I' does not decide anything. 'My known spiritual journey began on 20 June 1996, when I attended a three-day Workshop on 'Management by Human Values' organized specifically for the top managers of our company. It was held at the Management Centre for Human Values, Indian Institute of Management, Kolkata. From the moment I filled in the questionnaire sent to us before attending the Workshop, I became aware of my own spiritual and moral dimensions. 'I was more of a challenger and investigator than a believer. I did manage to test the patience of the facilitator, and on four occasions got seriously counter-challenged in return. I did go through the experiential process in the Workshop. On occasions they touched me at a deeper level; and I became surprised and bewildered at the intensity of my own absorption in and response to these initial experiences.

'A couple of months later the Quality Mind Process (QMP) became part of me. Soon its duration started reaching 30-40 minutes in the early mornings. I felt more clear-headed. I felt immense energy at my command to fulfil challenging assignments, and ask for more.

'My temperament in the workplace became more gentle and responsive. ... We were a cosy and effective work-team. 'I had also recently visited the Sri Siddhi Vinayak Temple of Mumbai with a colleague. The visit to the temple created a strong impression on my mind, and I began visiting the temple more frequently. My wife would accompany me almost every time, and the children too would join often. ... I submitted myself to the grace and service of my lord Sri Siddhi Vinayak. 'Meanwhile, my daily QMP continued. Its duration became one hour, as I could wake up at 4.30 a.m. I got deeply interested in some books by Sri Aurobindo. I added them to the one given in the Workshop. Apart from *Living Within*, I read *Looking from Within* and *Growing Within*. I read the *Gita* many times – initially with some reservations and a large number of questions, but later with increasing understanding and deepening fascination. Each verse was meaningful, complete, and a fundamental truth in itself'.

'My meditation continues through all my travels. So does my quest to reach, meet, and unify with the Divine. I have in my heart accepted Swami Vivekananda as my guru, and have great reverence for Sri Ramakrishna and Sri Sarada Ma – his guru and *guruma*.'

4. General Manager of a Thermal Power Plant

'I see my life in three phases. In the first phase, as a student, things were relatively under my control. Then too some stress was felt; but that was due to the hard work required for better results. Even at that time, to concentrate better and to combat tension, I used to repeat God's name and visit temples with like-minded friends. We used to sit there in silence for a while.

'In the second phase, at the start of my professional career, anxiety and stress sprang from the pressure of tasks assigned to me by my superiors. This meant spending extra working hours to master the job. Here *japa* proved very helpful. Reading good quality fiction was also a healthy tension dissipator. I would also sometimes share my difficulties with a few elders outside the office. They would listen to me and suggest some tips. One good method I practised was invoking the *gayatri mantra*. 'As I grew older and climbed up the organizational ladder, I entered into the third phase. I then faced the internal and external systems of the corporate world which are steeped in corruption, greed and jealousy. I had to live with them, yet ensured that I did not lose my own human values. The other major problem was that I was now neglecting my family — old father, young children, wife, and others.

'So, I decided to draw up a self-regulating charter: Not to initiate anything unethical from my side, regular prayers in the morning (20 min) and before sleeping (5-7 min), and so on. I also started practising written *japa* of *Rama-nama* in a specially reserved pad. My family members have been cooperating positively in such efforts.

'However, the turning point was attending the first in-house 'Human Values Workshop' in 1999. I then saw vividly that 'silence in solitude' is essential for introspection. This is the key to conquer stress.

'After attending the advanced modules of the Workshop especially designed for those in leadership roles, I was convinced that *svarat samrat bhavati* (master of oneself becomes master of everything); this is the one way to live well and without stress. I also now subscribe to the *nishkam karma* (unattached work) philosophy of the *Gita*. I try to imprint this upon my brain at the end of my prayers. Now I clearly realize that when one achieves success, one should be ready to take failures and brickbats in one's stride too. Listening to *bhakti sangeet* (devotional music) at home also leaves positive residues in the subconscious. A combination of such methods, coupled with the sincere belief that God extends his support for correct actions, makes me feel more secure and gives me peaceful sleep.

'Moreover, nowadays I prefer reading spiritual literature rather than fiction. I bring my family too into discussions. They compare my actual conduct against the sacred guidelines. With the grace of God, all this helps us to evolve together bit by bit.'

II

The following learnings 'to do' might be highlighted from the four narratives above:

- The spiritual approach in organizations presupposes the prevalence of a continuous, living tradition in the wider social matrix. This is borne out un-mistakably by all the four instances above. In the absence of such an overarching ambience, all superficial or intellectual attempts to incorporate spirituality in secular organizations will tend to be counterfeit. It will be wiser for cultures which lack such a tradition to proceed from the roots, and with humility and learn from those who treasure all the precious details and authentic experiences.*

- The *Gita* has been the one common anchor for all the four leaders. This gives the lie to the allegation by some renowned intellectuals, Indian and Western, that the *Gita* incites violence. Violence might be a strong emotion ruling the mind of such critics themselves! For people see what they are predisposed to or want to see in someone or something. Denunciation is their a-priori intention.* Yet, millions of common folk in India, even today, are devoted 'to doing' on the basis of the timeless 'essential' principles the *Gita* embodies.
- Yoga-Vedanta, or Hindu psycho-philosophy, has been rendered practical through concrete processes like deep breathing, silent *japa*, written *japa*, prayer, and meditation. This ensemble is clearly demonstrated by the self-imposed discipline in the daily routine of all the individuals cited above. Faith and sincerity are their hallmarks. Positive proof follows their ardent faith. This runs counter to populist scientific temper.
- Prevention or reduction of stress, equanimity of mind in success or failure, clear thinking, strength to take difficult decisions, ego reduction, heightened ethicality, better credibility among team members, trust in God or a higher Consciousness or Intelligence – these are the common positive fruits reaped by all of them. But these fruits flow as derivatives from the primary motive for abiding peace, like attaining *moksha*, or becoming an agent or instrument in the hands of the Divine.
- All the four individuals tend 'to do' as 'yogis'. That is, in their own ways, each one is striving 'to be' in yoga with the Divine Consciousness – a sort of plugging into a charger socket. Among them they illustrate the practicality of *yogah karmasu kaushalam* (yoga is the skill required to do work), *tasmaad yogi bhavarjuna* (therefore, O Arjuna, be a yogi), and *tasmat sarveshu kaleshu mamanusmara yuddhya cha* (therefore, remembering Me at

* It was refreshing to read, after this chapter was printed, Jeffery Long's essay on this theme of the Gita (Prabuddha Bharata, October, 2009). Whereas our intellectuals readily join the Gita–violence brigade, Long has the seeingintelligence and courage to state that their opinions are off the mark and a little hypocritical (p. 571).
However, he omits reference to Sri Aurobindo's categorical views on this issue in The Message of the Gita, 1977, pp. 13-4.

all times, fight) – the eternal verities of *Gita* (2.50, 6.46, 8.7). What a contrast between such true yoga of inner realization, and the false 'yoga' of laboratory or questionnaire research. Such latest fashion is degenerating the 'essential' learning-to- of the *Gita* into timeserving 'circumstantial' learning.

- The fulsome, unequivocal trust in the universal relevance and worth of the *Gita* from Emerson, Thoreau, Wordsworth, Griffiths *et. al.*, has been mentioned earlier. The reader may now be presented with a stark contrast. Twenty years ago perhaps we had spoken on a few Indian insights for management at a national conference organized by a certain professional body. The *Gita* was mentioned by us in this context. At the end the vote of thanks was given by a former IIM student (Hindu) of ours, presently a senior executive in a well-known MNC. At one stage in his delivery he snubbed us rather severely: 'Would you teach *Bhagwad Gita* to a Muslim or a Christian?' (at least 95 percent of the audience was probably Hindu). And that too in terms of the *nishkam karma* principle of the *Gita* in the land of its origin. This was the prize we got from an ex-student for discussing Indian ethos. Imagine, if you can, the kind of 'liberal' education delivered today by our society. It could be asked: Why did the student do so? One reason could be to project oneself as a holier-than-thou secularist. The other, and deeper one, might be that by denouncing the Gita etc., the way would be cleared for wholesale acceptance of Western thoughts and ideas as the true stuff. We of course had no chance to respond back.

III

'Life-long learning' is another phrase frequently heard or read these days. This is a truism which cannot be contested. But there is a need to recognize the vital distinction between: (a) life-long learning of *ever-changing* tools, techniques, systems etc. to earn one's keep; and (b) life-long learning of *unchanging* principles to build one's character. Education currently leans heavily and increasingly towards (a) Occasionally some lip service may be given to (b) But the scope and opportunity for character consciousness are rapidly shrinking. This is true as much in the home or school, as in the neighbourhood or in the street. Let a few examples be given. The time-less principle of *nishkam karma* (desireless or un-attached work), illustrated above, requires life-long dedication and striving. No crash programme can implant this attitude as an integral basis of one's work-life. The potential for existential happiness contained in this 'essential' principle of 'learning to do' had been explained by Swami Vivekananda to a Los Angeles audience in 1900[1]:

> 'Attachment is the source of all our pleasures now... What, again, brings misery but this very attachment? We have to detach ourselves to earn joy... That man alone will be able to get the best of nature, who, having the power of attaching himself to a thing with all his energy, has also the power to detach himself when he should do so. The difficulty is that there must be as much power of attachment as that of detachment.'

Failing to address this superordinate need at the fundamental level of education, exhortations for learning-to-do and life-longlearning in popular platforms tend to keep people tied to the hidden motives of change protagonists. Most of the latter tend to be professional de-stabilizers for reaping short-term gains e.g., recall the world-wide scare let loose by Y–2K change agents on the eve of year 2000. The Indian counter-parts of such agents are generally content to be ardent imitators, though proclaiming to be innovative.

Yet another 'essential' life-long-learning is to acquire, by degrees, the capacity to preserve equality of mind, *samatwa,* in success and failure, gain or loss, praise or blame, recognition or denial, victory or defeat in every arena of life. The ordinary rational mind, equipped with secular logic alone, is inadequate for this task. As for the 'essentiality' of such equanimity, it lies in the virtue of conserving psychological energy. Thus, the erratic emotional swings we experience when high exultation and deep depression are felt at winning and losing lead always to edginess, tension and dissipative stress. Sri Krishna never tires of emphasizing this learning to Arjuna 200 in the *Bhagwad Gita* (verses II. 38, 50, 56; XII – 13,17,18, 19; XIV - 24,25; XV 5: XVIII 26). And those few (including the one's cited above) who have striven for this 'essential' learning in their own lives have all admitted that without an emotional anchor in the sacred or spiritual or Divine, this endeavour cannot be sustained. Given only such an anchor, can

---

* Unfortunately, the 'yellow peril' is now becoming a fact – for India and Tibet at least.

the learner manage to sail above the turbulent dualities in their secular lives. It is such a temperament alone which can stay reasonably detached from the largely non-controllable circumstantial factors governing the events happening to us. Sri Aurobindo expounds the true basis of such learning of 'equality' in these words[2]:

'... we shall have the same equality of mind and soul towards all happenings, painful or pleasurable, defeat and success, honour and disgrace, good repute and ill-repute, good fortune and evil fortune. For in all happenings we shall see the will of the Master of all works and results...' The idea of the 'Master of all works' is the sacred seed of human work sprouting on the soil of Cosmic work. The known and unknown Universes are an infinite work-project of a Godhead. Just as an automobile and a book pre-supposes humans with will behind them, so must be the case for the infinite projections of objective and subjective, gross and subtle worlds.

The founders of *sanatan* culture had intuited and formulated principles for and attitudes towards human work in such a way that it could remain imbedded, consciously and harmoniously, in the cosmic canvas. Individualized, separative and competitive egoes were not given the final seal of approval. Instead, life-long learning was directed towards nourishing the feeling of being a conscious 'instrument' for the 'Master of all works'. The petty or 'unripe' ego of the individual, now beginning to breathe in the vast Ego of the Cosmic, suffers less and less from tensions and clashes. Both *nishkam karma* and *samatwa* learnings are strongly correlated with the life-long process of becoming *nir-ahamkara* (de-egoization). Arjuna was meticulously educated about all three inter-related tenets of 'learning to do' by Sri Krishna. And Arjuna was a superlative achiever in the secular sense also. A venerable monk* had once put all this across succinctly to one of his earnest devotees in these words: 'Work is the bridge between the world and God'.

A common advice tendered to beginners on this path is to mentally practise this formula: 'Remember and offer'. In the first instance, non-egoistic learning may have convinced someone that all mental, physical and nervous energies ultimately originate and flow from the One *shakti* (see chapter 10 of the *Bhagwad Gita*). Thereafter,

* Swami Gambhiranandaji (1899–1988), 11th President of the Ramakrishna Math and Mission.

one might develop the habit of collecting oneself at the start by a little deep breathing, remembering the above truth, and feeling that the task at hand will be done with the help of energies flowing from the One Divine fountainhead.

At the close of the work one should again stop for a few moments, and consciously offer whatever has been done to this One source of all empowerments. This is a fruitful method to 'bridge the world and God'. This is an outcome of sacred rationality, but denied by secular rationality. The former impels us towards life-ling 'essential' learning, making for a progressively firm standing ground. The latter compels us towards life-long 'circumstantial' learning which is shaky and fleeting. Neither of them is dispensable. But in our time the latter has almost completely overshadowed the former, ruining human culture and character. The sense of priority and proportion has been lost.

This tragedy has overtaken mankind because another great learning has not been learnt or has been ignored: 'Seeing before doing'. Technology–driven commercialism has been the dominant keynote for the last four centuries. And during the last four decades its pitch has become strident, deafening. The frenzy for 'doing' thus created has been turning us blind to human values. Witness, for instance, the steeply rising curve of frivolity in the most dignified and elegant of all games: cricket. Have we paused to take stock of what 'essential' values we have un-learnt, and what 'circumstantial' values we have swallowed in this process? Something similar is happening to *yoga* also.

The *sanatan* Bharatiya culture and society had been conceived, planned and structured by *rishis* during Vedic and Pauranic times. They were 'seers' (*drashtas*) of Reality and Truth from a supra-mental, supra-rational plane. It was a holistic vision across time and clime. What they had 'learnt by seeing' beyond mind and reason, was gradually formulated into 'learning to do' norms at personal and social levels. KM Munshi had thus expressed this first principle of 'learning to see' before 'learning to do'[3]: 'The Central Idea underlying the Vedic Culture, on which Indian culture is founded, is that *Rita,* the Cosmic order, is one and indivisible, operating in the material as well as moral and spiritual fields.'

The modern sci-tech mentality has however severed all connection with such holistic Realization of *Rita* or Cosmic Order. Although science these days sometimes speaks about unified field theory, consciousness, inter-connectedness of all creation and events, and the like, these proclamations have made no impact on the reordering of human outlook and society. This failure is inevitable because they are merely abstract theoretical notions. Without respect for the solid basis of Realization, as the *rishis* had, there can be no practical rendering of such post-facto scientific corroborations of eternal verities 'seen' by the Rishis of yore.

That is why the ideal for kings, emperors, leaders etc. in Indian culture has been that of a *Rajarshi.* The 'seer' plus 'doer', the 'monk' plus 'emperor', the 'sage' plus 'king'. Kautilya's treatise on administration (around 300 BC) contains classic delineations of this model for indispensable learning even to this day.[4]

A critical psychological discipline for 'seeing through' beyond 'looking at' is that of *antarmukhita* (interiorization or centripetalization). Our scattered, exteriorized awareness is excessively centrifugal. Cumbrous and explosive consumerism associated with modernity (malls and plazas and shoppes) is relentlessly fuelling our *bahirmukhita.* Cosmic Order, perennial verities, *ritam,* etc., cannot but sound as antiquarian and redundant to such a *bahirmukhi,* disintegrated mentality. The scope and opportunity for the essential life-long learning of *antarmukhita* are dwindling fast.

Moreover, during the post-renaissance sci-tech era learning for 'analysis' and analytical capacity has been the dominant credo of education. This has been associated with determined downplaying of 'synthesis' and synthesizing ability. Left-brain analytical learning in all fields has yielded many discrete objective benefits in the short run. But the abandonment of right-brain synthesizing power has made humanity destitute of integral, holistic perception of all work and existence. The simple, sincere, intuitive mind has been ousted by the clever, calculating, manipulating mind.

The cumulative pathos of such pathological obsession with 'analysis' is, however, quitepatent: Mounting social, psychological and ecological misery and chaos. Learning-to-do wholly on the basis of left-brain analysis, by the very nature of it, has been producing irreparable fragmentation and disintegration. The well-fed, long-life learned human of today is increasingly suffering from subjective penury in the midst of objective plenty.

And our innocent children too are being seduced into this path. The remedy common to both these correlated learning deficits is 'meditation'. This essential process has numerous methods and steps from low to high to suit individual temperaments. It has also a general, common approach available to all beginners. But, in either case, a fruitful start presupposes some minimal withdrawal from ceaseless externalizing on the plea of being active and dynamic.

This needs to be supported by learning that the real source of joy and bliss is already built into our inner core. The kingdom of Heaven is within, the musk is already inside the navel of the deer, *chidananda rupah shivoham, twamasi niranjanam* and the like. Such messages are the first birth-right of a human child; not humpty dumpty sat on a wall, or ba ba black sheep, etc.

A learned and spiritually elevated monk-scholar had once answered the question 'What is Education?' in a unique style[5]. 'Education is that by learning which one's whole life becomes happy. That learning by which the funs of adolescence do not turn into frustrations of youth, the pleasures of youth do not become the pains of middle age, and the enjoyments of middle age do not turn into misery in old age is called education.' In other words, learning of techniques and tools for material existence in the secular sphere has to be preceded or accompanied by subjective learning from the domain of the sacred.

The central hub of such learning for overall life-long happiness in our culture lies in *sanyam,* or self-restraint in its most comprehensive sense from childhood to old age e.g., *vak sanyam, drishti sanyam, shruti sanyam, ahaar sanyam, vihar sanyam* * and so on. It is easy to see how 'modern' society, and its champions are destroying these essential capacities by forcing upon us wanton indulgence in lower appetites. The few practical principles, starting with *nishkam karma,* dealt with earlier in this chapter are supportive of this one foundation, *sanyam,* for truly happy human development. Then 'doing' will undermine 'becoming' to a much smaller extent. This will contribute amply towards allround Highest Good, as Munshi emphasizes at length.[6]

---

* Vak = speech, Drishti = sight, Shruti = hearing, Ahaar = eating, Vihar = enjoyment, pastime.

IV

This chapter has drawn attention to a few fundamental subjective principles about the art of learning-to-do. While competency mapping of employees is now fairly widespread, it is unable to touch the core being of the doer. One of the major problems at this level is our incompetence to handle or manage success and failure in work and life. Our emotions tend to run high or low, as the case may be. Such inner afflictions enslave and bind us.

The liberating influence of attempting to do *nishkam karma*, etc., from such continuous subjective energy drainage has been captured well by Bede Griffiths[7]:

'The first condition is to do the work, but not to seek the reward, because seeking a reward means that you are putting your ego into your work. Work which starts from the ego – which is the false self, the persona, the mask – all such work will be impure and will bind you. 'You may be given... the charge of a school or hospital or other social work, and after some time you have built up quite a good organization.... and then you are removed. It may be that the whole thing then goes to pieces. Here you must reflect that you received your work from God, and you must leave the fruit of your work to God. You do not allow yourself to be disturbed.' Such a clear grasp of the 'essential' art of doing made Griffiths declare that the *Gita* 'can become a manual of spiritual guidance for the West. It has a universal message'.[8]

The above keynote of this chapter is also a basic working principle in the social design of Bharat's culture – a non-competitive society in spirit and action. Let us listen to Munshi again for a brief yet lucid exposition[9]:

'... to attain the Highest Good... society should be organized on a non-competitive basis so that the egotistic impulses resulting in untruth, greed and self-indulgence are progressively eliminated.' The Highest Good of mankind is in spiritual unfoldment of the free soul

---

* The common English rendering of yogah karmasu kaushalam Gita, verse 2.50) is 'skill in work is yoga'. This may be one impetus behind the recent creation of a strangely-named organization , 'National Institute of Skills Development'. The true meaning of the Gita postulate, however is: It is karmayoga or nishkam karma which is the essential skill for ethical and liberating work.

or *atman*. The competitive ethos is, however, naturally associated with *sakam karma*, or egotistic, desireful work.* The damaging ethical consequences of excessive *sakam karma* in present times are quite evident to those who can or will see.

Moreover, despite all rationalizations to the contrary, *sakam karma* violates *ritam* or Cosmic Order. The entire range of working agents of Nature – from sun and wind to water and earth to flora and fauna – functions on the principle of *nishkam karma*. God, the Master Worker, is *nishkam karma* in Itself. The human agent alone acts as a deviant, disempowered from this Cosmic, Divine rhythm. God and Nature have no axe to grind in their doings. The human being has just too many of them. Hence so much misery and chaos and trouble in an apparently progressive world.

Finally, lest one may doubt the power of *nishkam karma* philosophy for doing excellent secular work, here is the categorical assurance from Sri Aurobindo[10]:

'Such desireless action can have no decisiveness, no effectiveness, no efficient motive, no large or vigorous creative power? Not so... action [so done] is not only the highest, but the wisest, the most potent and efficient even for the affairs of the world....'

The four live exemplars highlighted in the beginning of this chapter provide unassailable testimony for Sri Aurobindo's faultless verdicts.

References

1. Vivekananda Swami, *Complete works*, Kolkata: Advaita Ashrama, 2005, Vol. 2, p. 3.
2. Aurobindo Sri; *Right Attitude To Work*, Pondicherry: Sri Aurobindo Society, 1991, p. 23.
3. Munshi K. M.; *Foundations of Indian Culture*, Bombay: Bharatiya Vidya Bhavan, 1974, p. 26.
4. Chakraborty S. K. and Chakraborty, D; *Spirituality in Management*, New Delhi: *Oxford University Press, 2008*, pp. 181-189.
5. Premeshananda Swami; *Atmavikas* (in Bengali), Kolkata: Belur Math, 2006, p. 14.
6. Munshi, op.cit., pp. 59–76.
7. Griffiths B; *The Cosmic Revelation*, London: Collins, 1983, p. 93.
8. Ibid., p. 92.
9. Munshi, op.cit., p. 74.
10. Aurobindo Sri; *The Message of The Gita*, Pondicherry: Sri Aurobindo Trust, 1977, p. 37, fn. 2.

CHAPTER 8

THREE DUTIES AND LEGITIMATE EDUCATION

तेजोऽसि तेजो मयि धेहि ।
वीर्यमसि वीर्य मयि धेहि ।
वलमसि वलं मयि धेहि ।
तेजो असि तेजो मयि धेहि ।
(य:- १९/९)

Thou art fiery spirit, give me the fiery spirit.
Thou art manly vigour, give me manly vigour.
Thou art power, give me power.
Thou art energy, give me energy.

(*Yajur Veda 19/9*)

(Ibid., p. 238)

I

An elderly (70+) European professor of a reputed university has been a close acquaintance of ours for about fifteen years. He has been coming to India regularly for many years to study and teach, staying on for three to four months at a stretch. It is India's *core culture* which captivates him. So he comes every year. During his visit in November 2005 – March 2006, at some stage he shared these critical insights:

'Whenever I come to India I make sure to glance through a cross–section of latest books in the field of social sciences written by Indian scholars. Most of them are full of disproportionately extensive and zealous references to writers and sources which do not synchronize with your cultural milieu.

'For instance, I have just finished glancing through a 600+ pages book on ethics and spirituality by a recently retired bureaucrat. The book seems to be at pains to quote with monotonous repetition a few categories of writers who are little-known even in India, except in one or two pockets. On the other hand, the most competent and widely acclaimed Indian authorities in the field like Aurobindo, Vivekananda, Ramana and so on are given scanty attention, even omitted altogether.

'Most of them have little empathy for your *core culture* disconnected as they are with its mainsprings. They may physically live in India, or elsewhere. But both groups prefer allegiance to cultures which have had aggressive, conquering relationships with India. Honouring them with copious references no doubt flatters and pleases them. But this only inflates their haughtiness. They do not reciprocate with respect and gratitude.

So far as I can assess, such one-sided efforts by your *core culture* for over sixty years since independence has failed to achieve India's avowed goal of national integration. And if my prognosis has any merit, this method will not be fruitful in future either. For, no matter how much the *core culture* concedes or tolerates, the stark truth is that cultures which keep their anchors planted firmly in epicentres outside India will not integrate with her. It is naïve, both intellectually and politically, to wish away this hardest of all facts. Who knows if this one-way traffic is not really the symptom of an ineradicable malaise of the literate Indian mind: Will-to-slavery! My apologies for saying this.

'There are several Western and Eastern countries too with plural societies. But scholars there do not indulge in emasculating prevarications about their respective core cultures. Authors and speakers in these places, where significant numbers of various denominations live (e.g. Germany where 30 percent are Turkish), do not lean over their backs to accord special recognition, far less parity, to the core texts or writers belonging to external cultural origins. In Malaysia, where the core culture constitutes just 55 percent of the population, only the sacred text of that culture is recited during inauguration of all government functions. Besides, deluxe copies of that text are gifted to visiting speakers from other cultures – without any qualms. These countries have solved the problem of cultural plurality by clearly laying down the order of priority. This has helped all concerned to know their respective places. Sadly, your country is in a mess of its own making due to shortsighted folly.

'British books on values, ethics, etc., for example, never quote the *Gita* or the *Upanishads* or Indian authors of world-wide standing. Yet, Britain has been deeply connected with India for over 250 years. Now I realize: Why should they? For, most Indian authors themselves deprecate, or are shy or afraid of owning up (far less asserting) their own *core culture,* and its greatest modern exponents who had not only thought, but also lived. The only plausible explanation for this may lie in the *enslaved subconscious* of the Indian mind.'

These candid views from a person with no axe to grind should serve as the right silhouette against which to project a few key issues about education in India today.

II

The second item in the ten duties listed for every citizen in the Constitution of India is: **'To cherish and follow the noble ideals which inspired the national struggle for freedom'.**

Clearly, parents and teachers are the primary sources for such cherishing, following and inspiration. It is their duty to resonate, to vibrate with these 'noble ideals', and then to animate the young minds it home and school with the same. Those teachers who were born after 1947, particularly after 1950, never breathed the air of selftranscending nationalism of the pre-independence struggle since 1905.

The *moolmantra* then, as coined by Satish Chandra Mookherjee (the Founder of the National Council of Education), was *Know India and Love India.** Today, although they are living off the fat of the glorious sufferings and sacrifices of Bharat's freedom fighters, large sections of ungrateful parents and teachers themselves are either ignorant or derisive about these noble souls. For them love for one's Motherland is chauvinism, jingoism, parochialism, etc. They claim themselves to be global citizens, and exhort their children or students to think likewise.

The following are some of the grave consequences of such disorientation in the two fountainheads of education:

---

* *More details have been furnished later in Chapter 9*

(1) Most parents and teachers, especially in urban areas, have become career-obsessed. Such 'careerist' teachers and parents are infecting the young minds with opportunism and greed for money. With *legitimate educators* thus becoming a vanishing tribe, what chance has noble idealism?

(2) Occasional and motivated references to Gandhiji apart, the heroic deeds of Netaji, Tilak, Lajpat, Aurobindo, Kshudiram, Surya Sen, Bhagat Singh, C.R. Das and many more, are being cast into oblivion, even disparaged.

(3) On the contrary, in several other countries which despatched conquerors and plunderers to seize the wealth and freedom of other simple-minded, trusting cultures, such *asuras* are lionized and kept alive in the memories of every generation as heroes. One may only look at our immediate neighbour on the West.

(4) When one visits China or Japan or Malaysia, one is struck by the powerfully active spirit of nationalism in their people. They all outpace India in almost all the tracks of development. This is because of the empowerment and unity derived from vibrant national sentiment transmitted to each succeeding generation by their parents and teachers alike. In the 2008 Olympic games, China stood at the top of the medals tally, whereas India was placed almost at the bottom. This glaring fact justifies our thesis. What are their counterparts in India doing?

(5) The European professor's perception about the elite Indian's 'will-to-slavery', mentioned earlier, appears so accurate. Here are a few instances from in and around Kolkata:

- The construction of Derozio Bhavan and Charnock City. An immature teacher of 17 years (died at 23), with boys ranging between 11 and 16 years as pupils, training them to abuse elders-parentsbrahmins, to drink, to eat beef, to disown and ridicule everything in their tradition as rank superstition or silly animism. This, in brief, was Derozio's chief contribution! And Charnock became the first British landowner through buying up three villages in this part of the country.*

---

* *Such celebration may be contrasted with the pulling down of KGB buildings of Stalin's time and converting the site into a big green lawn in Moscow.*

- The cleaning and sprucing up of an invisible, forgotten Christian graveyard within the compound of the erstwhile Bengal Engineering College, just opposite the clocktower. The names of Madhusudan Dutt and Krishnamohan Bandyopadhyay, who had become Christians, are now prominently displayed in the campus.
- A large white marble plaque facing the booking counter of Shrirampur, a suburban railway station. It proclaims the deeds of the missionary William Carey. What remains concealed is that, with his two aides, he had converted as many as 700 Hindus to Christianity in less than a year.

It is comical to witness such actions from quarters which cry hoarse on walls and platforms: 'Death to imperialism'. Some other parts of the country might also be following in these noble footsteps, haloed by the golden light of self-respect ! Thus, the natural conclusion is that it matters not whether one is an imperialist or communist. The only criterion for showering applause and paying homage to the above is: How much scorn had been poured by them on Hindu culture.

(6) Freedom cannot be reduced to a merely political notion. What about the freedom to be oneself — as a culture, a tradition? And that too a culture like Bharat's which is the longest living, and internationally the most peaceful tradition of the world. (And possibly also the bitterest sufferer for that reason.

This real, true freedom is under relentless threat from hostile forces and powers both within and outside the country. Is it not a paramount duty of every Indian parent and teacher to wake up and grasp the ominous implications of all this? Otherwise, how will the citizens of tomorrow stand on the firm ground of a *cause to defend* – with body and soul? If education continues its callousness towards this problem, the fourth Constitutional duty, 'to defend the country', might eventually become a mockery.

(7) Globalization – an euphemism for crafty neo-colonialism of unprecedented amplitude and penetration – is the new mode of robbing other nations of their true freedom. By breeding inferiority complex through catchwords like under–development, modernity, liberal education, human rights, etc., and by fuelling infinite greed in the name of wider choice and higher living standards, the literate Indian is being blown off by a glitzkreig. The will-power and moral courage to challenge and

resist this calamity is absent in our educational outfits e.g., compulsory purchase of Reebok shoes or Raymond garments as part of school dress.

(8) Here is an unsavoury fact to grasp by all legitimate educators in Bharat. Practically all the snowballing *global crises* of today – sociological or ecological, psychological or familial, moral or spiritual – can be linked with globalization triggered by a few greedy and rich countries. Over the last three centuries the *leadership* of the world, in all its facets, has been explicitly seized by sci-tech and businesscommerce from these countries. Logically, therefore, the *responsibility* for all the intractable problems of the world should also lie with them. Currently, besides the above, under the rhetoric of global development, the intangible, life-giving *cultural freedom* of the sustainable traditions too is being destroyed. Consumerist as well as armed terrorisms are ruining simple, integral and peaceful societies like Bharat's. Of course, her own self-serving elite are equally culpable for 'digging the canal and inviting the crocodile' (translation of a Bengali proverb). Students have to be trained to develop this sort of *critical aptitude* during their education.

(9) Several star universities in the West nurse wholly dedicated groups of academics who primarily create and supply theories, models, techniques etc., to their governments to tighten the stranglehold of powerful countries over the whole world. Various world bodies like the UN, IMF, OECD, World Bank etc. buy out our best bureaucrats and academics, irrespective of leftist or rightist inclinations, and in a few years brainwash them into their spokespersons. With very few exceptions, such self-centred, un-conscientious Indians have no second thoughts about denigrating or destroying their own culture and economy. In fact, some of the most influential universities and academic institutions in India are devotedly engaged in doing quite the opposite of what their Western counterparts are doing. China presents a sobering, dignified contrast. Our educators, if they wish to be legitimate ones, should seriously and urgently scrutinize these undercurrents and stand guard against, as well as oppose them.

(10) Now follows is a classic instance from the long unbroken tale of fifth-columnist betrayals and sycophancies by educated Indians. Bertrand Russell had written to his wife in 1916 about one evening he had spent as a speaker and listener at the Indian Majlis in London. "The man who spoke last was a biologist full of passion for science... 'I am going', he said, 'from this land of prosperity to the land of plague and famine, ... from this land of enlightenment to the land of religious bigotry ...'. ... It must be appallingly tragic to be civilized and educated and belong to such a country as India."

Dear educator, does all this give a wrench to your heart and make it bleed? Woe to our Tagore's, Vivekananda's, Gandhiji's *et.al.*! Did Sri Aurobindo live and study in England for fourteen long years from the age of seven, not knowing a word of Bengali or Sanskrit? Yet, was this the sort of ludicrously servile language in which he ever spoke about his Motherland after he touched her shores in 1893? Where do we turn then for our education: to the likes of the biologist above, or to the likes of Sri Aurobindo? In any case, bravo.

Mr. Scientific-tempered Indian Biologist – you must be rejoicing in Heaven to see that your tribe has multiplied a thousand-fold since you had spoken your nectarine words ninety years ago ! It is indeed a strange *leela* of *vidhata purusha* that the legacy of Mr. Biologist is apparently proving to be more enduring and pervasive than that of Sri Aurobindo – at least for the time being.

(11) Surrender of freedom, as mentioned above, has been occurring (at an accelerated pace since 1950) at the *high end* of the ladder. Complementing this, here are some instances of the same enslaving phenomenon pervading the *low end* of the ladder. They all flow from the author's personal experience:

- Sacramental marriage and *grihashram* as noble ideals are being recklessly whittled down. Instead, Western companionship is gradually gaining ground. Possible divorce is already a starting assumption of most marriages. Parents themselves often dissuade their daughters from living with their in-laws.
- Motherhood as the noble consummation of a normal woman now commonly meets with derisive laughter. Sameness is mistaken for equality. But medical science says that every single cell of the female is structured by Nature (God?) distinctively from that of the male.

- A class XI student has high estimate of her proficiency in English. She has already formed a clear view of her future career. She has rejected her father's advice to study English literature and adopt the sober teaching profession. Teaching doesn't have much money – she said. She would go, instead, for the more glamorous and lucrative job of journalism and mass communication. The mother supported her.
- Children and youth are often supplied with books which contain scornful allusions to apparently superstitious practices in the Sanatan Hindu culture of India e.g., *vrats* and *upavasas*, bathing and non-cooking during eclipses, the *upanayana* and *shraddh* ceremonies and so on.* The derisive label of 'brahminism' is used to tarnish these age-old practices which definitely teach *sanyam* (self-control), strengthen will-power, and purify the heart.
- School students are frequently told about the mischiefs of Brahmin priests and the caste system (carefully, perhaps fearfully, avoiding any mention of worse things amongst their equivalents in other communities). But they are never told about the cast eless *rishis*, the founding fathers of our frugal and holistic *sanatan* civilization which alone could address *shrinvantu vishwe amritasya putrah* and *vasudhaiva kutumbakam* to the whole world. This world-view has been poles apart from the commercially clever globalism being thrust upon us today from the West. It is never explained to them why Hindus have the *gotra* system of *sacred identity* named after *rishis* (about 24) – a feature perhaps without parallel anywhere.
- School children are now being imparted sex education. Woe to *sanyam* and *brahmacharya* – the rock-like pillars of the most sustainable of all cultures.
- The alleged faults of *sanatan* culture voiced by learned Westerners like Macaulay and Marx are regularly drilled into the youngminds. But positive assessments like the following are not:

---

* *Chapter 5 has handled this issue at some length.*

- Children are duly informed about inglorious *suttee*. But they are not told of *sahamaran*. Nor are they told about the great glory of *jauhar vrat* done by Hindu queens to protect their honour from lustful invaders.
- Governmental organisations are now producing school text books (August, 2006) which include the accounts of two or three very recent events of rightful retaliation, by the mainstream. They took place only during the last two decades or so. But centuries of unprovoked torture by alien or separatist forces are being rationalized, explained away or deleted. These alien hordes did not enter Bharat with love, but with sword and gun. The crucial question therefore before the legitimate educator of today, and more so for that of tomorrow is: How will they equip themselves with a grasp of the long chain of historical events, and educate the children about the truth? Will they, for example, take pains to inspire their wards and pupils with these words of Swami Vivekananda (*Complete Works*, III, 105-6). '... when history has no record ... even from then until now ideas after ideas have marched out from her, but every word has been spoken with a *blessing behind it, and peace before it*.'
- From sweeper to Chairman, student to Principal the mode of address now is 'good morning', and of greeting is 'handshake'. Gone are *Jai Hind*, *namaskar, namaste, suprabhatam* etc. Even the first lady of the country has been seen on the small screen to welcome foreigners at Rashtrapati Bhawan with a handshake, not joined palms.
- Valentine's Day is becoming a new snare. The other day an eight-year old boy handed a card to his girl classmate aged six. The girl took it home. Parents saw 'I love you' written inside it. The innocent girl asked: 'What does this mean?'
- A mother, walking back home after a school examination, was inquiring how her daughter (11 years) had fared in that day's test. After a few exchanges the mother was heard telling this: 'You should have been more smart. Why didn't you copy the answer from thestudent next to you?'

(a) 'India is the cradle of the human race, the birthplace of human speech, the mother of history ...' (Mark Twain)

(b) 'We owe a lot to Indians who taught us to count ...' (Albert Einstein)

(c) 'If I were asked under what sky the human mind has ... most deeply pondered on the greatest problems of life, and found solutions, I should point to India.' (Max Muller)

- Continued presentation of the false notion that India was never a whole nation until the British came. Gandhiji's forthright refutation of this falsehood, and Sri Aurobindo's meticulous affirmation of the *sacred secret* of Bharat, underneath the surface flux of Rajahs, Badshahs and Viceroys, are never shared with our budding citizens.
- Our children are not informed that Ahalya Bai, Rani Rashmoni, Rani Bhavani, Rani Laxmibai, Chand Bibi and many of their likes were not the secular, university-educated, computer-adept, jeans-wearing, mobile-dangling, male-aping, ego-inflated urban women of today (honourable exceptions notwithstanding). They had managed and led homes, estates, public works, armies, and temples – all with perfection. How? Through the sacred mode – that is the answer.*
- Children's education, within home or outside, has no room for the profound lesson that because pre-1950 India had glorious *jananis* or *sahadharminis* like Bhubaneshwari Devi, Prabha Devi, Kasturba, Basanti Devi, that we are blessed with freedom-winning personalities like Vivekananda, Netaji, Gandhiji, Deshbandhu Chittaranjan, Tilak and so on. Is there any hope of such a phenomenon recurring again in the womb of progressive, secular education as it is understood today?

---

* *The author is conscious of the adjectives he will attract when he says that en-masse study of law and management by our girls is wrong in principle. But let us listen to Carrel (a Nobel laureate quoted in chapter 5). He spoke against same education, powers and responsibilities for women because, ... woman differs profoundly from man...in every one of the cells...women should develop... in accordance with their nature without trying to imitate the males (p. 93).*

- Look at this milestone prophecy from Tagore (1919). 'We forget that the same weakness in our character, or in our circumstances, which inevitably draws us on to the slippery slope of imitation, will pursue us when our independence is merely of the outside. For then our freedom will become the *freedom to imitate* the foreign institutions.' With what fatal speed is India today fulfilling Tagore's prophecy!

(12) Here is a brilliant illustration of what defending freedom of culture means. It is extracted from a long letter to the editor by one Malaysian, K. J. John (*New Strait Times*, 28/06/99).

'I wish to express my disgust and total abhorrence of the proposal by a total stranger (a regional Director of Human Rights Watch) and foreigner regarding our national values and conduct of life. ... Can Jones take time to understand our world-view and values and thus respect us, and not try to deny not only our rights but, more importantly, our sovereignty?'

One wonders if any educated Hindu, not to speak of any Indian Christian or Muslim, has in recent times articulated such a spirited defence of Bharat's culture as John, a Christian citizen of Islamic Malaysia, had?

(13) Alas! What kind of freedom was it for which thousands upon thousands of fragrant, blooming Indian youth had offered themselves so utterly at the feet of Bharat Mata during the first half of the 20th century? There were hardly any non-Hindu martyrs among them. Parents and teachers of today – could you please pause and ponder?

(14) All parents and teachers who can consider it to be their first national duty to be *legitimate*, not careerist, educators have to outgrow the surface meaning of the 4th Constitutional duty: *to defend the country* i.e., defending the political boundaries of free India. Unless a view wider than this is taken by all civilians, only the jawans will be, and have been, doing such duty. But this duty must be understood at the deeper level of *defending the cultural and spiritual freedom of the country too*. It has been completely ignored, during the last two decades at least. If this callousness continues, we might all be charged for colluding with a sort of 'cultural terrorism' by posterity.

- Unlike the politically correct or his-master's-voice educators, legitimate educators should also carefully grasp the colossal difference between armed terrorists on the one hand, and freedom fighters or revolutionaries on the other. Here are the main points:

  (a) Terrorism now ravaging India is not for winning freedom from colonial rule. There is nothing noble about this scourge. Poverty as an excuse for such crime is unacceptable. For, poverty is not a monopoly of any particular community.

  (b) Terrorism perpetrated in India is aimed at innocent, helpless, common citizens in trains, planes, buses, bazaars, temples, pilgrim routes, etc. There are no exploiters or oppressors here to blast out.

  (c) Terrorism has been used in the recent past to secede from India and establish separate nations. This has involved, once again, the brutal killing of thousands of innocents of primarily one community, across several years.

  (d) Terrorism is being employed for planned ethnic cleansing in certain parts of the country – again for years. Freedom fighters never did that.

  (e) Freedom fighters or revolutionaries in France, Russia, China etc. are never branded as terrorists. They are simply worshipped.

- Therefore, it is ominous that a certain government outfit in India had recently (August, 2006) gone to the length of describing the likes of Tilak, Aurobindo, Bipin Pal et. al. as terrorists. What a topsy-turvy in the scale of values among education-pedlars in India. No better proof of our die-hard slavish mentality is required.

- September 7, 2006 had provided a golden opportunity to test the sincerity of all communities about national integration. It was the centenary of Bankim Chandra Chatterjee's song, *Bande Mataram*. It was sung publicly for the first time at the Indian National Congress meeting of 1896. Later, at the Varanasi Congress session in 1906, it was adopted as the opening song. Gandhiji is reported to have observed thus: 'The song is said to have proved so popular, that it has come to be our National Anthem.' Rabindranath Tagore himself had composed the tune for and sung it. It had continued to be magically inspiring during the long, arduous freedom struggle. No wonder, Sri Aurobindo had credited Bankim Chandra as having 'created a language, a literature and a nation'.

- Yet, opposition by certain communities, aided and abetted by the connivance of some top executive functionaries of the country, saw to it that the nation was divided on this most vital matter. We have it from Ram Jethmalani ('My Tryst With Vande Mataram', *Asian Age*, September 13, 2006), that on January 24, 1950, the President of India had declared in Parliament that Jana Gana Mana and Vande Mataram will both have *equal* status, though the former was chosen as the National Anthem because of better musical qualities. There was standing ovation from the MP's of both Houses to this declaration. Opposition or protest was unthinkable.

- Thus, if anything, the events around September 7 show that the bigoted opponents and the political dice-players, prompted by their imaginary fears0 and short-term self-interests, possess little allegiance to and affection for their Motherland, and the freedom struggle.

- So, the abiding post-1947 question, even after vivisection of the country, continues to haunt: When will the complementary communities begin to play *their due role* and discharge *their duty* tohonour the keynotes which constitute the very heart-beat of their land of birth? Are they not also the beneficiaries of Indian freedom, which was gained almost wholly at the cost of the life and blood of men and women belonging to the core culture? National integration cannot be a onehand clap. *Legitimate educators* have therefore a vital message to convey, with conviction: Reciprocity, adjustment and gratitude from the complementary cultures towards the core culture, is a *must*. They should take a leaf or two on this momentous issue from the books of experience in countries like Malaysia, China, Thailand, Indonesia, etc.

(15) Before concluding this section, a multi-criteria definition of *legitimate educators*, in contrast to careerist ones, is in order:

(a) They will regard their first obligation (irrespective of their specializations) as the creation of *shraddha* and love for its Motherland in the child's mind.

(b) They will care little about being politically correct and, therefore, prefer to shun homilies and platitudes.

(c) They will demonstrate *brahminic* virtues like patience, forbearance, forgiveness, acceptance, etc., but *not* at the cost of *kshatra* qualities like heroism, valour, combativeness, self-sacrifice – in short, *veeryam* – against diabolic forces, indigenous or alien.

(d) Their primary aim will be to inspire high and pure character in students who will value and sustain uplifting *freedom from*, and not to turn out 'marketable products' who will aggravate degrading *freedom to*.

Such indeed have been the qualities which had, and which will, make *acharyas* of our legitimate educators. Let them also rest assured that pursuit of such an ideal cannot invite the false accusation of fundamentalism.

For, fundamentalists insist that theirs is the only prophet, only valid creed, only right book. Others must either be converted to them, or exterminated or taxed (*jaziya*). Our core culture *acharyas* have never done so. Nor can they ever pursue such ignoble, barbaric missions in future. The core culture is 'genetically' incapable of achieving such feats.

III

The sixth duty in the Constitution stipulates this: **'To preserve the heritage of our composite culture'** Such a duty is beyond dispute. This is so insofar as plain reading of the sentence would imply. But careful scrutiny of this apparently short, simple statement exposes certain serious problems about education of the Indian mind. Obviously, by this we mean a sphere much wider than just school or higher education in the formal, careeristic sense. Here are some of these concerns:

- The word 'composite' means a compound of several separable parts. But the separable elements in a compound are not equiproportional. Like the pendant in a necklace of many gems, there is one preponderant, principal element in every compound.
- For quite some time the word 'composite' seems to have been used to deftly deny that Bharatvarsha's cultural heritage has an overwhelmingly distinctive ethos after her own genius. The latent message in 'composite' is that Indian culture is just an amorphous, un-definable concoction, shorn of a unique personality and flavour of its own. What then is the status of the **core** *sanatan* culture and *dharma*, which has come to be called Hinduism for more than two millennia (with its grand and partly corrective, offshoots like Buddhism, Jainism and Sikhism)?
- Legitimate educators in Bharat should be vigilant about the phrase 'composite culture' for another simple commonsense reason. A human body cannot stand erect without the vertebral column. What is true of the human frame is equally true of the nation. Without a robust *core culture*, which is the spinal support of Bharat, composite culture is no better than a misnomer, a myth.
- And what has been the perennial vehicle of this *sanatan* core culture? The Sanskrit language and the Sanskrit literature, both characterised as 'sacred' by Monier Williams (*Hinduism*, 1877, 1951, p. 9). Not all legitimate educators may be knowledgeable in Sanskrit. But every one of them should be full of reverence for this Mother language of their Motherland (called *deva bhasha*). And all their students too need to be inspired to cultivate the same healthy respect for it (as is done for Latin and Greek in the West — though, unlike Sanskrit, they are dead). To this day Sanskrit *mantras* are recited in every rite of passage, and in every significant event of Indian daily life. This is not true of Latin or Greek.
- S. P. Huntington, a Harvard University authority, has recently written thus (in *Who Are We?*; 2004): 'Americans have been extremely religious and overwhelmingly Christian throughout their history.' This emphatic declaration had come in the wake of the September 2001 terrorist attacks on New York and

Washington DC. Can anything similar be imagined in India after the Taj Mahal hotel outrage in Mumbai seven years later? Would anyone dare call Huntington a fundamentalist?

- America too is a plural or composite society hosting large numbers of Hindus, Muslims, Jews, Hispanics, Confucians, Buddhists, Sikhs and others. Yet this American authority does not engage in politically motivated obfuscation when it comes to upholding the core cultural genius of his country.
- The 1995 Education Act of Britain, while endorsing the teaching of five other religions in schools, had categorically declared that Christianity would receive predominant attention.
- By the standards of today's liberal, universal and secularminded leaders of education in India, both American and British educational authorities could be regarded as chauvinist and bigoted. But they cannot even contemplate saying so. Those parents, teachers and educators who tend to feel guilty and apologetic about uttering '*sanatan* culture' or 'Hindu *dharma*', in their *only* homeland in the world at that, may be informed about the following additional facts:

  (a) At the close of the 19th century, **Margaret Noble**, a brilliant teacher, journalist, writer, and above all an authentic seeker, had come to India with Swami Vivekananda. After consecration to Lord Shiva at Amarnath she became Sister Nivedita – offering all her life and soul at the feet of Bharatvarsha. Her *Footfalls of Indian History* and *Web of Indian Life* are monumental examples of 'Know India, and Love India'.

  (b) In the late 1920s, **Ronald Nixon**, a Cambridge science, engineering and philosophy scholar, an RAF pilot in World War I, joined the Lucknow University as a teacher of English literature. He later stayed on in a remote ashram off Almora, (called Uttar- Brindavan) and left his body as Krishna Prem — more perfect than the most perfect *Vaishnava*. All his life was dedicated to *vigraha seva* in the most meticulous orthodox style. And yet he could always surpass the most brilliant rationalist in his interpretation of *pooja* rituals. For example, once when asked what was the significance of *aarti*, he replied, 'the circular movement is the Divine movement'. Sri Aurobindo held him in high esteem.

(c) **JBS Haldane**, the famed biologist and geneticist, had come to India and opted for Indian citizenship in the early 1960s. His biographer informs us about two reasons why Haldane chose India to breathe his last: One, it was enough to have worn socks for five decades second, he was in love with Hindu philosophy and culture. One of his favourite boyhood heroes was Mahavir Hanuman. (Ronald Clark: *The Life and Work of JBS Haldane*, 1968.)

(d) The American thinker-scholar **David Frawley** has become Vamadeva Shastri. He has written comprehensively on every aspect of Bharat's history, culture and *dharma*, taking Hinduism as the core. (e.g., *Gods, Sages and Kings*). His books often remind one of Sri Aurobindo's writings.

(e) One **Dr. Jones** spent practically the whole of his life treating poor patients at the Ramakrishna Mission charitable hospital at Brindavan. The author had seen him many times, wondering how he endured the mercilessly blazing inferno that Brindavan is for most of the year. He had a small room with just an aircooler in the Mission compound. He used to sit every evening on a chair at the far end of the prayer hall and watch the *aarti* in its full sequence. The author once asked him: 'What makes you spend your whole life in such a place?' He replied: 'Yes, I perceive the meaning of human existence in this culture and atmosphere only. Although I have a family in Canada. I go there once in three years or so, and come back within a month.' His body was cremated at Brindavan in accordance with Hindu rites — as he had willed.

(f) **Bede Griffiths**, an Oxford scholar of comparative literature, lived in his ashram at Shantivanam near Trichy on the banks of Kaveri. The author visited him there twice. He passed away recently, having spent more than thirty-five years in India. His books are full of openness, sincerity and depth, (e.g. *Return to the Centre, Cosmic Revelation*).

(g) **Mirra Alfassa** , born of Turko-Egyptian parentage (1878) and brought up in Paris, lived in India for sixty years till she expired in 1973. She had also dedicated herself to this country as a protégépartner of Sri Aurobindo. Here is a small example of her estimate of Bharat's *core culture*: 'The future of India is very clear. India is the Guru of the world. India is the living soul. The government of India should recognize the significance of India in this sphere and plan their action accordingly.'

(h) Right now **Michel Danino**, a French scholar-thinker, is living in India. After twenty-five years of enormous labour and love for Bharat's culture and history, he too has become an Indian citizen. Several research works have been published by him in both English and French. He also addresses teachers and students all over the country about Bharat's *core culture*: They should put to shame those Indian scholars, celebrities and journalists who delight only in tarnishing *sanatan* culture at every turn. *The Invasion That Never Was* is one of his (with Sujata Nahar) many outstanding books.

- The eight examples given above (and there are others too like JJ Goodwin and Capt. and Mrs. Sevier – Vivekananda's British disciples; Nicholas Roerich, the Russian artist and painter; Annie Besant, the theosophist; CF Andrews, the friend of Tagore and Gandhi; John Woodroffe, the English *yogi*; Francois Gautier, the French journalist) prove that such individuals have not dedicated their lives and works to India because of her cosmetic 'composite culture'. It was, instead, the unique and enduring *Vedic* Hindu *core culture* of Bharatvarsha, which drew them to this land.
- One is not sure how many educators and intellectuals in India today are aware or take due cognizance of the *standing ground* of every individual born in Bharatvarsha. Let us have a glimpse of the extensity of this base:

(a) Between 1879 and 1910, under the general editorship of Max Muller, the Clarendon University Press had published a 50-volume series called *The Sacred Books of the East*. Barring the last volume of Index, the other 49 volumes comprise:

(i) Vedic/Sanatan Hinduism	23 volumes
(ii) Buddhism/Jainism	10 volumes
(iii) Zoroastrianism	8 volumes
(iv) Chinese	6 volumes
(v) Islam	2 volumes

Thus, more than two-third of the sacred literature of the East comes from Bharatvarsha alone.

(b) The above series, however, does not include the two Epics, the Puranas and the Shrimad Bhagavatam. Motilal Banarasidass have already published 72 volumes on the *Puranas* in a planned set of 100, edited by Shastri and Bhatt. A team of four Western scholars has published 7 volumes of translation of the seven *kandas* of the Ramayana. P. Lal is engaged in translating the eighteen *parvas* of the *Mahabharata* in as many volumes (Writers Workshop). At the time of writing we are not aware if a similar multi-volume English translation of the *Bhagavatam* is under way.

(c) At any rate, we have above a tally of at least 158 (33 + 100 + 7 + 18) volumes of sacred literature handed down to us by our *rishis*. It is the sacred duty of every *legitimate* Indian educator to meditate over the significance of this stupendous ancient labour of love bequeathed to us. This must be correlated to the deathless character of the *sanatan* Hindu culture. Every child in India, no matter which faith or race he or she belongs to, must be duly and reverently informed about this inexhaustible, life-giving treasure of his/her land of birth.

(d) Besides, with due modesty, but no apology, they must also be told: There is no parallel to this achievement anywhere in the world. If others can be proud and jealous of just one or two sacred books handed down over fifteen or twenty hundred years, why should Indian boys and girls not be quite as much at ease with the fabulous storehouse they have inherited from much earlier, and which, moreover, has never been forced upon others with sword and gun.

(e) Education about culture in India must begin with this *big picture* about Bharat's core culture. The mind of every Indian student needs to be poised to embrace the cultural panorama imbedded in the works cited above. Legitimate educators have to accept this responsibility without ado. They should diligently steer clear of the 'pussy cat mentality'. That is, ostensibly going to see the queen on the throne, the 'pussy cat' ends up by seeing the mouse under the chair. This is what most careerist teachers seem to be doing.

- But there are many smart persons, bent on writing off Bharat's *core culture*, who retort with questions such as these: If your *sanatan* Hindu culture is so great and unique, why are you then in such a plight today? And why has your country been enslaved and plundered times without number? The *legitimate educator* should be ready with these minimum answers:

(a) Pray, which country in the world is today not tumbling downhill, is plunging into the abyss – in its own way?

(b) I am a harmless, guileless, simple person walking down the road back to my home. Suddenly an armed ruffian descends on me, beats me up half-dead, grabs my belongings, then forces his way into my home and goes on ordering about or sermonising me. Surely, I am to blame for getting thus roughed up. What a rational and just way of looking at Bharat.

(c) Despite being thus mauled and bled for centuries, Bharat is still a *living tradition* at its base. Rome is not. Nor is Greece. Nor Egypt, Nor Babylon. Will Durant (*Story of Civilization*, Part I) had admitted that, while for several other ancient civilizations he had to write in the 'past' tense, for India 'present' tense had to be used. Pray, why? The much-idolized USSR, built on 'scientific materialism', could live hardly seventy years. But Bharatvarsha, founded upon 'wisdom spirituality', continues to be alive for close to seven thousand years. Why? Should not the 'spirit of inquiry' tackle this supreme question of all? Where are the legitimate educators to render this yeoman's service to our youth?

(d) When unprovoked violence is repeatedly committed by some members of aggressive cultures, intellectuals bend backwards to offer sophisticated psychological explanations, justifying such actions. But when mild and patient cultures retaliate once in a blue moon, out of sheer exasperation, loud orchestrated condemnation is unleashed. For the latter psychological explanations or justifications are ruled out.

(e) Moreover, such 'living' has not been sustained by conquering, butchering or looting other lands and peoples. Nor have the Bharatiyas ever imposed the diabolical law of penal taxes on the original inhabitants of a different faith in those countries where they went. Surely then Bharat's core culture deserves to be chastised for daring to deviate so much from the noble histories of other honourable, civilized cultures and nations.

- The bogey of *secularism* must also be appraised for whatever it is worth, and rejected by legitimate educators. The word has two meanings:
  - (a) A life-and world-view which denies anything subtler and higher than the material, sensual conceptions.
  - (b) The separation of church from government in Europe. The first view stands rejected everywhere — East or West. Thus, every US dollar note declares in print 'In God we Trust'.* The right-hand sentry gate at Moscow's Red Square is now a small church full of images and burning candles. The second view is entirely irrelevant in the Indian context. For, temple or priest hegemony over government has never occurred in Indian history.
- The real intent behind the cry of secularism in India is to deny the prime place to her spiritual core culture as enshrined in her vast literature, a corpus that has grown and flourished within the soil-air-water of Bharatvarsha. It straddles the whole range from the Eternal-Transcendental to the Cosmic-Universal, and then to the Individual–Society in utmost detail. Spirituality, religion, economics, government — the entire *sacrosecular spectrum* has been meticulously handled within a seamless whole. Yet, since 1950, all restrictions and denials have been directed towards the core culture alone. The subconscious will-to-slavery among a cross section of mindless Indians seems to be the reason for this death-wish. They have to be reminded that though each gem has its relative place in the necklace, but it is so never at the cost of the pendant in the centre.
- *Objectivity* is a precious but difficult quality expected of social sciences. India's composite culturists have apparently perfected this quality in their activities by adhering to the following formula:

---

* Even in secular India the ministers in the new government after the 2009 elections were heard to read out the oath beginning with the words: 'In the name of God...' !

(a) Always stretch ingenuity to find defects and distortions, mostly through alien lenses, in the *sanatan* core culture and keep harping on them.

(b) Suppress or mis-represent all that is high and noble, practical and sound in the core culture.

(c) Matching (a), strain hard to find a few apparently positive features of complementary or ancillary cultures and magnify them.

(d) Matching (b), conceal or cover-up the countless negative and ignoble practices in complementary or ancillary cultures. In other words, intellectual double-speak has been masquerading as objectivity for six decades.

Such travesty of integrity should be challenged by legitimate educators. They might know or recall that the historical writings of stalwarts like Dr. R. C. Majumdar and Sir Jadunath Sarkar are virtually banned from Indian educational institutions. Students are even threatened with penalty if they are quoted. At the same time, fictional writings by Salman Rushdie and Tasleema Nasreen have also been banned here. One can easily see, which way the wind of objectivity has been blowing. No wonder, *Bande Mataram* has today become a target of insult. And along with it our freedom fighters. Ingratitude, thou marble-hearted fiend.

- So, *legitimate* educators in India should carefully amend their outlook and convictions to preserve India's cultural heritage. The sooner, the better. 'Composite culture' may sound fine, but is vague and nebulous. It has to be remembered that preservation of *core culture* is the first duty of all responsible citizens. What is glibly called composite culture today could emerge only because this *core culture* has been gentle, forgiving, patient, all-embracing. If Bharat's core culture is forced to cave in or disappear, there will be no composite culture at all. Instead, some dogmatic, monolithic culture(s) could overtake. *Shraddha*, loving reverence, for the roots of Bharat's cultural genius is imperative. The whole world has a great stake in it.
- The above apprehension need not be dismissed as idle. The issue of *racial sub-conscious* is pertinent here. For, it stores the memories of all past experiences, bloody or benign, a race has

cumulatively undergone. On this ground the balance is heavily tilted against the *core culture*. Actions and behaviours of all the members of this core may not always have been impeccable over a 1,000-years span. Yet, as impartial historians like Will Durant (*The Story of Civilization*, Vol. 1, p. 459) have clearly told, there is simply no question about which race or community has been at the receiving end, and from whom. Legitimate educators must awaken to this major fact, and avoid being overly reticent. Members of the complementary or ancillary cultures or races from beyond India have a lot more to account and atone for. This is called 'coming to terms with history' e.g., Japan in relation to Korea, France in relation to Africa, and so on.

- It is relevant to recall here that in 1965 the new Burmese government had banned all foreign missionary organizations in that country. Even the Ramakrishna Mission, doing wonderful social service without proselytization, had to fold up. It did not care for world opinion. *Shraddha* for their own core culture was the only decisive motive. Myanmar had thus solved, once for all, its cultural identity issue in a self-confident manner.
- By contrast, India's pusillanimity on this score since 1950 has been continually inviting the prowling eyes of some of the aggressive cultures with epicentres outside India. The kind of effrontery they keep heaping upon the *core culture* of India (e.g., Vatican Popes) cannot be dreamt of by them towards Confucian China, or Shinto Japan. It is the softness, even connivance, of a 'core-less' composite culture which is the most probable reason for such public affronts to Bharatvarsha.

Not only that. India is a beleaguered country today, cornered or threatened at will, by the smallest to the largest countries surrounding her. It is reasonable to correlate this painful phenomenon with the *inherent weakness* of a wooly, core-less, composite culture image that India has been fostering about herself since independence. That is why, as one army Lt. Col. had told us in anguish (2004), India has always been 'reactive', never proactive, in most of her international relations.

That is why one sees a humiliating sight at the Nathula pass on the India-China border: a Chinese soldier standing on a peak on the Chinese side which is at least 1000 feet higher than the Indian outpost, pointing his bayonet at India. Our *legitimate educators* need to acquire the acuteness to grasp such demoralizing under-currents, and implant countervailing correctives in the student's mind. Delay may spell death.

- Sometime in early 2006 a final year M.A. (history) student of a major Indian university had sent an application for employment 234 against an advertisement by a newspaper on its website. It was a major all-India English daily, looking for trainee journalists.

The young man had a standard CV which was sent along with a request for interview. After two weeks he got a call. The first question the interviewer shot at him was: 'Why have you written Hinduism as your religion? Do you belong to the saffron brigade? Such information is redundant.' Stunned by this surprise attack on his identity, his subsequent responses were shaky. Yet, he was quite westernized in his dress, language, entertainment and reading habits.

Next day he narrated this unnerving experience to his closest classmate. The latter was quite skilled in across-the table talk. He told his friend: 'Look, if you were a Christian or a Muslim or a Sikh, the interviewer would dare not ask the questions or make the comments hurled at you. I would have told this to the interviewer on his face and immediately quit.'

- There are infamous artists and zealous preachers in this country who revel in painting obnoxious pictures or writing scurrilous accounts of Hindu Gods and Goddesses and the Epics. This is symbolic of the contempt such communities generally nurse towards India's *core culture*. And it is intellectuals again who give public support to such vulgar antics in the name of 'artist's freedom' or minority rights. There are, on the other hand, Education Ministers and other public figures who quit functions or seminars on education if a portrait or image of Goddess Saraswati is placed on the dais, or *Saraswati vandana* in Sanskrit is chanted. Thus, only the sentiments of the mainstream or core culture can be trampled upon with impunity. Such is their lofty secularism, and their contribution to 'composite' culture.

- During the last few years the author has encountered certain zealous pacifists or harmonisers or synthesizers (*samanvyavadis*) from the mainstream elite who brand anyone who has a word of praise or defence for Hinduism as 'fundamentalist'. This includes foreigners, and of course Hindus themselves. On this basis, Sister Nivedita and others of her ilk cited earlier, should rightly be held as 'fundamentalists'.

Quite a significant instance of the cowardice stored in the sub-conscious of such synthesizers has gone unnoticed: The deletion of the word 'Hindoo' from Swami Vivekananda's original Chicago photograph titled 'The Cyclonic Hindoo Monk of India'. This is a sort of insult to Vivekananda himself. Such *karmas* are now coming home to roost. *Samanvya* between fire and water, between honey and poison is proving to be a pipedream.*

- Certain English dailies, around April or May 2006, carried a full page open letter from an erstwhile Central Government Minister of Tourism and Culture pleading for the revival of the Saraswati Valley Civilization excavation project. This vital archaeological venture had been abandoned half-way through, perhaps instigated by the argument from a few eminent historians that such a civilization is imaginary and fanciful. The truth seems to be that these anti-*sanatani* or anti-core culture intellectuals are apprehensive that fresh archaeological discoveries from the Saraswati valley could open up more solid and authentic frontiers of correct education about our Motherland. This may not be to their relish. Nothing must be done which could boost the self-esteem of the *core culture.*

- In another instance a modern project has been launched at the same site as the *sethubandha* of the Ramayana at Rameswaram. Satellite pictures by NASA (late 2002) about this under-water bridge had yielded sufficient evidence of its antiquity – 17,25,000 years. Instead of protecting and preserving this ancient wonder of our culture, the state and central governments are trying to do the reverse (TRUTH, June 2, 2006).

- The examples given in the preceding paragraphs show how comprehensive and orchestrated are the ways in which the Mother culture of Bharatvarsha, including even her so-called composite culture, is being undermined. These bewildering cross-currents in the sphere of education need to be detected and checkmated carefully. *Legitimate* educators should uncover and expose how ill-motived 'detoxification' is actually turning out to be *de-factualisation* of Bharat's culture and history.

---

* Even mutual coexistence with respect towards the 'core culture' has not been achieved till today. Samanvya is a far cry.

- Alongside de-factualisation runs apace that process of *negative* education which Swami Vivekananda had bitterly criticised in his lecture, 'The Future of India'. What he had uttered more than a century ago has turned even more vicious today. Let us hear him*:

'A negative education, or training that is based on negation, is worse than death. The child is taken to school and the first thing he learns is that his father is a fool; the second thing that his grand father is a lunatic; the third thing that all his teachers are hypocrites; the fourth that all the sacred books are lies! By the time he is sixteen he is a mass of negation, lifeless and boneless' (*Complete Works*, Vol.III, pp. 301-302). Except for wide-spread hypocrisy among teachers today having become a standard trade mark, the other *negative* learnings are nowadays imparted with planned, made-to-order text books.

- Let us listen again to the words of Vivekananda: 'What we want is *shraddha*. Unfortunately it has nearly vanished from India, and this is why we are in our present state. ...Give up the awful disease that is creeping into our national blood, that idea of ridiculing everything, that loss of seriousness, give that up.' Even Swamiji could not have imagined, with all his *divyadrishti*, the extent to which, more than a century later, his beloved countrymen (and women), would do exactly the contrary of what he had implored. Do we aspire to remain a *free nation,* and to educate ourselves and our children with that supreme goal in view? Of course Swamiji was not entirely unaware about 'traitors', as much as Shri Aurobindo of 'betrayers', from within. Such persons are apparently having a field-day now. Perhaps our Constitution-makers could not foresee such a nullifying twist to their laudable emphasis on duty no. 6.

- Our legitimate educators should realize that India is now being hit by a trident: *collapsing* capitalism, *collapsed* communism and *alien* fundamentalism. They have to save their minds from this deadly blow. And then lead their pupils and children into the centre of Bharat's sustainable core culture.

---

* In all probability these words were his scathing rejoinder to the silly antics of the likes of Derozio. Yet certain quarters today, especially in Bengal, hail them as harbingers of renaissance, liberal education, etc.

IV

The Indian Constitution lays down the eighth duty for every citizen as: **To develop the scientific temper and spirit of inquiry:** In itself this duty too is unexceptionable. Like in the second and sixth duties, here also the Constitution should be taken as well-intentioned. Yet, this one too, over the years, has been used by certain sections of Indian intellectuals, scholars, journalists and politicians as a ploy to vilify or reject the subtle, deep-structure, sacred ethos of Bharatvarsha.

- What is 'scientific temper'? As events have developed over the decades, popular attitude towards it has become wholly concentrated in the material and sensual spheres. Within these limits marvelous things have been happening — from decoding the human genome to landing on the Mars, from instant communication to instant *samadhi*, and so on.
- Yet, the world is becoming more and more a fearful, unhappy, and potentially catastrophic planet. Emotional bonds in families are breaking up. The human family itself as the basic social unit might soon be extinct. With irresponsible free sex and vanishing family, the technology-led human world is descending closer to the animal world each day. And terrorists can kill you anytime, anywhere. Progress indeed.*
- Galloping *sci-tech* has let human greed get the upper hand through economics, finance and business. Expanding the range of 'choice' is an economic deception for fuelling rampant consumerism, reminding one of the plight of King Yayati. The *Hitopadesha* dictum '*I need your greed for my greed*' is the true face of globalised consumerism.
- World-class scientists like Einstein, Bohr, Heisenberg, Schroedinger, Carrel, Abdul Kalam, Eccles *et. al.*, frankly admit that science can contribute nothing to the development of morality, ethicality, character, etc. Science may be supreme in

---

* A common defence by the votaries of modernistic progress is : Things have always been bad. Each earlier generation blames the later one for all evils, as though the previous ones were spotless. So the caravan must move on as it is now. But a number of us can see in broadlight the great acceleration in the rate of erosion in all subtler and nobler human conditions over the last fifty years. Why not then take the darker side of the moon seriously too.

the domain of 'what is'. But it has no say in the sphere of 'what should be'. Radhakrishnan had once remarked about the scientific temper as fostering 'nuclear giants who are moral dwarfs'. Hence, scientists of the class of Einstein et. al., do not hesitate to leave room here for the Super-personal, the religious, the spiritual consciousness.

- However, this class does not include authors or scientists like Stephen Hawking (*A Briefer History of Time*), or Paul Davies (*The Mind of God*) who strive for a complete theory 'to know the mind of God', or to write copiously and teasingly about the mind of God. The spiritual path for *realizing* God is closed for them. So, they struggle in vain to write on something about which they perceive or feel nothing. The existential, moral emptiness of such rationalistic speculations will be readily perceptible to any *legitimate* educator who studies, for example, Sri Aurobindo's *Hour of God*. If someone can understand the Hawking or Davies-type of dry logical argumentation, there is no reason why that person cannot grasp Sri Aurobindo's rich thoughts – and get truly uplifted by them.
- This problem plagues most social scientists too. The principal agenda of Centres manned by them seems to be to hit at the foundations of our *core culture*. Their academic sophistry appears incapable of hardly anything constructive and enduring. They habitually employ western thought categories and idioms to interpret or appraise our culture which is radically different.
- Let Acharya Prafulla Chandra Ray (a D.Sc. from Edinburgh, a Professor, and the founder of the Bengal Chemical and Pharmaceutical Works) speak to us as a genuine son of Bharatvarsha:

  (a) 'All through my varied activities I felt the force of the saying: *Tvaya Hrishikesha hridisthitena, Yatha niyukthosmi tatha karomi* 'I commit myself to Thee, O Lord ! Make me thy agent'

  (b) 'Whatever field I have ploughed, I have ploughed as an humble instrument in the hands of Providence; my failures are my own. ... But my successes if any are to be attributed to the guidance of the All- Knowing who chose me to be His humble instrument.' Secular scientists of progressive India may be humbly 'inquired': What is your estimate of the Acharya?

- It appears strange, and also intriguing, that the 1976 duties list in the Constitution does not show the courage of conviction by laying down the duty ***to develop a spiritual and scientific temper.*** This would have demonstrated India's originality and uniqueness — an example to the world. May be, as usual, she is waiting to imitate some Western Constitution which might incorporate such a duty. For instance, she has done so long back by replacing 'Education Ministry' with 'HRD Ministry' at the Centre.

- But recently we also have begun to introduce a few such learnings. Why? Because, true to our apish mentality, 'yoga' of sorts is in vogue and practice today in the West. Or, such-andsuch UN body has referred to it.

- It is apt to cite here (on the basis of an eye-witness account) a revealing incident towards the end of 2005. Dr. Abdul Kalam was presiding over the 150th anniversary function of the three earliest premier universities of India. It was being hosted by one of the trio. The President had asked in advance for a separate list of questions from the Post-graduate students of each university. The teachers of the host university had, however, censored out all questions from its students on the socio-cultural aspects of India. (Their questions had 240 to be routed through proper channel as they say.

After the President read out this list aloud, he expressed his dismay, and reprimanded the highest authorities of that university who were present there. His intended charge was that the list reflected a *hyper-scientific pose* in the barrage of questions put to him exclusively on bio-technology, nano technology, virtual reality, space technology, etc. But the President had enjoyed responding to the deeper and more vital issues presented to him by the students of the other two universities. He himself had no problems with God.

- The legitimate educator's attention is invited to the appendix at the end which reproduces the various meanings of the word 'secular' cited in three well-known dictionaries. They are unanimous about its central import. The peculiar Indian nation of 'equality towards all religions' does not figure in them. Another word should be searched for it.

- Now to the component of *spirit of inquiry*. In brief, its real thrust is to accord implicit primacy and rectitude to the 'present', and hence confer upon it the untrammeled right to inquire or question the 'past' which is summarily considered as dark, obscurantist, superstitious etc. Educational outfits and social processes are thus being contaminated with contempt for enduring verities. Passing fads and vanities are at work to overturn the solid standing ground and superstructure built by the *rishis* over millennia e.g., disposable, contractual marriage instead of life-long, sacramental marriage; egoistic careerism abroad, mocking at healthy social traditions, leaving old parents in the lurch, etc.

- One of the manifestations of such a vain 'spirit of inquiry' is the cavalier manner in which many academic, bureaucratic and journalistic high-fliers frequently denounce *sanatan* ideals like *vanaprastha* or *upanayan* or *kshatra dharma* or supramental realization. Have such celebrities done their homework with *shraddha*, and 'inquired' into the true import of these ideals with a straight mind? Teachers and parents who receive or are provided with such negative stuff in tailor-made text books, are being unwittingly or unwillingly induced to vitiate the tender minds of their pupils and wards.*
- 'Spirit of inquiry', as proclaimed by the majority of intellectuals, thrives on the myth of linear ascent in the quality of human thought and perception. This is patently wrong. The present era is considerably more boisterous, convoluted and vulgar than the ones by-gone.

With silence and contemplation vanishing from the human sphere, and with the dissecting 'left brain' supplanting the integrating 'right brain', the capacity to perceive holistic and eternal TRUTH is becoming almost zero. But this the world's seers and Bharat's *rishis* had been able to accomplish in the calm serenity of *ashrams* and *tapovans* in the days of yore. Every now and then we come across

* *Amidst this gloomy view of education, the author was greatly delighted to recently read to his grand-daughter (6 years) the following* lines from a 2008-book from London: 'TOM is an old train. He is very very old and slow, but he is always happy. SAM is anew train. He is very new and fast. But he is not always happy. Often he feels sad.' This symbolic analogy perfectly sums up the gnawing sore inside sci-tech modernity. (Early Readers, by Gill Davies, Brown Watson)

contemporary reports about ancient norms of restraint regarding anger or sexuality or consumption being more foolproof than modern suicidal espousal of license in such matters. The sooner *legitimate* educators can seize this insight, the better will be their ability to turn the minds of pupils towards a 'spirit of inquiry about enduring Truths', and not merely about the 'transient facts' of restless change. It would rather be much safer for them to 'inquire into the present' in the light of the ancient.

- Your enslavement is celebrated, but your achievement concealed. There are several such instances cropping up across the country. What then is the sort of 'spirit of inquiry' the aggregate educational package of independent India trying to promote by such self-defeating manoeuvres? One may search in vain throughout the world for a second example of slavishness such as ours in matters of educating the minds of its young citizens.
- Steps taken by major all-India and state educational authorities often leave the lay public wondering about the extent to which prejudice against mainstream educational materials or models or institutions can go, e.g., the recent (May 2006) announcement declaring three Missionary colleges in West Bengal as Centres of Excellence. Among the rejected ones is the Ramakrishna Mission Vidyamandira at Belur. Similarly, scurrilous works get published, or cooked-up cases get framed against the venerated saints of only the mainstream community — all with the blessings of the ruling establishments. It goes without saying that crafty arguments will not be scarce to cover up the hidden agenda behind all this. Can these malafide 'inquiries' build up a positive and inspiring atmosphere of nation-building education by strengthening Bharat's nonproselytizing *sanatan* ethos? Will such stratagems contribute in any way to education for national integration by bruising and alienating only the mainstream sentiments? All this is anything but 'scientific'.
- Back to 'scientific temper'. Education in India, for the sake of Bharatvarsha, should accord *priority* to 'spiritual science' over 'material science'. This is both her right and duty, not only for herself, but for the whole world. Mundane, secular rationality

must be guided by *supramundane sacred rationality*. Our children and pupils have the right to be educated about the sacred/spiritual temper of their Motherland. Some examples of this temper are given below:

(a) The following verses from Bharat's *rishis* have called uponthe whole world, not just their own specific community, land or prophet -

- '*Asato ma sadgamayah, tamaso ma jyotirgamaya*'.
- '*Udarcharitanam tu vasudhaiva kutumbakam*'.
- '*Sarve bhavantu sukhino, sarve santu niramaya*'.

Why not begin educating the 5 or 6-year old child of every community with these mantras, instead of injecting *self-hate* in their minds with descriptions of suttee, dowry, distortions of caste system and the like? It is not known if any other nation or culture follows such suicidal practices by entering the mansion of national culture through the stinking backdoors used by scavengers. Yet, which culture in the world does not have its rotten backyard?

(b) In certain parts of India, the new-born baby is taken to a temple and offered to the deity there, seeking Divine blessings. What is regressive in such sacred rationality?

(c) The *Upanishads*, Epics, *Puranas*, etc., are replete with characters, stories, parables which can raise tender, untwisted minds to sublime heights, and also warn them against transgressions of *dharma*, or ethics and values. We believe the characters of boys like Nachiketa, Dhruva, Lav and Kush, Prahlad should constitute the *natural staple* of values education for all communities in Bharatvarsha. This method shall also coincide with one of the first principles of early and *legitimate* education: *from the near to the far, from the local to the global.*

(d) During 1956 Madras was gasping under relentless drought. All storages and reservoirs around the city had gone dry. C. Rajagopalachari, who was then the Chief Minister, sponsored a public Vedic *yajna* to propitiate the Divine to show mercy for His children by showering rains. The same evening clouds peeped across the horizon. By nightfall it started pouring. It rained and rained ... the whole night.

Next morning the city was seen flooded, and boats had to ply on the roads. Even in 2004 or 2005 a similar *yajna* was performed in Karnataka, with positive results. The so-called scientific mind may dismiss such events as just coincidences i.e., effects without cause, smoke without fire. This stance itself is unscientific. Rather, sacred rationality would read into these events the higher laws of man-Nature, terrestrial–transcendental, earthly–cosmic inter-relationships and inter–dependencies (see *Gita*, chapter IV, 14-5). Such examples of Cosmic/Divine responsiveness to sincere, humble human prayer conveys one of the most fundamental truths of sacred education. The imagination of tender minds should be elevated by such narratives told with *shraddha. This is holistic education too*.

(e) The sacred temper has also to be nourished by engaging with Epic characters through the reverential route, not by the path of debunking them. For instance, the correct way to educate about Yudhisthir's character is to narrate how, during the malafide exile of the Pandavas, it is he who had directed his brothers to rescue the scheming Duryodhana and his cohorts from the captivity of Gandharvas for playing mischief with their women. It is mischievous to dismiss the numerous lofty learnings from his character by just pin-pointing one half-lie he told during the war, and that too without disclosing that he had to pass at the end through 'hell' even for such a slight aberration. In any case, who are we – parents, teachers, and intellectuals — to pick holes in such characters? What is our standard of morality? The same remarks apply to the self-righteous debunking of Ram, Krishna and similar heroes who constitute the life-force of Bharat's culture. *Legitimate* educators must go to Tagore, Gandhi and their likes to realize the essential truth and power of our Epic characters.

(f) Yet another ubiquitous sacred feature of Bharat's tradition is to provide a place, however, small, within the home which is consecrated to the Divine. It is exclusive to the chosen symbol(s) of God, and provides an abiding, sacred anchor for the entire family, often across generations. Modern, secular, 'flat' culture, after the Western mode, is succeeding in uprooting this anchor — at least in metro areas. Even those who get their own homes designed by secular architects, are not advised, nor the owners inclined to provide for such sacred space. But such *scared rationality* is existentially wholesome and enriching. Scientific or secular rationality is destitute of this quality.*

(g) The most scientific of all scientific enquiries had been mooted and solved millennia ago by Bharat's unrivalled *tapovanic* tradition: Why am I born as a *human being*, not as an ant, a reptile, a fish, a bird, a dog, a tree and so on? What is the *special purpose* of human birth? Is it just an accident, or the high point of a very long evolutionary process? Does it imply an even greater, grander culmination? How do I proceed for it? Why should I proceed for it? Who is the Magician behind this Magic? Can I commune with Him? Such is the character of the 'scientific', inquiring temper of Bharatvarsha. Secular science has neither the capacity nor the courage to scale such 'scientific' heights. True scientists confess this, smart intellectuals do not.

- Most of the present masterminds of the sci-tech spirit in India appear to be equally poor in their grasp of both human psychology and supra-rational knowledge. Their smugness is often matched by their unconcern about these ultimate matters. Legitimate educators, teachers and parents alike, therefore ought to be duly cautious before giving a freeway to such individuals and groups in determining the direction of educational endeavours in our country. For, they do not (and will not) understand Bharatvarsha. They harbour alien minds in Indian bodies.
- With the type of 'scientific materialism' now being forced upon the world under the mask of 'development', all such processes of sacred living are under mortal threat. So, the *legitimate educator* is invited to judge the populist pedlars of 'scientific temper' in the light of this biting interlocution of Sri Aurobindo (*All India Magazine*, Pondicherry, July 2006). "When my

---

* Modern apartments, in India at least, often bring to the author's mind this sharp Biblical rebuke : 'Ye unto like whited sepulchres'—just a mass of dry bones and flesh covered with a tomb in bright white (St.Matthew). There is no room or space for the 'sacred'.

subjective experience tells him (the scientist, materialist, reasoner), 'I am hungry', he consents; 'Of course you must be so since you say so'. But let it tell him, 'I am full of bliss from an immaterial source,' ... and he answers, 'you are only fit for the gaol or the lunatic asylum'." (p. 13).

V

- Anyone who feels inspired to blossom into a *legitimate educator* for the youth of Bharatvarsha, would immensely profit by studying Swami Abhedananda's book *India and Her People*. It was first published in 1906 in New York. Abhedananda had taken up the work of teaching Indian culture and Vedanta immediately after his *gurubhai* Swami Vivekananda had launched this daring adventure of spreading *Sanatan* light and peace. Abhedananda's small but intense book comprises seven chapters delivered as lectures to elite audiences at the Brooklyn Institute of Arts and Sciences more than one hundred years ago. They are as incisive and dense as courageous and scholarly. To quote him:

'As early as the Vedic period, which dates from 5000 to 2000 BC, the ancient Seers of Truth asked the most vital questions, and discussed problems that have troubled the minds of the great philosophers of all ages. In those questions we can discern the development of their intellectual powers, and their insight in to the true nature of things' (p. 31, 1963 Indian edition).

- Apart from many such capsule evaluations of Bharat's cultural roots, he had also adduced solid corroborative assessments from several unbiased Western savants. A few instances follow:
  (a) Victor Cousin: 'India contains the whole history of philosophy in a nutshell.'
  (b) Julian Huxley: 'To say nothing of Indian sages to whom evolution was a familiar notion ages before Paul of Tarsus was born.'
  (c) Monier Williams: In his book *Brahminism* and *Hinduism* says, '... the Hindus were Spinozites more than two thousand years before the existence of Spinoza; and Darwinians many centuries before Darwin; and evolutionists many centuries before the doctrine of evolution had been accepted by the scientists of our time. ...'

(d) E. W. Hopkins: 'Plato is full of Sankhyan thought, worked out by him, but taken from Pythagoras. Before the 6th century BC all the religious-philosophical ideas of Pythagoras were current in India ... such coincidences are too numerous to be the result of chance.'

- All *legitimate educators* of India, whatever be their specific subject or profession or community, should therefore acquire sober and respectful confidence in the culture's past. Inwardly too they should confess that they are today *unworthy* inheritors of such a peerless legacy. No question of feeling guilty or apologetic to any quarter arises. So, while they need to devote their energies to revivify this legacy in their heart and head, they have also to pass on the baton to the future generations.
- In the light of the foregoing observations, we suggest **first** that autobiographies or biographies of Gandhiji, Netaji, Tagore, Tilak, PC Ray and Abdul Kalam should be essential study at school level. **Second**, stories from the Epics, *Upanishads*, *Hitopodesa*, *Panchatantra,* etc., ought to be the main corpus of English and vernacular prose selections. **Third**, tape-recorded dialogues with those freedom fighters who are still living e.g., the ones who suffered brutal tortures in the cellular jail of Andaman should be a regular feature of student study circles. **Fourth**, it should be the moral duty of all Semitic cultures settled in India to respect and honour India's mainstream core culture. They would be well-advised by the leaders of their own communities to shed notions of superiority over the *sanatan* culture. This will be a constructive step towards national integration, if it is genuinely desired. Besides, this gesture will also be a welcome recompense for the many wrongs done by them to this land.
- The **Parsees** are the best example in this respect. They had migrated into India to seek shelter, not conquer. National integration and preservation of cultural heritage calls for *reciprocal* duties by ancillary cultural streams also, as demonstrated by the Parsees. Countries like Britain and USA (Christianity), China (Confucianism), Malaysia (Islam), etc., are firm and clear in this crucial matter. The educational systems there recognize all non-mainstream cultures, but unambiguously accord top place to their respective *core cultures*. Everyone thus knows one's rightful place in the aggregate social mosaic. Vote-catching politics, or pliable judiciary, or foreign patronage

and awards do not cloud the central cultural focus while educating their citizens.

Here is a moving example of what *shraddha* for one's Motherland and preserving its heritage means (as narrated by Prema Nanda Kumar): "I meditate upon that hero as a publisher, Pratap Chandra Roy, who published Kishori Mohan Ganguly's English translation of the Mahabharata in eleven volumes more than a hundred years ago. Just when the last volume was to be made ready, Pratap Chandra fell seriously ill. He told his wife Sundari Bala:

> 'The book must be finished. Don't spend money on my funeral rites if it is needed for printing. Live as simply as you can so as to save money for the *Mahabharata.*' Sundari Bala faithfully completed the task, and a year later the eighteen *parvas* of the epic were available to the world of scholars abroad."

- Early in the year 2006 an English national daily reported that the former Principal of a prestigious school in North India had become an educational consultant after retiremsent. One of his tasks is to identify Principals from Britain for heading the businesslike elitist 'international' schools now mushrooming in India.* Compensation packages are no hurdle. Woe to Mother Bharat— no Principals among your 110 crore children ! What a mighty fall for the Bharat of Takshashila, Nalanda, Varanasi, Nadia, etc.,
- In his Foreword to David Frawley's book *Hinduism and The Clash of Civilizations* (Voice of India, 2001), Rankin speaks of the 'great injustice done to Hinduism by Islamic and Western invaders, by missionaries old and new, and by an Indian elite who have made a new religion of secularism' (p. x). Later in this perceptive book on 'Indian or Bharatiya' civilization, Frawley himself declares: 'Though battered by time, Indian or Bharatiya civilization has better survived the onslaughts of time than any other culture. It has done so not through military force or missionary zeal – like the fierce opponents it has had to resist –

* Big business houses are building 'International Baccalaureate Schools' which charge ₹ 100,000 or so per month from each student. From architecture to infra-structure, there is nothing Indian in them.

but through the dedication of its people to the spiritual practices set forth in the region during ancient times. India is the *perennial civilization* of the planet. ...' (Chapter 12).

- Here is a moving tribute from the Korean poetess Kim Yang-Shik, Chairperson of the Tagore Society of Korea (*India*, TSK, Seoul, 1993)

'My life and its values underwent a major metamorphosis in 1975 when I visited India. The visit gave me the opportunity to acquaint myself with the soul of India's spiritual heritage. I do not know how futile my life would have been had I not known India, because life without knowledge of the fundamental truth of humanism which India symbolises, has perhaps no meaning. Truly speaking, India offered delectable pabulum to my starved soul. 'India also proved to be a mirror for me in which I could see my bloated vanity and ambition. India taught me the ideals of mankind. ...' (pp. 1-2)

- By honouring the hopes and goodwill of the likes of Frawley, Yang-Shik *et. al.* In their heads and hearts, through their words and actions, our *legitimate educators* would also honour themselves and the ancient *rishis*. There is no question of fundamentalism in such dutiful defence of Bharat's *core culture*. For, in this endeavour no conversions or massacres or taxations of the members of other faiths are implied. But our Mother and our Mother Culture must be defended at all costs. This has to be the ultimate purpose of true education.

- It will be fitting towards the close of this chapter to hear N. A. Palkhivala's (the renowned Parsee Jurist) pregnant words in regard to education about India's *core culture* (1980).

'The old faith and the old culture referred to by Rajaji (C. Rajagopalachari) is not merely for Hindus, not merely for India, but for the whole world. 'Schelling, in his old age, thought the *Upanishads* the maturest wisdom of mankind. Today that wisdom is essential not only for the rebirth of the Indian nation, but also for the *re-education of the human race*.'

- There can hardly be a better-articulated redemptive impulse than the above to the time-serving policies, measures and institutions our country is being subjected to since 1950. It will be chastening to recall that on April 3, 1986, Prof. Richard Gombrich of Cambridge had bluntly told the elite National

Library audience in Calcutta that 'most middle-class intellectuals of India knew next to nothing about their culture.' (*The Telegraph*, April 4, 1986). Things have worsened since then. Let therefore, all *legitimate educators* arise and awake to prevent such future indictments from those who wish India well. Never for a moment should it be forgotten that Bharat has to be saved from the enemy within — that is India. *Legitimate educators have a duty to become 'intellectual kshatriyas'* as Frawley has proposed.

- In a sitar recital by Pt. Ravishankar there are many categories of accompanists. This is true of a sarod performance by Ustaad Amjad Ali Khan too. There are other similar instances. All of them constitute different kinds of *composite* performances. Yet, there is not a moment's doubt or confusion in the mind of any member of the audience who the *core* player is. If an accompanist cannot accept his duty in a supportive role in the performance, he should gracefully quit the stage. The symphony cannot be allowed to degenerate into a cacophony springing from the vanity of false equality among supporting players in the team.

APPENDIX

'Secular' in three dictionaries

(A) *The Concise Oxford Dictionary:*

1. concerned with the affairs of this world, not spiritual or sacred.
2. (education) not concerned with religion or religious belief.
3. not ecclesiastical or monastic, not bound by a religious rule.
4. occurring once in an age or century.
5. lasting for or occurring over an indefinitely long time.

(B) *Webster's Comprehensive Dictionary:*

1. of or pertaining to this world or the present life, temporal, worldly, contrasted with religious or spiritual.
2. not under the control of the church, civil not ecclesiastical.
3. not concerned with religion, not sacred.
4. not bound by monastic vows.

(C) *The New Collins Concise Dictionary:*

1. of or relating to worldly as opposed to sacred things.
2. not concerned with or related to religion.
3. not within the control of the church.
4. an education having no particular religious affinities.
5. not bound by religious vows to a monastic or other order.
6. occurring or appearing once in an age.
7. lasting for a long time.

References

1. Sri Aurobindo: *Prison Tales* (1972)
2. Chakraborty S. K.: *Against The Tide* (2003)
3. Tagore Rabindranath: *The Centre of Indian Culture* (1988)
4. Tagore Rabindranath: *Human Values: The Tagorean Panorama,* translated by Chakraborty, S. K. and Bhattacharya, Pradip (1999)
5. Gandhi M. K.: *Selected Works*, Vol. II (2001)
6. Gandhi M. K.: *My Experiments With Truth* (1972)
7. Tagore Rabindranath: *Reminiscences* (1980)
8. Sri Aurobindo:*The Foundations of Indian Culture* (1998)
9. Huntington S. P.: *Who Are We?* (2004)
10. Sister Nivedita: *Complete Works*, Vols. II and IV (1996)
11. Clark R.: *The Life and Work of JBS Haldane* (1969)
12. Frawley D.: *Vedantic Meditation* (2002)
13. Krishna Prem: *Initiation Into Yoga* (1976) 252
14. Griffiths B.: *The Cosmic Revelation* (1983)
15. which charge Rs. 100,000 or so per month from each student. From Michel: *The Invasion That Never Was* (2001).
16. Danino Michel: *The Indian Mind – Then and Now* (2000).
17. Swami Vivekananda: *Complete Works,* Vol. III (1962).
18. Einstein A.: *Ideas and Opinions* (2003).
19. Heisenberg W.: *Quantum Questions* ed. K Wilber (1985).
20. Radhakrishnan S.: *Recovery of Faith* (1976).
21. Ray P. C: *Autobiography* (1932).
22. Kumar Prema Nanda: *Indian Epic Narrative: Alive and Vibrant* (2004).
23. Abdul Kalam A. P. J.: *Ignited Minds* (2002).
24. Basham A. L.: *A Cultural History of India* (1997).

25. Palkhiwala N. A.: *India's Priceless Heritage* (1980).
26. Russell B.: *Autobiography* (2000).
27. Kersten H.: *Jesus Lived in India* (2001).
28. Swami Abhedananda:*India and Her People* (1906, 2000).
29. Hawking Stephen: *A Briefer History of Time* (2005).
30. Davies Paul: *The Mind of God* (1993).
31. Frawley D.:*Hinduism and the Clash of Civilizations* (2001).
32. Williams, M. Monier: *Hinduism* (1877, 1951).
33. Bose, A. C.:*The Call of The Vedas* (1970).
34. Rowland, W.: *Greed Inc.* (2006).
35. Epps, W. M.: *Terrorism and Personal Security* (2005).
36. Spar, D. L.: *The Baby Business* (2006).
37. Schumacher, E. F.: *Small is Beautiful* (1977).
38. Rifkin J.: *Entropy* (1981).
39. Kim Yang-Shik: *India – Selected Poems* (1993).
40. Mukherjee R. Kamal: *The Sickness of Civilization* (1964).
41. Basu Durgadas: *The Constitution of India* (1995).

CHAPTER 9

EDUCATION ACROSS A CENTURY: A Bird's Eyeview

भद्र कर्णेभिः श्रृणुयाम देवाः ।
भद्र पश्येमाक्षभिर्यजत्राः ।

(*Rigveda*)

Let us hear with our ears all that
which is auspicious;
Let with our eyes we see
all that is auspicious.

(Sw. Yatiswarananda,
Meditation and Its Methods,
RK. Math, Chennai, p. 289)

I

The National Council of Education was born in March, 1906. Its birth had followed soon after the infamous Bengal Partition in the previous year. Later in the same year in August, the National College of Education, Bengal (NCEB), too was launched. The moving spirit behind this saga was Acharya Satish Chandra Mukherjee. Its first Principal was Sri Aurobindo, who had left Baroda for this act of worship at almost one-third the salary. The magnetic power of the NCEB had attracted numerous great teachers as well as authentic students of the time. Among the visiting and regular teachers Rabindranath Tagore's name appears on top, followed by Annie Besant, Sri Aurobindo, Sister Nivedita and many more. The galaxy of students included Benoy Kumar Sarkar, Rajendra Prasad, Triguna Sen, Radhakumud Mukherjee and several others. All of them had kept alive and alight the Indian mind in Indian bodies. The inspirations and aspirations of the NCEB had been distilled into this *moolmantra:*

Know India and Love India. Mukherjee himself was a legitimate educator * par excellence. By divine dispensation, as it were, the NCEB had witnessed a confluence of *acharya devobhavah* and *chhatranaam adhyanam tapah* – the twin perennial streams of educational philosophy in Bharat's *sanatan* tradition.

The year 2005-06 was the centenary of such an epochal labour of love, of *shraddha*, for the Motherland. The NCEB and Sri Aurobindo Samiti had, therefore, put their heads together and conceived a National Symposium on the Philosophy and Practice of Education for India, as a precursor to the NCEB's centenary celebrations. Country-wide participation by eminent academics and professionals in other fields was arranged. The Symposium was held at Kolkata during November 26-27, 2004 at Sri Aurobindo Bhavan. It received ample support from the Indian Council of Philosophical Research.

Several months of preparatory thinking by the Symposium Committee** emerged with the following diagnoses of some thorny issues and problems, and their visible manifestations besetting education in India today. Although the sample of facts cited below may not appear smooth and suave, yet honesty to the NCEB legacy had induced genuine acknowledgment within the Committee about these matters. They are deeply connected with education. Silent aloofness in this regard borders on meek acquiescence, even abdication. Such apathy among educators is turning education insipid, uninspiring and unwholesome. When posterity attempts once more to cast off the current spell of hypnosis, it will not forgive the irresponsibility of the present.

- From around 1950 onwards the Indian mind has been gradually de-educated from 'Know India and Love India'. Instead, education has been gravitating towards something like 'Forget India and Berate India'. This trend seems to have accentuated since the start of the 21st century.

---

* Legitimate educators are those who: (a) Set their first aim as the imprinting of abiding shraddha in the minds of students for their Motherland, and (b) Do not care to be politically correct — unlike the careerist ones.

** The author was its Convener.

- Commissions, Committees, Councils and Counsels have been galore. Yet education in India has been drifting to nowhere, without a compass and anchor relevant for her. From the assessment year 2005-06 the Indian tax payer is being required to pay a surcharge of 2 percent on the total tax payable. It is called 'Educational Cess', and is intended to promote better education!* This could be a unique fiscal innovation in the world. So, the Committee proposes to present below a series of diagnostic pictures about the 'State of Denmark' i.e., the state of affairs in the realm of Indian education at this moment.

- Almost every ounce of energy of our educators (parents, teachers, leaders, media and policy-makers) is being consumed in obligingly responding to shots called from distant shores. Indian society is thus getting mis-educated into cyber-porn, juvenile crime, crass consumerism, old age homes, crèches, stress, divorce, school sex education, beauty parades, law courts, etc., India is progressing and modernizing at cyber-speed as it were.

- Essentially *sattwic*** India, but presently *rajaso-tamasic*,** hardly pauses today to realize that she is gobbling all the disruptive stimuli from restless, expansive, *rajasic* cultures. The folly of a mature and sustainable culture in this imitative rush is poignant.

- Compared to China, Japan, Malaysia, Korea, Singapore etc., Indian education has been failing to galvanize her post-independence generations for self-transcending national causes. The very foundations of such a higher call are being struck down in India. No wonder then that these Asian countries outperform India on most counts. The national spirit there is strong and virile. In India the situation is dangerously contrary. *Egoistic* and *personal individuality* is today asserted vehemently as 'emancipation'. But *cultural and national individuality* is rejected summarily as 'fascism'.

  Yet, the latter ascription is squarely contradicted by the record if Bharat's history and culture. It tries to slay a ghost that never exists. Bogeys such as these need to be banished

* It has now been withdrawn.

** Sattwa is the psychological energy of illumination.
Rajas is the psychological energy of action.
Tamas is the psychological energy of darkness, inertia.

from all discourse on education for India. Though ceaselessly sinned against, from around 400 B.C. till today, Bharat has not done so towards any country. She does not have to apologise to any other nation for Plasseys and Chittores, for Romanias or Hungarys, for Hiroshimas and Vietnams, for Auschwitzs and Bosnias, for Chechnayas and World Trade Centres, and a lot more. Yet, the irony is that national education in these countries never condemns such misdeeds before their young minds. Rather, such events are usually portrayed as heroic achievements, or slurred over. The situation in India is reverse. It therefore becomes a moral responsibility of legitimate educators in India to impart such big-picture perspectives to our daughters and sons.

- Recently a grandfather was conversing with his 10-year old grandson. He was a pupil of class five in a reputed English medium school of a metro city. One afternoon the former asked, 'Do you know who was the first Indian winner of the Nobel prize?' Prompt came the answer: Mother Teresa. Further exploration with the boy could not elicit a single Indian name – Rabindranath Tagore onwards.

- Our children are told about Copernicus, Newton and Marconi. But they hear not about India's Bhaskaracharya, Aryabhatta, JC Bose *et. al.* They are informed that Europe gave us printing press, grammar, dictionary, etc., But they are not told that Bharat gave zero and the decimal system to the world — the basis of all mathematics. As if there have been no *vyakaranas* and no *shabdakoshas* in Sanskrit, Tamil, etc., Today we all are supposed to be getting enriched by 'information capital'. Yet our children are growing up as paupers with either noninformation or mis-information about their own country and culture.

- There is a well-known tourist spot to the north-west of Delhi. A family of four went there in July 2004. The two 60-plus elder members had visited the site a few times earlier also. Amidst numerous tombs and towers stands a tall iron pillar – at least 1,600 years old, dating back to Chandragupta II's time. It is a marvel of ancient Bharat's iron-making technology, rustless to this day. Unlike during their earlier visits, the two elders were amazed this time to find no signboard around the iron pillar. Yet, every other later structure displayed large red sandstone plaques with detailed information about each. Meanwhile, a few busloads of school children arrived. Reaching the iron pillar, they were clueless about it. Nor the few accompanying elders (perhaps teachers) were of any help. Thus, the younger generation is being left 'uneducated' about the nation's past glory achieved by indigenous craftsmen. Again, in 2007 and 2009 the same family had visited the Ellora caves. The very first massive and marvellous rock-hewn Kailash temple had no Government display board at the entrance, though it is the oldest (7th century) monument there.* But for the other caves a little away appropriate information boards right in front told the visitors that they were Buddhist and Jaina caves (11th and 13th centuries). Similar 'malpractice of education' could be discovered in other parts of the country also.

- We had been invited in June 2005 to address a group of twenty-eight IAS officials at the National Academy of Administration, Mussoorie. During our three-day stay we observed that everyone was greeting one another in the mornsian country. Phrases like 'hyper-nationalism' and 'illegitimate nationalism' have been coined to belittle any emotional disposition to own up the enormous positive stock of Indian culture.
- Most major universities in North America have a Department of Chinese Studies, but very few for Indic Studies. They are now usually clubbed with South Asia Studies (e.g.; at York University, Toronto). The plea: India is a sub-continent, not a nation. How then can there be a British nation with Ireland, Wales, Scotland and England who are not so homogeneous or friendly with one another as might be supposed? At several places courses on Islamic studies, even Sikh studies are offered. But it is rare

---

* We were later told by some other visitors that a sign board was there, but tucked away quite afar on the right side of the main entrance – liable to be missed by most visitors.

nowadays to find any on Hindu Studies or Hinduism. (Incidentally, many large US cities have China Towns, but none has an India Town.

- Indian Embassies abroad cannot celebrate Deepavali or any similar national festival. But the Gregorian New Year fete is in order. No other plural society in the world, from Britain to Malaysia, puts the mainstream on the defensive like this. Here, too, politicized education in India is on a fatal track. Some of the tributaries also need education about their duties and loyalties to Bharat. For this task we need *legitimate*, not *careerist* educators.
- The Committee wondered about the character of education that induced orchestrated denunciation of a religio-cultural tradition which has never invaded or persecuted any similar system beyond its borders, by its own learned scholars. In the process, terms like Hindu and Hinduism seem to be on their way out. It is forgotten that these terms have imparted an indispensable component of identity for mainstream Indian citizens, coexisting with a rich variety of indigenous sub-cultures and sub-traditions, for two thousand years and more. These latter include Buddhism, Jainism and Sikhism. Yet, articulate intelligentsia and media are often seem to be keen to avoid these two words. Thus, in May 2005 a two-line announcement for a public lecture on 'Hindu Studies: Its Problems and Prospects' by a non-resident Indian scholar was sent to the major newspapers of a metro city. The two English newspapers which received the notice did not publish it. Such partisan behaviour by the professional media of this country must be a unique phenomenon in the world. Reconstruction of educational philosophy for India should address such critical grassroots issues.
- It also bears mention here that if the word 'Hindu' is an ascribed one, not found in our ancient texts, then so too is the word 'India'. Why then, from the Constitution onwards, we steadfastly cling on to India? Bharat is the word for this land in ancient texts. But this word too seems to be on the way out e.g. Indo-Bangladesh Cultural Forum. How to reconcile such double think? Every country around ours has adopted its own indigenous name after independence. India is the only exception. The names of some cities only have been changed here. Such anomalies

carry deep implications for the education of a national 'common' mind as Sister Nivedita had advised us.

- The local newspaper incident just mentioned, and the contraction of Indic/Hindu studies in Western universities could be joined up to yield a big picture. And such linkages can be extended. Thus, this author was approached twice (in 2000 and 2002) to write on 'Ethical Concepts in Hinduism' from North America and Australia. But immediately after he had consented, all communication from them stopped — mysteriously.
- In 2004 two Vice-Chancellors in a certain State were involved in fraudulent recruitment and false written declarations about academic qualifications. However, quite different methods were adopted for handling the offenders, guided by whether one was on the wrong side of the political fence or the right. This, for the Committee, was another telling domestic evidence of the virus eating into India's educational structures and systems.
- During Olympic games or other international athletic meets the national anthem, *jana gana mana*, is not played when the Indian contingent parades, or an Indian mounts the victory stand. Another song is played. What sort of education leads to such a national sin? It is impossible to imagine any other country committing such a sacrilege.

A prestigious Central Indian university does not have a department of Sanskrit Studies. But there is one for a non-Indian, non-Western language. Similarly, in the new reading hall of one of the largest and oldest Indian libraries the reader sees an exclusive display rack right in front for magazines — not in Sanskrit, nor Hindi nor English even. In both cases one can easily guess what might be the highlighted language. Politicians with ulterior motives, are thus precipitating disintegration by denying the gentle mainstream its due, and pampering the aggressive ones with what is undeserved.

- Till this day the *Ramayan* is recited by priests at the time of childbirth in many Indonesian homes — Muslim and Hindu alike. The belief is, if it is a boy its character would resemble that of Ram, if a girl that of Sita.[1] In Thailand Kings still proudly proclaim their lineage from Sri Ram. Whither education in India today?

- Increasing non-terrorist violence in Indian society is due directly to the menace of imported and domestic serials and films portraying raw sex and violence. It is a travesty of truth to attribute this scourge to our Epics of lofty idealism. Fights and battles therein, following strict codes of conduct, being incidental only.
- Certain United Nations agencies have assumed the role of world educators, global teachers. In a recent personal communication to us, a Western writer has remarked that many of the UN reports 'smack of deceptive sophistry'. This observation is as honest as it is apt. For instance, the Human Development Report, 2000, is an elaborate exercise in forcing upon all cultures such notions of 'human rights' (HR) and 'human development' (HD) which have not been tested on the anvil of time.[2]
- The elimination of 'home', coupled with the booming business of 'old age homes' at one end and 'baby creches' at the other, is just one telling instance of the devastating consequences of the kind of HR and HD education being thrust upon the world. Fashionable ideas, with moth-like lifespans, from cultures which have hardly a few centuries of history, are displacing or being allowed to displace, the wise, sustainable and proven principles of HD through 'human duties'. In Bharatvarsha a person is born with duties or debts (*pancha rin*), not rights. All-round duties by all produce the ultimate fruits of rights for all. Duties cannot be politicized, whereas rights can be. This is the perspective in all oriental cultures e.g., Japan.[3] Emphasis on rights creates or aggravates conflicts in the social fabric e.g., British kids are already taking their parents to the court in a snow-balling 'compensation culture'. This may suit professions like politics or law. But this is not education for HD. Besides, *the paramount HR of all* — a nation like Bharat's right to be and to develop her true self, her true culture — *is getting smothered by the poison pills of 21st century education*. Careerist intellectuals should be clearly distinguished from *Rishis* and Seers. The former can only 'look at'. The latter can 'see through'. So, education has been and is always safe in the hands of 'seers'.

II

- A certain day during the early months of 2001 had witnessed this painful incident. A research scholar, holding a Master's degree in philosophy, was working on Sri Aurobindo. She was berthed in a vintage research institute of international standing, specialising in Sanskrit and Indology. That day she reached the Institute around 10 a.m. and was walking into her cubicle. A senior faculty member saw her in the corridor, and she said 'namaskar'. The teacher informed her about a lecture by him on the *Gita* scheduled at 11 a.m. in the large seminar room, and asked her to come. She had some urgent writing to finish, and politely pleaded her inability to attend. But the teacher insisted that she must come. Reluctantly she agreed. As the lecture unfolded it turned out to be a vitriolic attack on the *Gita*, its motives, its assumptions, its enunciations. As for Sri Krishna, he was far from being a role model, an avatar. He was a diabolical schemer and inciter of violence, etc., Unable to bear any more, she quietly slipped out of the hall.

Full of agony, almost tearful for being forced to hear such abuse of Gita-the-mother, she pondered: 'Why did then Charles Wilkins take the pains of translating the *Gita*? How could Wordsworth, Keats, Emerson, Eliot *et.al.* get captivated by the *Gita*? Inspired by the Gita, how could Shelley pour out the following lines in his poem 'Stanzas Written in Dejection': "... and that content surpassing wealth, The sage in meditation found, And walked with inward glory crowned?" Was this not the *atmarati*, or the *atmany eva atmano tushtah* of the Gita? She recalled the wisdom: You see only what you are predisposed to see — in someone or something. Otherwise, how to explain Ronald Nixon, a Cambridge science scholar and RAF pilot in the first world war, coming, living and dying in Bharat as Krishna Prem — by adoring the same Krishna who was a villain, a trickster to the Hindu apostle of peace in the seminar room? Such were the thoughts crossing her bruised heart in the silent cubicle.

- Continuing with the pathos of the wounded researcher, the following also is in order. The latest leader of this Gita-Krishna demolition brigade appears to be one Indian (Hindu) academic of world renown, but torn from his roots. So was Sri Aurobindo–– fourteen years in Manchester-London-Cambridge. He had returned to and settled in India in 1893, knowing not a word of Bengali or Sanskrit. Yet in a few years he became an epitome of 'Know India, and Love India'. The magnitude of difference between a *careerist educator* and a *legitimate educator* is nowhere better illustrated than by these two instances. Krishna Prem had written thus about Sri Aurobindo's *Essays on The Gita*[4]: 'Every Indian who loves the Gita should read it. For his commentary breaks new ground and is more inspiring than any other, thanks to his resplendent intellect and yogic intuition.' The anti-Gita-Krishna-Rama Indian messiahs of peace may be asked: What advice would they have tendered to Churchill in the face of Hitler's aggression? And what did Krishnaprem himself tell Dilip Kumar Roy about Krishna?: 'See Krishna, think of Krishna, act for Krishna...'[5] The bulk of our self-appointed champions of internationalism just mentioned above, to whom the *bansidhari* Krishna is sheer lust and *chakradhari* Krishna pure violence, may be informed also of these thoughts of Krishnaprem about India, expressed to Dilip again in 1942[6]. 'What I feel is, that the wealth of tradition which is a nation is too precious a thing to be merged into a common hotch-potch... *When the traditions of a nation die, then that nation is dead.* ... History is a symbol, it signifies something more precious than a mere piddling adherence to a sequence of so-called "facts". It is to be prayed that this magnificent insight, echoing Nivedita, into the deep-structure ethos of Bharat awakens a small spark of *shraddha* in the iconoclastic educators of today.

- It is pertinent to observe here that seekers like Nixon and Griffiths, observers like Reymond and Raine, historians like Basham and Toynbee, scientists like Einstein, Heisenberg, Schroedinger and Haldane — to name only a few — have proved their power of entering into the *core* of India's culture, seize its *essence*, and acknowledge it with honesty and humility. They candidly admit the narrow limits of secular science. And most of them agree that Hindu Yoga-Vedanta philosophy is the best educator – for the body-life-mind triad and much more beyond. This phenomenon prompts a fundamental question: Why is it that social scientists, in almost all branches e.g. economics, sociology, political science, psychology, anthropology, etc., demonstrate either a studied avoidance of, or a trained incapacity to penetrate into the eternal heart of Bharat? Most Indian historians, social scientists and technocrats also evince a crude, distorted view of things. Hence is the enigma:

How is it that several outstanding scientists and other thinkers of the West are able to grasp Indian ethos far more accurately and passionately than the majority of their Indian counterparts? Yet policy and practice of education today are entirely in the hands of the latter.

- It was, therefore, a rare inspiration in 1997 to hear from R. K. Talwar (former Chairman of SBI and IDBI) the following declaration of profound conviction[7]. 'Indians have to became true Indians. Their whole tradition and heritage has all the answers to today's ills and problems?' He could assert this because his feet were planted on the ground. Intellectual acrobatics had not robbed him of his faith-led experiential insights. He was a practitioner of *nishkam karma (Gita, II.47)* from boyhood.

- Here is yet one more instance of the cumulative harm caused by rudderless education in post–1950 India. An authentic NGO had invited this author as the main speaker to talk about 'Sustainability and Human Values'. It was an afternoon in May 2005. The assembly was inside an air-conditioned hall. One of the key ideas the speaker had tried to explain was that of *tena tyaktena bhunjitah*. One might engage in legitimate external *bhoga*, subject always to the control of internal *tyaga*. Such ingrained education is the best antidote against rampant consumerism which is unsustainable — both psychologically and ecologically. After all the proceedings ended, the audience and the speakers were treated with snacks and beverages.

While this informal mingling was on, one member of the audience (in his late forties probably) accosted the speaker and told him with an air of authority: 'Just now you had been talking about *tyaga*, renunciation. Ever since 1947 India has been bleeding over Kashmir. Why can't India renounce Kashmir and be done with the cancer?' The shocked speaker stood speechless! Ladakh, Bengal, Assam, Meghalaya, etc., may be similar other 'objects' of *tyaga* in the agenda of such large-hearted educated persons.

Woe to Bankim Chandra that he had composed 'Bande Matarm'. Woe also to the thousands of mainstream youth of Bharat who had sacrificed everything, courted incarceration, deportation, torture, and death during 1905-1947 for the freedom of the Motherland. What a recompense awaits them through such mighty seminar-attending renouncers. As the rush of such thoughts subsided, the speaker asked the questioner: 'Dear, friend, would you be prepared to 'renounce' even a tiny corner from your portion of parental property if your younger brother were to force his way into it — by means fair or foul? And later, what if he were to plot for grabbing more and more?' Not a tinge of *tyaga* now played on the fellow's face.

III

- During the year 1997, the 5th anniversary of India's political independence, the author had interviewed a score of top industrialists and business leaders. S. P. Godrej (a Parsee) was then the patriarch of the Godrej group. The conversation started by our asking him how he felt about the 50th anniversary of freedom. His quiet, slow reply, tinged with sorrow, was. 'We did not celebrate independence day on August 15, 1947. My father and myself withdrew into a small room, unnoticed by anyone. We spent the whole night in darkness, weeping silently over the partition of India. Is this what all of us had struggled for?' A few years before his death we had read a letter-to-the-editor where the writer had informed that JRD Tata (a Parsee again) had once said that he would wish to be born again — in India. For it is such an interesting and lovable country.

  Thus, both SPG and JRD teach us what 'knowing India, and loving India' could mean. They were not brain-washed ideologues. Let them be compared with the mighty 'renouncer' mentioned above.

- A few years ago the four oldest universities of the country had been advised to forge a comprehensive scheme of collaborative research and education. Given the foregoing facts and cross-currents, this move creates misgivings about its latent agenda. Sometime soon, who knows, IITs, IIMs, etc., may also be drafted into this grand alliance. What for? For, we already have some knowledge about the active discouragement of students by professors in some such institutions to own up and be proud of their indigenous culture.

- For quite sometime India has been witnessing the purposeful misuse of the title 'Gandhi' by generations of descendants of a idely–known Indian family. Such is the state of education in the country that one has hardly heard any condemnation of it. Careerist educators obviously cannot or will not speak up.

- We have it from two authentic verbal sources (one Indian, one American) that, according to both Megasthenes and Marx, 'India has no history'! One cannot escape the inference from this verdict that history has to mean invading, plundering, destroying, converting other lands and cultures beyond one's borders. Thus, an Alexander or a Genghis Khan makes history, not the naked Sadhu who advised Socrates that one should know God before knowing man. You cruise along the banks of major European rivers, and you see only forts and castles on them. But you sail along rivers in India to discover only *ashrams, tapovans* and temples. The children of India have the right to be educated about such vital facts regarding Bharat.
- Your children and youth are entitled also to the important insight that, among all the cultures of the world, Bharat's history demonstrates the *closest alignment* between what her scriptures have laid down, and how she has actually behaved with the rest of the world. We know also how some major world cultures have actually behaved with other countries in ways quite opposite to what their basic religious texts advise. '*Udarcharitanam tu, vasudhaiva kutumbakam*' of Chanakya has, on the other hand, been practised by Bharat almost literally. The Hindus and Buddhists, the Jains and Sikhs have implemented this principle through the centuries. Yet, this is no history. It is they, especially the Hindus, who have to be educated to behave.
- K.M. Munshi, as Governor of UP, had visited Sri Aurobindo at Pondicherry in July 1950.[8] He had been the Master's student at Baroda College in 1904, and was profoundly influenced by him. Munshi had discussed Indian culture, the present crisis etc., and expressed his anxiety thus: 'The younger generation is fed on theories and beliefs which are undermining the higher life of India'. Sixty years later today Munshi's worry about 'undermining' is bordering on 'destruction'. The kaleidoscopic range of events in the sphere of education in India, gleaned above from the primary to post-graduate levels, points towards this conclusion. Of course the Master's response to Munshi was very much affirmative: 'Our culture cannot be undermined.' But should the *legitimate educators* of 2010 continue to behave like lotos-eaters, sunk in a kind of *tamasic* stupor, simply because the Master had prophesied so? For, he had warned us too against our lack of anticipation and our inertia.

These compelling instances, are but a few pieces in a chaotic jigsaw that post-1950 education has superimposed on India's nationhood. As pointed out above, education is not conceived here in the conventional narrow sense of what is done by certificate warding schools, colleges and universities. *Cultural de-nationalization pervades these venues as a parallel to the damage at home*. The situation is more tragic today than it was upto 1947, because there is no alien ruler who could now be treated as the scapegoat.

- We were seized by another necessity of going back a hundred years in search of the fountainhead. This was the rationale. Personalities involved in the National Education Movement were not self-servers. Instead, they had acquired, through *sadhana* and *tyaga*, varying measures of *transcendental insight and integral vision* into the chain of continuity from the past to the present to the future. Most individuals associated today with education are destitute of all these primary qualities. So, it is the earlier set of personalities who alone can serve as trustworthy and reliable guides for education in India. As already cited previously, they alone deserve to be approached as *legitimate educators* again and again.
- All the savants in the vanguard of the National Education Movement had plunged deep into Bharat's culture. They had recovered the gems in it, and had brightened their own lives with their perennial lustre. Yet, they were equally forthright in condemning the distortions and wrongs in several visible dimensions of our society. But their criticisms had sprung from love for Indian culture. They all had *earned the legitimacy* to warn about and chastise us for our many evils (pray, which society in the world does not have its own pile of rubbish in the backyard?). But the post-1950 de-constructing educators of India do *not* possess such legitimacy. Imposed or borrowed structures and categories of thought hold sway over their intellect. *Careerist educators* are unable to evaluate such stuff from the perspective of the Indian worldview. They cannot do so because they have not *lived* Bharat's *sanatan* thought even for a day. Perhaps they get personally rewarded for such apathy, even scorn. But the nation loses out. So, if they do not transform, it would be wise to ignore them in living our life and educating our children.

- Let us therefore glean some warnings and counsels from a few of those legitimate educators for India mentioned above. The sage-poet Rabindranath Tagore, who used to lecture occasionally at the National College, had captured the *central problem* about education in India in these words[9]. 'But this nation was very much in existence when the aliens arrived. Otherwise what could have given birth to Kabir, Nanak, Chaitanya, Tukaram – *even* in those turbulent times? It was not that only Delhi and Agra had existed then – Kashi and Nabadwip too were there. ...

But unfortunately our children have to learn such history as to make them forget these very facts. It appears as if we ourselves are nobodies in Bharatvarsha; those who have come from without are all. *Wherefrom* shall we then draw our energy and strength – if our minds are trained to treat *the link with the country itself with scant respect?*' (emphasis added). That is why Tagore's foresight had shot out this rapier-thrust question:

'How can there be history where there is no politics?' The pertinence of this question is unquestionable today. Tagore had expressed these views on education for India in 1902 – the year Vivekananda died. In this very essay he had also strongly advocated the concept of *swadeshi shiksha*, and the need for dedicated teachers whose principal plank would be a *complete history* of Bharat, the living and true Bharat. He was bemoaning the absence of such an over-arching atmosphere in India – the very opposite of what prevailed in Oxford and Cambridge. In contrast to these places, in India, he observed, '... the whole situation is *negative*, what is learnt is *negative*, the methods by which all is learnt are *negative*, those who teach are also *negative*.' Amazing indeed is such prevision about the state of affairs today. Most secular Indian intellectuals of today are being in such negativism with much vigour. Chemical fertilisers are now known to destroy the intrinsic organic powers of the land. The current Indian brand of secular education is causing such havoc to our mental soil. The likes of Tagore *et.al.* may not thus be born again in Bharat. Can future Bharat do without such lighthouses and survive? Tagore was unsparingly critical of the increasing number of teachers who did not appreciate this imperative for Indian education. '... their ways have become reprehensible, they are not contented with their material lot, they do not treat *vidyadaan* as a religious obligation. They are trivializing *education as a commodity* and thereby vulgarizing

themselves too' – thus did he vent his anger.* Yet, he had not lost all hope. During the few decades following the NCEB, his dreams were partly fulfilled. But if Tagore were to have lived today, would he not be a very sad person – infinitely more mortified than what he had been in 1902?

- Then again, Sri Aurobindo, ninety years ago, had expressed this lofty hope[10]. 'Our leaders and followers both require a deeper *sadhana* ... it is the spirituality of India, the *sadhana* of India, *tapasya, jnanam, shakti.* ... *Shakti* is more than strength – it is the universal energy which moves the stars made individual.' Post-independent India has turned her face away from an appreciation or apprehension of this Shakti, this 'deepest self ' of Bharatvarsha. Indeed, the last few decades have been recklessly rejecting this irreducible, ultimate psycho-philosophical keynote of education for India.
- Let us also savour a sample of cautionary words from Swami Vivekananda, a classmate of Satish Chandra Mukherjee, and perhaps the *first father figure* of the National Education and also the Freedom Movements (emphasis added).[11]

'On one side, New India is saying "If we only adopt western ideas, western language, western food, western dress and western manners, we shall be as strong and powerful as the western nations." On the other, Old India is saying, "Fools ! *By imitation others' ideas never become one's own*: nothing, unless earned, is your own. Does the ass in the lion's skin become the lion?" '

'On one side, New India is saying "What the western nations do is surely good, otherwise how did they become so great?" On the other side Old India is saying, "The *flash of lightning is intensely bright*, but only for a moment: look out boys, it is dazzling your eyes. *Beware* ." But most careerist educators, bereft of self- respect, prefer to continue as dazzled imitators today, perhaps even more avidly than in Vivekananda's time. Although a few sincere thinkers and scientists in

---

* For thirty-two years at IIMC we never attended Faculty meetings which discussed salaries etc. Our gross monthly emoluments were ₹ 46,000/- only when we retired in January 2003. During these last years we often used to tell our family that so much money was really not needed.

the West now admit that their social and moral capitals are eroding fast, that their society is more risk-prone and unhappy today than yesterday, yet our educators shun such honest and sober writings. 'We realize what we are doing is out of sheer compulsion; but all this is harmful' — one can sympathize with such a stand. But going out of the way to openly espouse all imposed notions is unacceptable — especially from educators.

IV

• That die-hard habit of our careerist educators – be it professors or media – to evaluate every facet of Indian history and culture through alien categories and constructs had been tellingly exposed by Mahatma Gandhi (emphasis added)[12] . 'We were one nation before they (the English) came to India. One thought inspired us. Our mode of life was the same. It was because we were one nation that they (the English) were able to establish one kingdom.

> 'What do you think could have been the intention of these *farseeing ancestors* of ours who established Setubandha (Rameshwar) in the South, Jagannath in the East and Hardwar in the North as places of pilgrimage? You will admit they were no fools. ... they saw that India was one undivided land so made by Nature. They therefore argued that it must be one nation. Arguing thus, they established holy places in various parts of India, and *fired the people with an idea of nationality in a manner unknown in other parts of the world*.'

Learned educators might muster some humility to assimilate this masterly articulation of India's sacred, deep-structure nationhood. Western categories and definitions are misleading and harmful for us. Gandhiji's grasp of the *sacred secret* of India's unique nationhood could be amply substantiated. Of course, this requires 'insight', mere 'outsight' is of little avail. Here is one insight for educators: the mantra '*Om Ganga cha, Yamune chaiva, Godavari, Saraswati, Narmade, Sindhu, Kaveri jalehasmin sannidhi kuru*' is a mandatory recitation in all pujas, sacred rites of passage etc. Here is another: if one travels from Gangtok to Thiruvananthapuram one will discover that the same deities or Gods are celebrated through the entire length of the land – Lord Ganesha and Mahavir Hanuman for example. This is how our 'seer educators' had forged India's nationhood. *This kind of education for India's children is imperative.*

- To Sri Aurobindo we may turn once more for yet another impeccable insight into what it means to possess a sound philosophy of education[13]. '... I would certainly repel the formula of taking good and leaving the bad as a crudity ... Obviously if we "take over" anything, the good and the bad in it will come in together pell-mell. If we take over for instance that terrible, monstrous and compelling thing ... European industrialism ... assuredly *we shall get too its social discords and moral plagues and cruel problems...*'* So, sometime during 1919, a little more than twenty years after Vivekananda had thrown his dramatic challenge at Indian educators, Sri Aurobindo had reiterated the same warning with greater sophistication. And Gandhiji too, in his own simple language, had asserted that all criticisms about unchanging stolid India were really directed at her merit. For, '*she dare not change what has been tested and found true on the anvil of experience*'. But afflicted as we educators are with the deadly 'pied piper-rats' syndrome, such convictions and warnings from authentic educators are treated as regressive or chauvinistic.
- This is a Himalayan blunder of our teachers and educators today. Flouting the above flawless insights from our *tapaswi educators*. The fatal folly lies in thoughtlessly judging a sustainable culture and its enduring processes by the standards of unstable and self-serving cultures. Turning Hinduism into a pejorative term is a sin that selfserving universalists amongst present-day educators are committing. In the process, education is discarding all that had made India the Bharat of at least four or five millennia before the onset of the second millennium. *She needed not a single borrowed idea to create her unique and complete civilization*.

Hence, constructive education should checkmate these destructive moves with courage and honesty. The State machinery will not and cannot do this. Alternatives must be adopted without further ado. The sample of quotations offered above indicate the intrinsic nature and direction of educational philosophy which Bharat

---

* The Times of India (Kolkata, July 3, 2010) published a survey-based report on 'City Kid Syndrome' with the title 'Young, Pampered and Reckless'. The contents make for blood curdling reading. This then is the end-result of 'taking over' of sci-tech–driven economic globalism!

must accept as a trust from her no-axe-to-grind educators. The golden quartet of Tagore-Vivekananda-Gandhi-Aurobindo were the tallest among all the lighthouses along the shore line of education in India – – during 1860-1950. These unsurpassed exemplars of 'Know India, and Love India' cannot be charged with berating any other faith or culture. While loving Bharat, they were in true love with the world as well. They were grand forgivers. Yet, being free from self-seeking, they were not genuflecting apologists for the wrongdoers, however aggressive or powerful might they be. So, with education in India rekindling such a flame anew, neither Bharat nor the world has anything to fear about. Will the 'educational cess' contribute towards this goal?

- Yet another issue of capital importance, is that of the 'secular' approach to education in India. Grave confusion prevails in this respect. English dictionaries tell us that the secular outlook is solely a materialist world-view. It rejects the sacred and spiritual aspects. But the consummation of the spiritual is Bharat's genius, if not India's. It is the raison-d'etre of her perennial culture. The Government could be secular in the sense that there is no State religion. But the nation and its people in India have always been very much religio-spiritual. In the future too Indians will never be secular in the dictionary sense.

With all the faults, here spiritual religion (not a monotonic dogma or an inflexible creed) holds the key to the immense sustainability of *sanatan* Indian culture. Let us listen to APJ Abdul Kalam. In June 2001 he had put the following question to a Swamiji[14].

> 'To realize this great dream (building *apara vidya* or secular knowledge on the foundation of *para vidya* or spiritual knowledge) three types of people are needed – *punya atma* (virtuous people), *punya neta* (virtuous leaders), and *punya adhikari* (virtuous officers). If the population of all the three were to increase in our society, then India would become the *jagadguru. How can their numbers be increased?*'

The word *punya* means sacred — as we all know. A *legitimate educator* that Dr. Kalam has been, he is not scared of the sacred. Nor does the scientist in him hesitate to nurse the vision of *jagadguru* for his country – as so many others like Sri Aurobindo did a century ago. And where lies the road to this goal in education? Does education in India today minister to this *vision*?

- When an eminent American scholar–thinker, defining his country's cultural identity, states forthrightly that it is extremely 'religious' and overwhelmingly 'Christian' in character, it gives a firm and clear lead to the undertone of education there.[15] India lacks this. For him neither 'religion' nor 'Christianity' are untouchable words. Whosoever can think a little seriously will be able to grasp that such affirmative, unequivocal convictions amongst educators will would and strengthen the over-arching spirit and the underlying base of the 'philosophy and practice of education' for America. Such candid articulations serve an inestimable function for education: *To instil in the people a high and abiding sense of cause beyond the selfish ego*. The number of Jews, Muslims, Confucians, Hindus, Buddhists, etc., in America is significant. Yet, this American scholar (and others like him) has not indulged in the confounding cant of 'composite culture'. But in India this is a pet fascination of the intelligentsia. As a result, education in India has no central hub where all the spokes can converge and integrate.

There are numerous signs in the present Indian educational system and process which show that the phrase 'composite culture' is being employed to subvert, even erase, all consciousness about the essential and unique *core culture* of Bharatvarsha. This *sanatan 'core culture'* (also called Hindu *dharma-sanskriti* for more than two millennia) has always been non-exclusive, all-embracing, all-forgiving — without reciprocation or appreciation. Holger Kersten 'gratefully' informs us that the fabled Biblical King Solomon had came to India and taken with him a lot of material wealth — and 'wisdom' as well.[16] This wisdom was clearly drawn from the fully matured, pre- 1000 AD *core culture* of Bharatvarsha. It has to be remembered also that in more recent times Sister Nivedita and JBS Haldane, Nicolas Roerich and John Woodroffe, Ronald Nixon and Bede Griffiths, Alfassa Mirra and C F Andrews had all come to and lived and died for Bharat's luminous *core culture*, not India's nebulous composite culture. Hiouen Tsang and Fahien had also written about this core culture only.

- As for the future, our educators should realize that if this *core culture* crumbles, the so-called composite culture shall also vanish. Instead, some brand of intolerant, monolithic cultural paradigm could hold sway over this *devabhumi*. The key learning is.

Core culture is the *cause*, composite culture the *effect*; hence the cause cannot be trifled with. Voices raising such vital questions should not be muzzled into silence. *A great duty of education is to rescue Bharat from India.* America is America first, Malaysia is Malaysia first, China is China first, and so on. The practice of education in these nations firmly imprints this allegiance in their people. The Indian note is the only jarring one in this symphony. Neurotic self-doubt and debasing double-standards in the practice of education have been robbing India of sincere respect in the comity of nations. The contrast between reporting on India and China in international news media is mortifying.

- Once a young admirer of Swami Vivekananda had implored him to join politics and help the cause of the country's freedom. After a little reflection Vivekananda looked at the young man with fiery eyes and asked: 'So what? Will you be able to preserve the country's freedom? Where are the men?' This was so prophetic.

Today politically independent India is mentally enslaved. Education, or rather mis-education, is the main cause of this plight. Institutionalised education is making Indians lose their cultural, spiritual freedom — the essence of their national freedom. Unless therefore the principles of human education, as perceived and practised in Bharat for several millennia, is kept in clear view in every phase or era in the march of time, all hasty reformation, innovation and renovation at the ground level will be abortive. Impressive though at times in appearance, they will be missing out on coherence, wholeness and sanity. A confused, intoxicated, manipulative, directionless global milieu cannot provide the compass for education – not only for India, but even for the world. Not that India and her children will not have to live now. But that cannot be the sole inspiration. India and all of us have to live tomorrow and day after, and on and on. But how? On what principles? By denying the wisdom of the Valmikis-Vyasas to Tagores–Vivekanandas— all legitimate educators par excellence?

V

- This is how another latest *maya* has begun to grip India's academia. Research is now a big craze. All college and university teachers are now mandated to do a Ph.D and publish, both before and after getting the degree. They are the chief criteria for ascending the career ladder. Consequently, every Ram-

Shyam-Radha is now scrambling on to the Ph.D bandwagon. In the process, all sorts of bizarre, often unspeakable things are occurring. They involve the researchers as well as their guides (better called groping remote controllers). Just about three decades ago, and before, we had scores of world-class teachers in our colleges and universities. Many among them had neither Ph. Ds nor publications. Still, they were all legitimate educators. Cherished, adored and venerated by their pupils to this day, they were also character-makers. But nowadays getting Ph.Ds and publishing books are becoming a child's play, honourable exceptions notwithstanding. And about character-making – the less said the better!

It may not be much out of place to recall here that Swami Vivekananda had once averred that the world possesses at best only four or five original and beneficial thoughts or ideas. The rest are all just repetition or noise. A few decades later Mahatma Gandhi too had aired an equally blunt opinion[17]: 'Formerly, only a few men wrote valuable books. Now anybody writes and prints anything he likes and poisons people's minds.'

- One cannot help recollecting, in the light of what Vivekananda and Gandhi have said, Shakespeare's stinging sarcasm. 'Life is a tale told by an idiot; All sound and fury — signifying nothing!' Perhaps 'life' could be replaced by 'research'. In any case, perceptive observers will be able to detect a clear positive correlation between research on the one hand, and riskcatastrophe- unhappiness on the other. If the rush for such net results through research is not *maya*, what else is?

A sad climax to this fancy for research is now manifested in socalled 'Consciousness research'. As usual, here too the impetus is of Western origin. Already a few international conferences have been held on the subject in exotic locations. The purses of Conference organisers, and the egos of new-age presenters – both may have been bulging considerably. Unfortunately, even some outstanding spiritual organisations in India are getting lured into this futile engagement. They should have known better. It was for them to avoid receiving cues about this theme from cultures where spirituality is not a living tradition. Let not the tail wag the dog ! Let not 'Consciousness' be either asked to prove its credentials or seek corroboration before the tribunal of physical science or business management or statistics. This is the puzzle: How is it forgotten, in

Bharat of all places, that 'Consciousness' is to be *realised*, not *researched?* The school drop-out Rabindranath had told his American audience in his profound lecture 'What is Art?', that the word consciousness in English had yet to emerge out of its 'cocoon state'[18]. Not so for the Sanskrit word *chaitanya*. This insight is as much valid today as it was eighty five years ago. And what about one hundred and twenty years ago, when the 'illiterate' Guru of Vivekananda was heard to plead helplessness on so many occasions about expressing his experience of Consciousness of *Brahman* in words – however earnestly he might struggle?

- Has not Sri Aurobindo also tirelessly emphasized that intellectual effort, and that is what research is, is too fragmented hence incapable of realising the whole, the pure Consciousness?[19] Above all, have not the Upanishads confessed time and again the futility of trying to objectify by mind and words the ultimate subjective Consciousness – that which is *akhanda*, hence *avyakta*? All authentic educators may therefore wish to ponder upon the following proposition.

The more we rush into research, the farther we recede from Realization, and the greater becomes the misery of humanity — especially *existential misery*.* The world needs, for peace and wholeness, not *rajasic* research but *sattwic* realisation. Consciousness research will, however, mean struggling to *quantify the spiritual*. Consciousness realisation, on the other hand, always means *spiritualizing the measurable*. Research tends towards *analysis*, Realisation leans towards *synthesis*. Research is primarily *experimental*, Realisation *experiential*. Research is really *apara vidya*, Realisation essentially *para vidya*. Our priorities in education for the future should therefore be clear and sound. It may be noted that quantum physics has concluded that everything in the Universe is *interconnected*. This notion has been around us for several decades. A lot has been written too. For all this, however, is the world today a better place to live in? So, that is what research boils down to. But interconnectedness is nothing else than the Yoga-Vedanta Realisation of *Oneness* — from the level of feeling, not merely of reasoning.

---

* The following aphorism attributed to Albert Einstein fully supports our argument: 'Not everything that can be counted counts, nor verything that counts can be counted ?'

- In search of links more immediate than those of Tagore at all. one could lay one's hands on some pertinent extracts from the Radhakrishnan Commission on University Education, 1948-49.
  a) 'If we exclude *spiritual training* from our institutions we would be untrue to our whole historical development.'
  b) 'All educational institutions to start work with a few minutes for silent *meditation*.'
  c) 'In the first year of the Degree course lives of the great religious leaders like Buddha, Confucius, Zoroaster, Socrates, Jesus, Sankara, Ramanuja, Madhva, Mohammad, Kabir, Nanak, Gandhi be taught.'*
  d) 'In the second year some selections of a *universalist* character
  e) 'In the third year, the central problems of the philosophy of *religion* be considered.'

The Constitution of India was adopted in 1950. It later declared India as a 'secular' republic. So, the Radhakrishnan Commission's Indiaspecific recommendations for the philosophy and practice of sacred education, beside the secular, received an unlamented burial. And since then the entire educational process in India, except for superficial tinkering now and then, has been a shameful tale of mimicry.

Little wonder then that seventeen years later the Kothari Commission, 1966, had to lament about the rootlessness of education in India, and the consequent alienation of the educated from their own culture. It added.

'The old values which held society together have been disappearing... (hence) innumerable signs of *social disorganization* are continually on the increase...'

Within forty-five years after the Kothari Report the situation has come to such a pass that the problem of *rootless education* is not even raised at policy making levels in this 21st century. The moment the theme is raised, it tends to be summarily dismissed by branding it as chauvinistic, parochial, even fundamentalist. After all, though unseen, the tree stands or falls by its roots. A tree, which has weathered six millennia of storm and stress, yet is still alive and continues to live,

---

* It is strange that while even Gandhi is included as a 'great' religious leader, Chaitanya, Ramakrishna, Vivekananda, Aurobindo and Ramana are omitted. from the scriptures of the world be studied.'

must yet be having solid roots. Those who are unwilling to know Bharat and love Bharat, can do precious little about education for India. We should recall here the sober warning by the philosopher K. C. Bhattacharya about the *shadow-minded* Indian educator in pursuit of *rootless universalism*.[20]

VI

- Many often ask: 'If you claim India to have such a rich culture and civilization then, pray, why are you in such a mess?' This question is correct, on the face of it. It is indeed humiliating to constantly see our leaders' integrity, our civilian behaviour, our private morals, our professional ethics, etc., crumbling to dust. We today are really unworthy of the inheritance bequeathed to us by our *rishis*. Nevertheless, our legitimate educators and conscientious parents should repeatedly, with full conviction, explain this truth to their pupils and children: 'India is today in a mess *not* because we have such a culture, *but* because we are ridiculing and discarding its fundamentals at the promptings of those who possess not the least understanding about Bharat.' But for the eternally valid core of *sanatan* Hinduism, with its robust details about daily life, and its supportive streams, India would by now have become a dead civilization.
- Infantile fascination with the pretence of parliamentary democracy, human rights, liberalism, secularism etc. etc., is pushing the country into a 'no man's land' – neither here nor there.* The diabolical manner in which TV is being used to smother cultural variations is thoroughly undemocratic.[21] It is time we educate our children that India has always been a truly democratic culture in the deepest, intrinsic sense. Just one example: Look at the variety of chosen deities worshipped by different individuals in a single home. Similarly, the *varna* system, despite its deformities, has in principle been a ladder for the ascent of all. Moreover, our society has remained bonded on the principle of reciprocal duties among the *varnas*. But now we are being mis-educated by the rupturing gospel of human rights. The reasons for the mess do not lie therefore in adhering to our culture, but in abandoning it.

---

* It is often claimed that we are better off in terms of say, freedom of speech, than the Chinese. This is a childish way to cover up our many worseoffs in other respects e.g. discipline, national pride, etc.,

- It is one thing to admit that we are feeling helpless under pressure from more powerful agents, and so being compelled to adopt ideas inimical to India. But it is quite another to see nothing but merit in them, to become their ardent protagonists– out-Heroding Herod as it were. It is not because such champions have independently and dispassionately scrutinised these ideas and methods before advocating them. The pity is that most of our vocal academics, bureaucrats, politicians, technocrats, managers, doctors, lawyers etc., are career–and money-seeking persons. They are in a hurry to oblige.

So they tend to swallow the many lollipops dangled be9fore them by the economically powerful and/or militarily strong players in the world. This is the unsavoury truth. How to save education from their stranglehold? Legitimate educators should understand these complex problems, and caution themselves and the youth of India against the irreversible harm arising from them. Let us respectfully listen to Kathleen Raine (a notable British literary critic, not a fundamentalist Hindu Brahmin)[22].

'... as one looks around the world it is evident that the [spiritual] light has been extinguished in one country after another. But that treasury of universal wisdom, however, imperiled by other influences, is still India's. *And if India is lost, all is lost*. For the greatest economic prosperity, the most prestigious and profitable multinationals cannot sustain a civilization in the absence of wisdom.' There could not be a more touching and true cry of the heart for legitimate educators in India. Shall they let down the 'Indian mind in Western body' that Kathleen epitomizes?

References

1. Saran M and Khanna, VC; *Ramayan in Indonesia*, Ravi Dayal: New Delhi, 2004, pp. 197-199.
2. *Human Development Report*, New Delhi: Oxford University Press, 2000, pp. 19-28.
3. *Chikuro Hiroike*, The Institute of Moralogy: Kashiwa (Japan), 2005, p. 399.
4. Roy D. K. and Devi, I, *Pilgrims of The Stars*, Mumbai: Bharatiya Vidya Bhavan, 2002, p. 95.
5. *Ibid., p. 110.*
6. *Ibid., p. 106.*

7. Chakraborty S. K., *Wisdom Leadership*, New Delhi, Wheeler, 1999, p. 40.
8. *All India Magazine* (Pondicherry), December 1997, pp. 5-6.
9. Tagore Rabindranath, *Rabindra Rachanavali* (Bengali), Viswabharati: Kolkata, 1975, Vol. 4, pp. 378, 386 and 387 – translation by the author.
10. Aurobindo Sri, *On India*, Pondicherry, Sri Aurobindo Society, 1973, pp. 12-13.
11. Vivekananda Swami, *Call To The Nation*, Advaita Ashram: Kolkata, p. 57. Also in *Complete Works*, vol. 4, p. 477.
12. Gandhi Mahatma, *Selected Works*, ed. Shriman Narain, Navjivan: Ahmedabad, 2001, Vol. III, pp. 124-125.
13. Aurobindo Sri, *The Foundations of Indian Culture*, Pondicherry: Sri Aurobindo Ashram, 1998, p. 438.
14. Abdul Kalam, APJ, *Ignited Minds*, Viking: New Delhi, 2002, p. 76.
15. Huntington S. P., *Who are We?*, Penguin, 2004, p. 83, pp. 348-351.
16. Kersten H., *Jesus Lived in India*, New Delhi: Penguin Books, 2001, p. 49.
17. Gandhi M. K., *Selected Works*, op. cit., p. 101.
18. Tagore Rabindranath, *Personality*, New Delhi: Rupa, 2002, p. 21.
19. Aurobindo Sri, *The Synthesis of Yoga*, Sri Aurobindo Ashram, 1988, pp. 294-302.
20. Bhattacharya K. C., 'The Swaraj of Ideas' in *Four Critical Essays* ed. S. K. Ghose, Jijnasa: Kolkata, 1977, pp. 16, 21.
21. Mander J., 'The Tyranny of Television', *Resurgence*, July 1994, pp. 5-8.
22. Raine Kathleen, 'India And The Modern World', *Ibid.*, p. 2.

CHAPTER 10

DEAR STUDENTS, MIND YOUR CHOICE TO TRUST

आहारशुद्धौ: सत्वशुद्धि:
सत्वशुद्धौ ध्रुवा स्मृति:
स्मशतिलम्भे सर्वग्रन्थीनां विप्रमोक्ष: ।
(छान्दोग्योपनिषत् - ७/२६/२)

With pure food intelligence
becomes pure;
With pure intelligence indelible
memory arrives;
With indelible memory the
individual gains liberation

(Translated by the author)
(*Chhandyoga Upa* –7/26/2)

I

It is widely known that, demographically speaking, our nation is comparatively 'young'. 'Old' Bharatvarsha happens to be a relatively 'young' India. A rather interesting paradox. It is also frequently pronounced that the future of a nation is held in trust which is entrusted to its young. A whole lot therefore depends on what you young people are made to believe in, have faith in. This, in turn, revolves around what you see and experience in your homes and external surroundings, and what you are told and not told in the corridors of schools, colleges and a wide range of other higher and supposedly progressive institutions. And, of course, media and press are there to complete the package. We may begin by high–lighting a few crucial things you are *not* told, and some voices you are conditioned *not* to trust. You should know that you are denied your right to a true and integral understanding of the roots of 'old' Bharatvarsha, the standing ground of 'young' India. Without a positive grounding in the panoramic and practical framework of your *sanatan* 'core culture', you possess no yardsticks to sift the grain from the chaff of those cultures which throw themselves aggressively at you. The opium of modernization and breathless change is making you tipsy. Without knowing, you may be taking dangerous false steps. 'Short term gain, Long term pain' is the bargain you are being seduced to strike. Agents of selfishness are masquerading as benefactors.*

Yet, many voices of high purity, integral vision, and true love are available who have been reminding you of the abiding truths and norms of a sane society. These noble souls have been imploring us to recognize the indispensability of the many change-less ideals and characteristics of 'old' Bharatvarsha for the heady, young, modern India and the world. They hail from both India and the West. You students should open up and listen reverently to a few such supraorbital, free spirits. Our comments will follow these presentations. (All emphases are the author's).

Ronald Nixon (1943)[1]: Nixon was a professor of English literature at Lucknow and Banaras Universities in the 1920s. A Cambridge scholar, he had left England after the First World War and lived the rest of his life in India. He got his Hindu-Vaishnava name, Krishna Prem, after initiation by his *guruma*, Yashoda Mai. He died in 1965 at Uttar Vrindavan off Almora. Here are some extracts from his thoughts as recorded by Dilip Kumar Roy, a disciple of Sri Aurobindo, and himself a student of Mathematics at Cambridge, while being a bosom friend of Netaji Subhas.

(a) '... after my initiation the scales fell from my eyes and a new vision was born overnight. What I saw was this that in India alone – of all the countries in the world — *a long and unbroken dynasty of saints* had reigned on, venerated by all. The change came only recently, at the turn of the century, when, though the common man in India has stayed loyal to her hoary wisdom and spiritual ideals, a

* Among the better methods of values-inspired man-making education encounters with the lives and minds of good and great personalities are probably the best. But it has no place today in our homes or schools. It seems we do not want to be inspired nobly.

sonorous section of your modern intelligentsia began to *mouth unthinkingly the Western shibboleths*, branding the Hindu religion as medieval...

(b) '...these cock-sure Daniels constitute but a small minority, and they...know *nothing* of the soul of immemorial India...'

(c) Referring to *Kumbh Mela* and the caste system he said, '... the foundation of the bulk of your social structures, unlike ours, rests still on religious sanction and *not* on any secular power.'

(d) '... [Divine] Grace will, assuredly, come down once more to your rescue *if only you firmly repudiate this disastrous Western gospel* of godless materialism and scientific agnosticism [with all its] deplorable results.'

(e) 'Often while meditating, I catch *myself praying to Krishna* that he may never let India's immemorial soul be swamped by the rational, robustious, God-deriding, scientific agnosticism of the blatant West..'

A J Toynbee (1976)[2]: Toynbee was probably the most widely appreciated Western historian of the previous century. Below are a few of his candid appraisals:

(a) 'The action required for coping with the evil consequences of power is ethical, not intellectual. But science is an intellectual activity that is ethically neutral. ... *Evils produced by science cannot be cured* by science itself.'

(b) 'Science will be used for *destructive* purposes if we act on the assumption that nature exists for man ...Religion is ... the only faculty of human nature that is capable of inspiring human beings to *master themselves*...'

(c) 'The greater man's power, the greater his need for religion. If the application of science is not *inspired and directed by religion*, science will be applied to the *indulgence of greed*, and it will *serve greed so effectively* that it will be destructive.' *

(d) 'I hold that the *goal of education ought to be religious*, not mercenary. Education ought to be a search for an understanding of the meaning and the purpose of life and for discovering the right [spiritual] way to live.'

(e) 'At present co-education is creating a very serious problem of *sexual promiscuity* among students of ages from thirteen to eighteen.'

(f) 'It [science] has only recently ventured to begin the *exploration of the subconscious*... which Indian philosophy was exploring about two and a half millennia earlier... psychic events at the subconscious level are probably the most important for us, and the most elusive for science.'

(g) '*Manipulation is technology*... Technology is facilitated by quantification, and though quantification intellectually misrepresents and aesthetically defaces the object to which it is applied, its serviceableness for technology makes it a generator of power over both non-human nature and people.

Bede Griffiths (1976)[3]: Like Nixon and Toynbee, Griffiths also hailed from Britain. Moreover, like Nixon, Griffiths was an Oxford scholar of comparative literature. And he too had settled in India, living on the bank of Kaveri near Trichy, as a monk in *gerua,* for forty years or so till his death. A small sample of his judgements follow hereunder:

(a) 'Young people now come to India from the West, seeking to recover the sense of the sacred, the inner meaning of life which has been lost in the West. But India too is losing it rapidly. Wherever *modern civilization* spreads, all holiness, all sense of the sacred, all awareness of transcendent Reality disappears. This is just another *Fall of Man*.'

(b) 'In ancient India there were four "ends" of life, pleasure, wealth, duty and liberation. The modern world recognizes the first three but has lost sight of the last; yet without this goal of *final liberation*, of ultimate transcendence, all the other goals lead to *frustration*.'

---

* It is becoming sad to notice how our 6-year old grand-daughter is gradually expecting more 'things' than before. Uptil about 3 ½ years or so she was very much self-contained and autonomous. A broken pencil, a piece of paper, an old spoon or a discarded toy were all that she needed to be joyful. But now the 'loving gifts' of birthday parties, school fetes and the like are gradually making the inwardly whole child into an externally need– ful girl. Is this a sign of higher human development compared to our own non–commoditized barefoot childhood days?

(c) 'This is the root cause of the *failure of modern civilization* – it has lost touch with the Centre, the Ground of reality and truth, and therefore it is doomed to destruction... [For] this is the world which is *maya* [as] the *Katha Upanishad* says...'

Kathleen Raine (1994[4], 1997[5]): Raine had been a renowned contemporary English poetess and literary critic. William Blake's poetry was her forte. She had spoken to the modernist in these words 'from the heart'.

(a) '*India is infinite and inexhaustible*...what is unmatched elsewhere is that in all traditional Indian art there is that infinite dimension... The severance of "art" from the sacred did not in India, as in the West, take place at any level or only since Western influence reached India.'

(b) '...the light has been extinguished in one country after another. But that treasury of universal wisdom, however imperilled by other influences, is still India's. *And if India is lost, all is lost.* For the greatest economic prosperity and profitable multinationals cannot sustain a civilization in the absence of wisdom.'

(c) '...do not reject or forget the *sacred heritage* of your civilization of the mind... Never has the *world needed India* as now.'

(d) 'For the *materialist world "nothing is sacred"*; we ourselves are mere biochemical mechanisms in a universe without meaning or value.'

(e) 'For all its triumphs, modern materialist science and technology is creating a world we are finding *increasingly uninhabitable*... because destruction is already upon us in many ways.'

(f) 'For our technology we in the secular West have lost the *secret of beauty*.'

(g) 'Tagore's *Gitanjali* ...poems display in their thought a world I have dreamed of all my life long.' (quoting Yeats)

(h) '*The world needs India as never before*. The great civilization of the "India of the imagination" remains intact, but is in grave danger from the imperialism of a materialist civilization.'*

(i) '... I believe that the time may have come when the learned world will have to study not Greek but *Sanskrit as the language of knowledge*.'

Stafford Beer[6] (1974, 1994): Beer, a Briton again, was an early pioneer in cybernetics, systems theory and operations research. Invited to deliver a lecture at Delhi, he had bluntly spoken thus. 'I was appalled when I first arrived in Chile, to find the whole middle class already held tight in the *grip of consumerism*, so that the worth of life was already to be measured in terms of cars, television sets and refrigerators. The *devastation* wrought in the quality of life in the advanced industrial countries by such use of *science and technology* is plain to see. *Do developing countries wish to follow the same road*?

David Frawley[7] (2002): Probably the most profound living Western authority (experiential, not just intellectual)on Bharatiya culture, Frawley belongs to New Mexico, USA. Exhaustive and authentic writings by him on his chosen theme are aplenty. Like Ronald Nixon becoming Krishna Prem, Frawley has also been honoured by the Vedic name Vamadeva Shastri. Students may savour a bit of his flair for looking through our culture. 'Because of its emphasis on the Self and its recognition of many forms of theism, Vedanta lies behind the tolerance and syncretic tendency that exists in the Hindu religion. ... Hinduism has always defined itself as *Sanatana Dharma*, "the universal or eternal dharma"... *Vedanta, therefore, is not a closed but an open system that honours the Self in all beings*, and does not reduce it to any particular formula, personality or dogma.'

Max Muller[8] (1896): He had edited the colossal 50-volume *Sacred Books of the East*. Forty-nine volumes of textual materials (the 50th was the Index) comprised 2 volumes from Islam, 6 from Confucianism etc.; 8 from Zoroastrianism, 10 from Buddhism and Jainism. The remaining 23 volumes represented Hinduism. Max Muller did not fail to acknowledge this unparalleled labour of the sacred while, for example, addressing the new ICS recruits at Oxford before they left for India. Is anything similar communicated to you, Indian students, at any stage of your education? Are your teachers aware of this fact?

---

* Mis–communciation is an essential aspect of mass–communication. For instance, only the other day we saw a student wearing a T-shirt with 'competition' printed on the chest and 'attitude' on the back. Another student wore a T-shirt announcing: 'Chicago – The Windy City'. Raine would have felt elated, not depressed, if she saw 'Banaras – The Holy City' in lieu. One of the horrid things we saw in March 2011 was 'Enjoy the most glamorous casino' on the chest of a 6-year old girl.

S. K. Ratcliffe[9] (1915): During early 20th century Ratcliffe was the editor of *The Statesman*. In his Preface to a book by Sister Nivedita he had quoted at length a piece by Lord Haldane on 'Higher Nationality'. Haldane, confessing the lack of a suitable English word, cited the German word *sittlichkeit* which provided for an extensive system of restraints in daily life and behaviour for building up an 'instinctive sense of obligation that is the chief foundation of society'.

Taking off from this, Ratcliffe commented: '*Dharma is a finer and more satisfying word for the living principle of conduct and society*... than the conception reached by the people from whom Lord Haldane borrowed his word.' Ratcliffe had indeed lived worthily in India to be able to draw the above comparison. Our educators and their pupils remain starved, as it were, of such mental nutrients abounding in their own culture, their own sanatan *dharma*. The above gleanings, dear students, transmit the feelings and thoughts of eight Western minds, spanning over a century. You may have often been advised to develop 'open minds', 'spirit of inquiry', 'flexibility' and similar attributes by your elders, teachers or wellwishers.

Surely you possess enough of them, we assume. So, you ought to direct these very qualities towards the above symphony from Western thinkers who have dared to transcend the sci-tech-dictated regime of modernist globalism. As for us, the following appear to be the common keynotes emphasized by them. This summary may be of some help to you in your choice.

(1) Each authority above has meant authentic Bharatvarsha while using the word India.

(2) Their grasp of Bharat's culture is crystal clear. For none of them it has meant a superstitious, non-descript, hotch-potch, composite culture. Uniformly have they implied the 'core culture' of *sanatan dharma* or Hinduism in their authentic expositions.

(3) Unflinching devotion to the 'sacred', not secular, has always been the central driver of Bharat's core culture. All secular activities have been placed under the governance of the sacred. This is the foundation of sustainability.

(4) Secular sci-tech has unleashed soul-and nature–killing consumerism and greed with deadly effectiveness throughout the world.*

(5) Religion of the sacred is the only answer to the destructive and dangerous impacts of sci-tech. The latter has no concern or capacity to support man's education for self-mastery for subduing wickedness.

(6) The sacred, simple yet transcendent Bharatiya core culture is held as the last hope for an otherwise doomed modern civilization (especially Nixon and Raine).

(7) Practically all of them are praying or asking the India and Indians of to-day to resist and defy Westernized secular modernism so that the essential Bharatvarsha may live on for all.

(8) All the eight thinkers have been able to overcome the vanity of the so-called 'white man's burden' of civilizing the alleged barbarous or idolatrous peoples of the planet.

II

You should also feel a confident poise, dear students, that some of the greatest universal minds of India had *accurately foretold* many decades ago, every single deplorable outcome of the modernistic Western project cited above. The following few such prophecies/ diagnoses by them await and expect your 'open minds'.

Swami Vivekananda (1897)[10]

(a) 'Race after race has taken the challenge up and tried their utmost to solve the *world riddle on the plane of desires*. They have all failed in the past – the old ones have become extinct under the weight of wickedness and misery, which lust for gold and power brings in its train, and the new ones are tottering to their fall.... We have solved our problems ages ago. ... Our, solution is *unworldliness – renunciation*.'

(b) 'Social life in the West is like a peal of laughter, but underneath it is a wail. *It ends in a sob*. The fun and frivolity are all on the

---

* The author knows from personal experience that in Singapore, TV does not operate before 3 p.m. Channels like MTV are banned. Similar restrictions on internet broadcast and TV channels apply in China. National character, values, culture, etc., are given top priority by them. Contrast with this the impotent liberal democratic pose of India today.

surface, really it is full of tragic intensity. Now here it is sad and gloomy on the outside, but underneath are *carelessness and merriment.*'

(c) From an unfinished manuscript by the Swami, *India's Message To The World*. 'I am grateful to the lands of the West for the many warm hearts... love... pure and disinterested souls..., but my life's *allegiance is to this my motherland*...And what a land ! Whosoever stands on this sacred land, whether alien or a child of the soil, feels himself surrounded – unless his soul is so degraded to the level of brute animals – by the living thoughts of the earth's best and purest sons. ...*The very air is full of the pulsations of spirituality.*'

Rabindranath Tagore[11,12,13] (1919)

(a) '...dualism in [man's] consciousness of what is and what ought to be. ..What *is desired* dwells in the heart of the natural life which we share with animals; but what *should be desired* belongs to a life which is far beyond it.'

(b) While launching the Vishwabharati in 1919 Tagore had castigated teachers and students alike for being anaemic in intellect, lacking intellectual courage, *borrowing* a foreign culture and a foreign standard of judgment, and *losing the historical sense of all ideas.*

(c) 'We in the East have had to arrive at our own solution of the problem of life....I do not seek to glorify poverty. But *simplicity is of greater price* than the appendages of luxury. The simplicity of which I speak is not merely the effect of a lack of superfluity; it is one of the signs of perfection.'

(d) 'Luxury was a thing almost unknown in the days of my infancy. The *standard of living* was then... much more simple than it is now. Apart from that, the children of our household were entirely free from the fuss of being too much looked after. ...Our food had nothing to do with delicacies. A list of our articles of clothing would only invite the modern boy's scorn.'

Mahatma Gandhi (1938)[14, 15]

(a) 'When I read Mr. [RC] Dutt's *Economic History of India*, I wept... It is machinery that has impoverished India. It is machinery that has begun to desolate Europe. ...Machinery is the chief symbol of modern civilization; it represents a great sin....It would be folly to assume that an Indian Rockefeller would be better than the American Rockefeller....We therefore say that *the non-beginning of a thing is supreme widom*. ...Machinery is like a *snake-hole* which may contain from one to a hundred snakes.'

(b) 'The *Gita* is universally accepted... It has hardly any effect on custom. *Hinduism is like the Ganges*, pure and unsullied at its source, but taking in its course the impurities on the way. Even like the Ganges it is beneficent in its total effect ... *Purity of Hinduism depends on the self-restraint* of its votaries.'

Sri Aurobindo (1912)[16,17]

(a) 'Man has created a system of civilization which has become too big for his *limited mental capacity*... and his still more limited spiritual and moral capacity to utilize and manage, a too *dangerous servant of his blundering ego* and its appetites.'

(b) 'Our call is to young India. It is the *young* who must be the builders of the new world – *not those who accept the competitive individualism*, the capitalism or the materialistic communism of the West as India's future ideal, ... but all who are free in mind and heart to accept a completer truth and labour for a greater ideal.' The above sample of truths uttered in the late 19th and early 20th centuries by four Indian *rishis* of our era may be well-employed as benchmarks to assess the validity of the pleadings, warnings, and hopes voiced later by the eight Western minds. Here are a few attempts:

(1) For instance, compare Vivekananda's 'solution of renunciation' with Toynbee's 'indulgence of greed', or Raine's 'grave danger from' 'materialist imperialism'.

(2) Tagore strikes the same note as Vivekananda's – 'arriving at our own solution of the problem of life' through the 'perfection of simplicity'. Comparable are the observations of Griffiths about 'loss of inner meaning of life in the West', and of Beer regarding 'devastation wrought in the quality of life' in advanced industrial countries.

(3) The student should hark back to Krishna Prem's criticism of a section of India's intelligentsia who 'unthinkingly mouth

the shibboleths of the West'. Vivekananda too had detected the same malaise, but alluded to it in a veiled manner, 'souls so degraded to the level of brute animals'. Tagore, however, was more direct while rebuking about 'borrowing of a foreign culture and a foreign standard of judgment'.*

(4) Toynbee has charged 'technology for manipulation through quantification'. Much earlier Gandhi had bluntly told, 'machinery represents a great sin'. Deriving from our *shastras* he had proclaimed: 'non-beginning of a thing is supreme wisdom'. We had recently seen (September, 2009) a newspaper headline to this effect, 'Scientists fear that robots may begin to revolt against their creators'.

(5) Krishna Prem had been able to discern, and correctly so, that Bharat's social structures rest on 'religious sanction', unlike those in the West. Toynbee was emphatic about the indispensability of religion and spirituality in education to direct and control the increasing 'power of man' through 'application of science'. And Frawley has declared that Vedantic *sanatan dharma* of Hinduism is the most universal religion, free from dogma and personality. All this had been captured by Gandhiji by employing the sacred simile, 'Hinduism is like the Ganges... which is beneficent in its total effect'.

(6) Both Krishna Prem and Raine have almost literally shed tears and prayed for the survival of the sacred keynote of Bharatiya culture. They have torn asunder the veil of phoney secularism. Thus, 'Often while meditating... I pray to Krishna that He may never let India's immemorial soul to be swamped... by the blatant West'; or.

'If India is lost, all is lost..., Never has the world needed India as now'. The ground, the basis for such touching affection for India (of course they mean Bharat and her core culture) had been foreseen much earlier by Sri Aurobindo. He had given the devil its due. At the

---

* A few more words from Vivekananda on this point: 'Oh! India, this is your terrible danger. The spell of imitating the West is getting such hold on you... Whatever ideas, whatever manners the white men praise or like are good... Alas! what can be a more tangible proof of foolishness than this?' (Thus Spoke Vivekananda, R K Math, Chennai, 38-9)

same time he had sternly warned about the immense problem of having created too big and complex a civilization which science and man are now finding much beyond their mental and moral capacities to manage. The resultant tone of desperation in some wise and seeing Western minds comes out loud and clear. Students with willing and inquiring minds should be able to discover more such illuminating linkages besides those we have mentioned above. Let them therefore take a few dips into the wide confluence of saving thoughts flowing from the twelve spiritual humanists with *antardrishti* (insight) and *doordrishti* (farsight) cited here.

III

And now you may savour a little of the things told and voices trusted. Reports from different UN bodies, economics-finance business writings, etc., are always advising, and frequently compelling, the people of the 'developing' nations to embrace the 'modern mentality'. And our students and teachers are unhesitatingly falling in line. This gospel is blindly trusted. But those who have the ability to stand beyond the apparently golden cage of modernism, perceive it to be an alarming phenomenon which chains humanity down, instead of liberating it up. Its loud noise about 'problemsolving' is deceptive. Sci-tech modernity has been consistently a 'problem-creating' process across the whole of twentieth century.

Problem-solving is really a face-saving mask, a nasty sequel. For instance, we recall a Western newspaper headline some twenty years ago: 'Environmental Problems To Generate a $500–billion Industry'.

So, environmental problems are created in the first place, and then snow-balling global catastrophe is seen as a 'business opportunity'. This is broadly the character of problem-solving. All the four new cardinal sins pronounced by the Vatican in 2008 (drug pushing, obscene richness, environmental pollution, genetic manipulation) could be causally linked with the modern secular mentality. While it may solve one problem for now, it creates two or more problems for the near or far future. Yet our students are being conditioned to treat problem-solving progress as the un-challengeable fact of modern times. The *Bible* had cautioned thus: 'For, wide is the gate, and broad is the way that leadeth to destruction.' Besides, it had also put the modern man in his place, as though in anticipation.

'Having eyes he seeth not, having ears he heareth not.' Sometime in June 2009 the teaching of ethics was being discussed in the Board meeting of an all-India post-graduate institution. At one stage we said that there is a good case to correlate falling ethics with rising technology. Instantly the Director, a Ph.D in mathematics, cut short our point saying, 'There is no data to support such a correlation.' The latest Lehman-Satyam scandals are brushed asideby the guardians of public interest as 'aberrations'. Our students trust these brave individuals and become complacent. Even Paul Samuelson, the first Nobel winner in Economics, was forced to this honest admission: 'No "lost decades" for us smart guys. ... these *fiendish* new financial engineering tools no CEO you will ever meet truly [understands them]. Instead of controlling riskiness, the new tools — swaps, puts and calls, securitized packets of mortgage loans — diminished transparency all led to damaging hyper-leveraging,...an *ultra-fragile financial system*...'[18] But academic courses and teachers in our upto-date, highly-ranked learning institutions doggedly insulate themselves from such penetrating appraisals. 'Ignorance is bliss' – yes and no both. Even lesser is their chance to encounter the mind of a Toynbee who had sadly confessed way back in 1976[19].

'The readiness with which we allow ourselves to be greedy and the poorness of our ethical performance is made still more humiliating by its contrast with the brilliance of our technological performance. ... the disparity between our technology and our ethics is greater today than it has ever *been* ... it is mortally dangerous.'

Yet, you students are being continuously indoctrinated with the myth of endless linear progress. So you are being forced or cajoled to trust un-trustworthy gospels. Here is a sample of exhortations of this tenor from some recent annual convocation addresses in a top rung post-graduate, government-created, academic institution. These addresses have been delivered by heavy-weight, elderly (60+) captains in bureaucracy, business, finance, information technology etc. The year 2000 address declared that a 'new world without barriers' was being ushered by 'business @ the speed of thought', B2B commerce growing exponentially, customers of e-toys bulging from only 10,000 to 1m. in two years, 1997-99, etc., As a consequence, the omniscient consumer is becoming a reality. Leaders are needed to move towards 'desired' (not desirable) goals so as to contribute to the 'growth of human kind'.

Next year too the graduating students were exultantly told about the 'highly dynamic new world order' of which they are a part. The 'demands' of this 'global world' have to be met. Hence students have to 'run faster than anybody else' in an era which has been able to 'conquer destiny'! You must 'move ahead' matching with technological change. The 2002 convocation address advised the graduates to manage change 'positively', to 'think future backwards', to acquire 'killer instinct', etc.,

The above as well as the 2003 addresses emphasized that 1991 was a landmark in the economic framework and history of India. The 2004 speech had begun by highlighting the 'rule of three' i.e., only the top three in any field are worthy of survival; the system of performance-related variable pay; the imperative of e-learning in an era of rapid change. In the later part of the address the thoughts suddenly tended towards the subjective and the sublime e.g., mention of 'eternal Reality', removal of 'mental dirt', tranquility, silent witness self and the like. Curiously, the speaker seemed to be oblivious of the fundamental contradictions between 'rule of three', 'variable pay' etc. on the one hand, and 'eternal Reality', 'inner tranquility', etc., on the other.

Of all the convocation addresses (ten in all) scrutinized by us, that for 2005 alone had stood out for the normative and the subjective. Here, students were told that smothering of their intuitive power, omission of values and integrity, neglect of character and culture, inducements for competitive rat race etc. were commonly associated with education in such institutions. It concluded with this question: 'Should we allow ourselves to be so obsessed with winning, with becoming the *numero uno* at any cost, as is the nature of modern society?' (The speaker was a PSU CMD).

The 2007 address, by a giant Indian private sector boss, reverted back to the previous long trail: You are part of the 'performing elite of India', you are to create a 'new India', you should redefine the 'concept of Indian elite', the world today is run as a process of 'continual value addition' and so on.

'Very exciting times' was the inaugural theme of the 2008 address. With 'knowledge and intellectual capital', India had 'arrived' in the 'globalized' world with shifting 'life-style aspirations' of new culture. Another PSU CMD was the speaker in this instance.* It is not hard to contemplate that young listeners would have been swayed by the 'brave new world' rhetoric of all the above convocation addresses, barring the honourable exception for 2005. All the lessons of Bharat's cultural history, stretching over several millennia, seem to have been written off the mental maps of these top Indians of today. Yet it is they who are entrusted with the role of mind-making of our youth. The yearnings, hopes and laments of Nixons, Raines, Griffiths *et.al.* go unheard and unheeded. In fact, many avant-garde modernizers of India suspect in their thoughts a design to hold India back from prosperity and enlightenment. So, when asked by such trustworthy well-wishers: 'Does India have to commit all the mistakes we (the West) have done?', one of our elites asserted: 'Yes, all of them.' This in fact had happened with Raine in 1997. We too have heard such responses, be-speaking the penchant among Indian intelligentsia for trusting 'false prophets'. This had been termed by Tagore as a major weakness of 'insularly modern minds'. The reason for this habit appears to be the temptation of some personal gain, or cheap acclaim and flattery from 'false prophets'.

It may have been 2005-06. A Padma-awardee, former Director of an Institute of 'national importance' told the large audience of a conference, including many students and teachers: 'We all are to-day citizens of a global world, one world. It is no longer valid to talk about Indian citizens, or about indigenous culture.' What sense does 'national importance' carry then? No wonder India gets clobbered by China and other smaller nations in the north-east, north-west etc. at their sweet will. A widely-known, non-agerian writer has adopted for long the brand tag of 'malice'. A couple of decades ago or more he had chastised Sri Krishna (in an English national daily) for having crafted the crooked caste system (in the *Gita)*. And as recently as in september, 2009 he wrote a piece for another daily complaining that 'he was losing his sleep for nights trying to figure out how "Basant Panchami", "Janmashtami", "Ramnavami", etc., had come to be so associated with given dates'. All sorts of pundits and classical scholars of Sanskrit had failed to satisfy him. So he was seeking help from the readers of the daily. Significantly, he chose certain dates of the Hindu calendar only for the fling — the easiest way in India to attain the status of enlightened intellectuals. In the same month and year an essay on 'India – Hope and Reality', by a former well-known bureaucrat, now a columnist, had appeared in the in-flight magazine of an airline. As

* The 2006 speech was by an expatriate CEO where no subjective exhortations were made. The 2009 address has already bee mentioned in chapter 1.

expected, the essay contained euphoric references to India's democracy, diversity, composite culture, plurality, secular ethos, inclusive society and so on. All this was possible because of the foresight of the leaders of the nationalist struggle. But the author offers no hint or acknowledgment of the over-arching fact that every outer trapping highlighted by him has been developed and nourished on the foundation of the 'spiritual, *sanatan* Hindu ethos' of our core culture. This is what Nixon, Raines and others of their ilk admit, admire and accept about India, standing on the foundation of Bharatvarsha. But they are also quite apprehensive because Indian intelligentsia itself has closed its mind to this supreme key note. And the young are expected to repose their trust in this category of people — convocation speakers, academics, and columnists who float with the tide of shiny shibboleths, with no compass or anchor to guide or hold.

IV

Just six 'realities' concealed by the above glossy external wrappings now follow. *First,* even after sixty three years of independence, the members of two significant minority communities usually declare their identity by first mentioning their particular monolithic faith. Sometimes when asked about their nationality, even then many of them are heard to mention their particular faith only.

Yet, India's vote-based democracy has been providing them with many concessions and privileges by dipping into our purses through taxes etc. Have the beneficiaries responded by better integration? Continuous terrorist outrages with local collusion, or clandestine tribal conversions tell a different story. *Second*, in the year 1998-99 (probably) one of the topmost corrupt politicians of the country, and a the-then Union Cabinet Minister had installed his spouse as the dummy chief minister of a State after conviction by the CBI, and underwent subsequent cosy imprisonment for some time. Yet, in the year 2007 he was reportedly invited by two highly-rated academic institutions, first in India, then in the USA, to address their academic communities. (It might be added that this person with his clownish mannerisms, is a sort of platform entertainer). Dear students, would you go on blindly trusting this breed of people, their promoters and supporters, and a democracy which legitimizes such sordid dramas over the years?

Even top-level educational institutions joining in? *Third*, the highest national honour, Bharat Ratna, is tending to become farcical.

For, you have a Sarvapalli Radhakrishnan and a Satyajit Ray as its recipients on the one side, and M.G. Ramachandran and Rajiv Gandhi on the other. How can the kind of exhortations of numerous opinion-makers quoted above help you to make honourable choices, voice your honest views? *Fourth*, by utilizing a certain technical flaw in the Constitution, a few years ago India was on the brink of being saddled with a national CEO completely alien to this country and culture. Is it possible even to dream of such a bizarre possibility, a foreign person as PM, in China or Arabia or France or Myanmar? Just the freak of a foreign marriage by a Chinese or French national, engaged in politics, paving the royal road to the top seat for the spouse, subsequent to the local person's death? So, here is a democracy where the deepest sentiments and yearnings of the majority are worth not even a penny.

We request all our youth to contemplate multi-faith nations like the USA or China leveling down Christianity or Confucianism to the status of equality (even inferiority) with other faiths and cultures existing there – in the name of a 'composite culture'. Should they try this with an open mind, they will fail. And add to this the latest injury: The foisting on the country of a President who, with the entire family, has been riddled with multiple, widely-known corruption cases. Woe to Rajendra Prasads and Abdul Kalams. There is no room for quality in the minds of highly positioned, self-serving, secularist champions of 'plurality' and 'inclusiveness'. The rampant abuse of quota system seems to be the best way, according to them, for such ends. Our students and youth have a right to be aware about the consequent ruinous social fractures.

This is just the opposite of what the special-privileges-cum-reservation advocates claim as being attained. It may be recalled that earlier Raine had been cited as espousing the learning of Sanskrit, not Greek, by the learneds of the world. Nixon also was heard praying to Sri Krishna that the culture of this land of *rishis* might always be saved by Him whenever ultimate destruction seemed to be imminent. So, our 'Core Culture' has little need for sermons from any quarter, even in 2009, about 'inclusiveness' and the manner of going about it. But the deeply-rooted trust of Raines and Nixons is nullified or betrayed by most educated Indians at every turn. Here is therefore the *fifth* reality. Less than a year ago we saw a course outline on 'History of Management Thought' to be offered to MBA students in a National Institute. The first topic was 'Early Pioneers — Tzu, Machiavelli'.

We could not figure out, despite consulting the *Encyclopaedia Britannica* (EB), which Tzu was meant because there were several Tzu's in it. Machiavelli (1469-1527) of course was amply covered (eight pages). What appeared striking to us was the omission of Kautilya or Chanakya as a 'pioneer' (in the course outline). The EB, however, fared better – about half-a-page was granted to him. He had flourished in the fourth century BC. Though he had preceded Machiavelli by about 1800 years, and had left behind management/ administration classics like *Arthashastra, Chanakya Niti,* yet our scholars are in the habit of referring to him, if at all, as 'India's Machiavelli'. A similar fate meets another Bharatiya classicist, (there was no India in his time, as it did not in Chanakya's time): 'Kalidasa is the Shakespeare of India'. Kalidasa had also preceded Shakespeare by many centuries. Kautilya, the 'Hindu Statesman and philosopher', as the EB characterizes him, was the moving spirit and inspiring architect of the great Mauryan Empire (321 BC to 238 BC), which stood out as a model of efficient government. According to Brown, a California University scholar, although the *Arthashastra* bears the stamp of both utilitarianism and realism, nonetheless it is 'thoroughly grounded in Brahmanical doctrine'[20]. The crux of this doctrine is the *rajarshi* model of leadership and management, presented in some detail by us elsewhere.[21]

- In the EB one finds some interesting observations about Machiavelli: His *The Prince,* mostly concerned with princes, is viewed by many as 'dangerously wicked'.
- Kautilya too had written on princes, which is a study in contrast to what Machiavelli had.
- Machiavellianism is 'the teaching of worldly success through scheming deceit'. This is what rules the world to-day. *Arthasashtra* is again a vivid contrast to such secular ethos.
- Machiavelli had proclaimed one of the keynotes of secular modernity — the conquest of nature and fortune in the 'interest of humanity'. To-day, through the eyes of Toynbees and Griffiths, we know now the fall-out of this gospel.
- Modern notions of 'irreversible progress', 'public good through private interest' etc. are also fully present in his works. They too, for whatever they are worth, have been leading to rapid ecological decay, steeply climbing inequities and brazen unethicalities.

The end of Machiavelli, as the EB notes, came like this: 'Denied the post [under the free republic after Medici], he fell ill and died within a month.' Kautilya, on the other hand, completed his last duty by getting Chandragupta married to the daughter of Selucus, thus cementing the bond between India and Greece. No craving for any 'post'. Instead, he repaired to the forest for *vanaprastha,* the traditional sacred phase for every individual in Bharatvarsha after due discharge of secular duties. Whom should you then study and trust, dear students?

Could your teachers give you the right guidance, the honest perspective? And here follows, for the time being, the *sixth* 'reality' about education in India today. In January 2010 we were the guest of a high-reputation, autonomous M.Ed. training college. During the week whenever we went to the Principal's room, his big table was found cluttered with some fifty books received for inspection for the library. All of them were from the West, and a few had strange titles. One day a History teacher had come in and we asked him if he was still using books which taught the 'Aryan invasion theory'. 'Yes' was his prompt answer. And yet, over the last five decades, thorough and extensive excavations in western and north-western parts of India, by both Indian and Western researchers, have been yielding mounting evidence against the AIT theory.

Danino[22] and Agarwal[23] have recently collated and summarized all such findings, exposing the hidden agenda of denying Bharatvarsha its power to create a stable, multidimensional, original culture from within. Vivekananda, more than a century before modern researchers, had scornfully dismissed the AIT thesis by his *antardrishti*, and had thundered against 'monstrous lies' that were being told to our boys[24].

V

You would have studied carefully some of the thoughts culled from twelve superlative minds of the East and West quoted above. Six of them have been independent 'thinkers'. The other six were 'realizers'. None of them was a scholar or columnist with minds subservient to petty or politicized aims. We appeal to you to trust them because all of them were un-contaminated by the dirt of politics and the opportunism of intellectuality. They could also transcend the snares and compulsions of the immediate and the measurable. You should profit by reposing trust in a few more indispensable, principled guidelines from two of them:

1. During an interview by the *Hindu* in 1897, Swami Vivekananda had said[25]: 'The Japanese are ready to sacrifice everything for their country, and they have become a great people. But you are not, you cannot be; *you sacrifice everything, only for your own families and possessions.*' Let us to-day quietly reflect on this rebuke and judge where we stand.

2. To the question, if India should become like Japan (in the same interview), Vivekananda's reply was equally forthright, 'Decidedly not. India should continue to be what she is. .. In each nation, as in music, there is a main note, a central theme upon which all others turn. ...*India cannot be like Japan.*' Is not this categorical imperative worthy of your trust? Ought you not be creative in working it out? Is not this what the eight discerning Western minds also are expecting of us? Or, would you still continue to trust those who advise us that 'India should become a second-hand copy of the West'?

3. Rabindranath Tagore must have had premonitions, a *rishi* that he was, about malafide cultural globalization ninety years ago. He had uttered therefore these warnings[26].

'Until we are in a position to prove that the world has need of us and cannot do without us, that we are not merely hangers-on of the worldculture — beggars who cannot repay — so long must our sole hope lie in gaining others' favours.' (Global culturists may note).

'...when natural differences find their harmony, then it is true unity; but artificial unity leads to lifelessness.' (modern i.e., Western mentality protagonists may note). 'The use of English inevitably tends to turn our mind for its source of inspiration towards the West, with which we can never be in close touch of life, and therefore our education will mostly remain sterile, or produce incongruities.' (Educators may note). 'The main river of Indian culture has flowed in four streams — the Vedic, the Puranic, the Buddhist and the Jain. It had its source in the heights of Indian consciousness.' ('Composite culturists' may note).

4. Subhas Chandra Bose had written an autobiography which narrated his development upto the age of twenty five.[27] In a letter written by him in August 1915 – he was only 19 years then – he had stated that his 'mission to be a man' comprised three strands:

- Embodiment of the Past,
- Product of the Present, and
- Prophet of the Future.

Yes, he had the priceless boon of a *legitimate educator* par excellence, Beni Madhav Das, who could mould the youthful mind of Subhas towards such a glorious vision. *Legitimate educators* of today can receive a fillip to their own endeavours from this splendid *gurushishya* bond. The 'triplet' above also exemplifies Nivedita's 'national mind' at its best (chapter 3). Bose's (later Netaji) uncompromising fight for India's freedom is now a peerless legend. His character and actions epitomise the Vedic- Epic ideals of valour, strength, heroism and self-sacrifice i.e., *kshatra veerya* (A. C. Bose, *The Call of the Vedas*, 1970, pp. 234-240). The core culture of Bharat has not been merely ascetic, mystic and effeminate. If it were, it would have gone under several millennia ago. But the way education is now being imparted in India, this possibility cannot be ruled out. Legitimate teachers need to consider this vital issue with the seriousness it deserves. Note also the all-important thought — the 19–year-old Subhas had aspired to be an *embodiment of the past*. What was this 'past' for him? Not the sum-total of (suttee + dowry + infanticide + superstition + caste distortions + untouchability + women's suppression) and so on. Yet, this is how Bharat's past is largely being presented now to our children and youth by academics and media persons. The *legitimate educator* has the duty to stand up and ask such careerists: Where has your conscience gone? For how long will it stay exiled? Except for tarnishing the child's priceless heritage, and caving the ground under its feet, what your positive contribution?

Moreover, the brilliant IIM-IIT students also should humbly learn from Subhas what *shraddha* is. He was not less brilliant than them. He had cleared his ICS examination in eight months, securing record marks in the English essay paper. Severed from all such moorings, Indian teachers are to-day generally incapable of offering any wholesome guidance. Rather, the latest signals are depressing, even ominous. Academics of the most highly paying national educational outfits have resorted to hunger strikes and other demeaning exercises in 'rationalised lunacy' (vide Bertrand Russell) for pay hikes in 2009. They have got approved for themselves cash rewards of ` 1,00,000 and upwards for papers published here and abroad. This is much like many earlier similar steps taken by MPs in Delhi. All this is happening in a country where the model teacher, Vishnusharma, the author of *Panchatantra*. had declined to 'sell education' for grooming the sons of a King. Students have the right, therefore, to be alerted in their choices for trust with the help of the following further forewarnings, born of transcendental, self–negating love for the country, from Vivekananda.

For, just as this year is proceeding with the 150th birth anniversary commemoration of Rabindranath Tagore, so perhaps will be the year 2012-13 with that of Swami Vivekananda. Dear students, treat it therefore as a humble *seva* from the author as he offers you below a few of the Swami's wisest pleas to his countrymen. They have been sifted from some of his most prophetic addresses after his return from the West during 1897-end. Our comments are added in parenthesis:

- 'Forty million English people can rule India because they have one will. In India, three hundred million people live and each has a separate will.'[28] (The end-less number of political parties in India, unlike just two or three in the USA or UK, is the greatest proof of Swamiji's diagnosis.)
- *Chittashuddhi*, purity of the heart, is the most important necessity.'[29] (That is, noble unselfish emotions; not clever and selfish intellect).
- Temples like Somnath suffered 'a hundred attacks and regenerated a hundred times. So we have a national mind, a national life-current. Give it up and you die. ... Political, social [and technological] improvements are secondary needs.'[30] (Recall Sister Nivedita in chapter 2. Politically beleagured India to-day proves to the hilt that India's genius for glory does not lie in politics etc. Every country, near or far, outplays India in political trickery. Tall talks of secularism, moon-landing, democracy, tolerance, nine per cent GDP growth etc. notwithstanding, every country plays foul with her and gets away).
- 'Materialism and its miseries can never be controlled by materialism.'[31] (We might easily add today technology to materialism because they are indispensable to each other. And as for miseries, a few un-opiated souls can only watch their explosion in helpless horror.)

- 'Are we to take always, to sit at the feet of the Westerners to learn everything, even religion [spirituality]?'[32] (Without having read these words of Swamiji at that time, our book *Spirituality in Management,* OUP, 2008, had emphatically argued the same point. Anyway, Swamijis' question has to be answered to-day with an unambiguous 'yes'— see chapter 2 above. What a shame.)
- 'For instance, if as a fisherman, or a student, or a lawyer you can think you are the Spirit, then you will be a better fisherman, a better student, a better lawyer... conquest of the world is to be done by Spirituality. ... If you believe yourselves to be Sages, Sages you will be to-morrow.'[33] (This then is the panoramic, all-encompassing Vision offered to each student of India by our own Swamiji. Choose you 'trust' now.)
- 'Today perhaps through your own fault this (national) boat has become a little damaged, has sprung a leak. Would you therefore curse it? ... If there are holes in this national ship, this society of ours, we are its children. Let us go and stop the holes. Let us gladly do it with our heart's blood, and if we cannot then let us die. ... Say not one harsh word against this society. Condemn it never.'[34] (Do your heart-beat, pulse-rate, eye-lids become fast, moist having read these words — dear students? If 'yes', then Bharat can hope to re-emerge out of India.)

January 12 had been officially declared as 'national youth day' some years ago. Only the Ramakrishna Mission Centres and Institutions observe the day with seriousness as it coincides with Swamiji's birthday. But in other educational institutions hardly a murmur is heard. In the national press and media not even a whisper seems to go around. Shall the new-born International Baccalaureate Schools ever take note of this day of consecration? Add to this, calling the utterly self-less freedom fighters as 'terrorists', insulting the national flag or anthem or song at will, falling flat for cash and career — and we have the perfect backdrop for national nemesis. Shakespeare's bleeding Julius Caesar had exclaimed thus: 'Et, tu Brute? Ingratitude, thou marble-hearted fiend !', when the latter had stabbed him mortally on the back. Our Vivekananda's too should be sending out such a cry to the post-1950 youth. To be sure, *Karmaphala* or *Karmic* retribution or poetic justice is inexorably beginning to take over. The hapless state of India vis-a-vis China, Pakistan, USA and others on the international political chessboard is a tell-tale story. *Karmaphala* and *karmic* network operate across a much wider canvas than we frothy folks can comprehend. So, dear students, instead of discarding or forgetting these great souls, return to them with love and respect. You and your country will both be truly re-empowered then in all respects. This will help you to discharge your *deshrin* (see chapter 1).

The human ideal or human value of *desh rin* is the kernel of patriotism in the *sanatan* tradition. But the world over, in all nations big or small, rich or poor, patriotism of an aggressive kind is often the ultimate civilian value for empowerment from within. Trust not, therefore, the red brigade (and other similar groups) of betrayers of India when they denounce patriotism as yet another mask for nationalistic hegemony. India has never done so. She is indeed genetically conditioned against such brutality. Instead, you ought to repose full trust in our A's and G's, T's and V's (amply quoted above) for moulding your minds for self-transcending (not self-liquidating) causes. The nation is in desperate need of such benign strength and vitality. Then only everything else — science, technology, business, ethics, civic discipline and the rest — will begin to fall in place in right proportionautomatically.

Dear students, you also often hear these days about the value of holism, holistic view of things etc.. Here again you must trust and follow what 'realizers' like Sri Aurobindo have instructed e.g., 'In this *silence*, *right* knowledge *comes*'. Silencing of stormy thoughts, calming the over-excited brain is a pre-condition for holistic perception (not thinking). Non-stop, serial mental thinking is inherently fragmented, fractional -- stimulated as it is by our outgoing senses. When you progress gradually towards even a modicum of such *brain-stilling*, only then you begin to appreciate that the whole is integral. Dis-integrated intellect cannot do this job, howsoever superlative might it be. A silent, calm, still, *ekagra* mind is like an empty, clean glass. The self-existing whole can then 'come' into it- as Sri Aurobindo has put it. This is exactly what Narendranath as a student (before becoming Vivekananda) had pathetically cried out to Master Mahashai (the chronicler of the world classic *Sri Sri Ramakrishna Kathamrita* or *Gospel of Sri Ramakrishna*): 'Sir , how I wish if I could get some medicine from somewhere, and be saved. For, I desperately want to forget everything that I have learnt so far.' Within a year or so thereafter he had reached the peak— *nirvikalpa samadhi*.

In the *Bhagwad Gita (BG)* too, *Acharya* Krishna instructs Arjuna towards holism, albeit in a veiled manner. Verse II-28 tells the 'student' that none of us is aware of anything prior to or after this present manifest, bodily existence, which is but a single link in a very very long chain. Yet, we all modernists indulge in mounting fuss and raging storm in the tea-cup of this life — just one link blown out of all proportion, blacking out all else. 'The world is too much with us'- Wordsworth's Pippa had cried. Hence, determined and steady contemplation of this power-packed insight can inaugurate a transition towards holistic perception. Why? Because, unlike much of the powerless teaching of today by power-points in dark rooms to faceless audiences, the BG was instructed in broad daylight face to face.

While the *Upanishads* may be 'ideational', the *BG* is primarily 'instructional'. Sincere students can truly reap enduring subjective gains from its application. The sooner they begin the better. The *BG* is simultaneously three-dimensional – profound depth, lofty height, followed by wholesome breadth. Within the span of this life itself there is a 'long chain' of holism. Students of today will became parents of tomorrow, and then grandparents of day-after-tomorrow (provided they do not opt for some modern brutish options). The author has a grandson (16 years) by the daughter, and a grand-daughter (6 years) by the son. As grandparents we have been observing striking differences in the mental make-up of the two children. For instance, it is remarkable that while one of the favourite declarations of the boy is: 'I don't believe in God', the girl fervently affirms: 'I love God v-e-r-y much'. The boy has no paternal grandparents at home, while the girl has. Except for a fancy career, the boy has been getting hardly any other life-making inputs in his mother tongue. The father is totally immersed in his heavy-duty, big corporate job — 8 a.m. to 10 p.m. The uninspired mother (fortunately not employed outside) tries her best to fill the gap, without much impact though. On the other hand, the girl receives regular enrichment through a daily routine at home beyond the school. The small set of disciplines set out below constitute transcultural, intrinsic human development. The statistical pugilism of Human.

Development Index cannot corner or capture the outcomes of such development. They constitute true 'enlightened citizenship', rather than negative shouting against so-called superstitions. The caring and devoted grandparents attempt to instill finer ideals through story-telling, reading of epics and great lives, visits to ashrams, religious rituals etc. Sometimes the twilight sky with the bright evening star and the moon, or towards God, the Cosmic. Or, assigning to her the duty of watering two flower pots twice a day. Or else, to accustom her to scatter some grains on the terrace for the birds before her own breakfast. Holistic living depends on such a complete process. Can you accept this holistic model of leading a life besides earning a living? This will need the urge to choose to put your 'money in trust', rather than the rage to put your 'trust in money' — as someone had said so aptly.

Let another vital facet of education for 'holism' be added to your repertoire of life and living. As students you are being ceaselessly prodded to 'strategize'. The *zeitgist* of the times seems to be 'strategizing' about almost every aspect of your functioning. Yet, the paradox that escapes all of us is that none of us cares for even a moment about 'strategizing' for the one certainty of life — death.

What is your and my 'strategy' for managing the moment of last breath? The scientific-tempered modern mind simply avoids this inquiry of all inquiries. But ancient Bharatiya thought had thoroughly probed this inevitable finality, and has left for us invaluable guidelines. Among the best of them are those in the *BG*, chapter 8, verses 5,6,9,10,12,13, and 16. Complementary verses occur in chapters 6, 14, etc., The strategic (?) principle encapsuled in these verses is this: You become what you think; things are thoughts. Recall Sri Aurobindo on Ashok Nandi's last moments (chapter 1). The Mother had once told a student that the most judicious way to pass away in neutral peace and calm is to live the whole life in such a way that unfinished desires, duties, debts, disputes, preferences or abhorrences etc. do not overburden the body-leaving consciousness. Thus freed, one's subtle being rises to higher states of evolution for a new birth. Gandhiji's death with 'Hey Ram' on his lips was the result of life-long spiritual 'strategy' adopted by him. This is the real meaning of 'life+death' holism, much like the 'head+tail' holism of a coin. If the above inspirations begin to vibrate in you, very well and very good. If not, let us be reminded of the following:

(a) Referring to the near-fatal folly of Shri Ram's enchantment with the chimerical 'golden deer', Chanakya had warned: "*Vinashkale viparit buddhi*" [35] (i.e, when destruction is nigh intelligence turns topsy turvy).

(b) In *Sri Chandi or Devi Mahatyam* too we have the humble submission: '*Ya devi sarvabhuteshu bhranti rupena sansthita*' (O ! Mother Goddess, thou art pervadeth all as folly).

APPENDIX

'Rishis': What and Who They Were

Rishis have been mentioned several times in the text above. Here are some extracts about them from a few *rishis** of our own epoch.

(A) Swami Vivekananda

(a) 'And we must remember that the leaders of our society have never been either generals or kings, but Rishis. And who are the Rishis? The Rishi as he is called in the *Upanishads* is not an ordinary man, but a Mantra-drashta. He is a man who sees religion, to whom religion is... actual realization, a coming face-to-face with truths which transcend the senses. This is Rishi-hood. ... May the Lord help us, each one of us here, to realize Rishihood for our own salvation and for that of others.' (*Complete Works,* vol. 3, p. 175)

(b) '... the Rishi-state is not limited by time or place, by sex or race'. (*Ibid.*, p. 252)

(c) 'Not belief in doctrines, not going to thousands of temples, not bathing in all the rivers in the world, but becoming the Rishi, the Mantra-drashta – that is freedom, that is salvation' (*Ibid.*, p. 255)

(d) '... the truth came to the Rishis of India — the Mantradrashtas, the seers of thought — and will come back to all Rishis in the future, not to talkers, not to book-swallowers, not to scholars, not to philologists, but to seers of thought.' (*Ibid.*, p. 283)

(e) 'When in the ancient times this knowledge (*Jnana*) and this feeling (*Bhava*)... blossomed forth simultaneously in the heart of the Rishi, then the Highest Truth became poetic, and then the Vedas and other scriptures were composed'. (*Complete Works,* vol. 5, p. 419)

(B) Rabindranath Tagore

(a) '... in ancient India we find that the circumstances of forest * Etymologically, *Rishi* means a person who is beyond the three gunas, is *nirdwandwa* and *samyak-drashta.* life did not overcome man's mind ... but only gave to it a particular direction. ... His aim was not to acquire but to realize, to enlarge his consciousness by growing with and into his surroundings. ...

To realize this great harmony between man's spirit and the spirit of the world was the endeavour of the Forest-dwelling Sages of ancient India'. (*Sadhana,* Macmillan, 1989, p. 4).

(b) 'What were the rishis? They who having attained the supreme soul in knowledge, were filled with wisdom, and having found him in union with soul were in perfect harmony with the inner self; they having realized him in the heart, were free from all selfish desires, and having experienced him in all the activities of the world had attained calmness. The rishis were they who having reached the Supreme God from all sides had found abiding peace, had become united with all, had entered into the life of the Universe'. (Ibid., p. 12)

(C) Sri Aurobindo

(a) '... the Rishi, the man of higher spiritual experience and knowledge, [was] born in any of the classes, ... exercising an authority by his spiritual personality over all, revered and consulted by the king... and in the-then fluid state of social evolution able alone to exercise an important role in evolving new basic ideas... It was the work of the Rishi to put [the spirituo-religious] stamp enduringly on the national mind... And in later ages we find the Brahminic schools of legists attributing their codes... to the ancient Rishis'. (*The Foundations of Indian Culture,* 1998, pp. 336-7)

(b) 'The Indian mind holds ... that the Rishi, the seer of spiritual truth is the best guide not only of the religious and moral, but also the practical life. The seer, the Rishi is the natural director of society...' (*Ibid.*, p. 61)

(c) 'The spiritual man who can guide human life towards its perfection is typified in the ancient Indian idea of the Rishi, one who has lived fully the life of man and found the word of the supraintellectual, supramental, spiritual truth. ... he has the complete inner knowledge and the higher surpassing knowledge. Therefore he can guide the world humanly as God guides it Divinely... (*The Human Cycle,* 1985, p. 169).

(D) Mahatma Gandhi

'... our forefathers were satisfied with small villages. They saw that kings and their swords were inferior to the sword of ethics, and they, therefore, held the sovereigns of the earth to be inferior to the Rishis. ... A nation with a constitution like this is fitter to teach others than to learn from others.' (*Selected Works*, Navjivan, 1969, vol. 4, p. 151).

(E) Sri Sri Santdas Maharaj

(His original name was Tara Kishor Choudhury, a leading member of the Calcutta Bar in the 1920s and 1930s. He used to command an extent of honour which was second only to that of Sir Rash Behari Ghosh. Later he became a leading Vaishnava Saint, heading all its sects and settled at Vrindaban).

We have this gripping scene from one of his short biographies: 'In his last year of earthly life Santdas Maharaj had been invited to Guahati to address the Harisabha audience. Local devotees had requested him to explain the contribution of the Rishis to Bharat's culture and civilization. He agreed and mounted the stage. As he took his seat he was found struggling for words. After a few minutes of such wordless and motionless sitting, the audience saw tears rolling down his eyes. He could not contain the increasingly rushing torrent.

Not a word could be uttered by him. Then the tear-stricken devotees realized what had happened. Some of them came near him and said: "Maharaj, your silent tears have told us so much about what we wanted to know as no amount of words could have. Our pranams, obeisance to you, Maharaj." And the *sabha* or meeting ended. (*Bharater Sadhak*, in Bengali, by Shankar Nath Roy, Karuna Prakashani, Calcutta, 1975, vol. 2, pp. 310-1)

References

1. Roy D. K; *Yogi Sri Krishna Prem,* Mumbai: Bharatiya Vidya Bhavan, 1992, p.89.
2. Toynbee A. J; *Choose Life,* Delhi: Oxford University Press, 1987, pp. 44, 45, 45, 61, 66, 84, 85.
3. Griffiths B. ; *Return To The Centre,* London: Collins, 1987, pp.17, 66, 68- 9.
4. Raine K.; 'India And The Modern World', *Resurgence,* July 1994, pp.22, 23, 25.
5. Same, 'The Voice of the Sacred In Our Time', *Vihangama,* Vol.V, 1997, pp. 2, 3, 4, 12.
6. Beer S.; *How Many Grapes Went Into The Wine?*, Chichester: John Wiley, 1994, p. 321.

7. Frawley D.; *Vedantic Meditation;* Delhi: Full Circle, 2002, p. 5.
8. Quoted in *Spirituality in Management: Means or End*; Delhi: Oxford University Press, 2008, chpter 10.
9. Nivedita Sister; *Religion and Dharma*,Kolkata: Advaita Ashrama, 1998, pp.vii-ix.
10. Vivekananda Swami; *Complete Works*, Kolkata: Advaita Ashrama, 2005, Vol. 4, 314-5, Vol. 8, 261-2, Vol. 4, 312-3.
11 Tagore Rabindranath; *Personality,* Delhi: Rupa, 2002, p. 86.
12. Same; *The Centre of Indian Culture,* Kolkata: Vishwabharati, 1988, p. 12, pp. 6-7.
13. Same; *Reminiscences,* Delhi: Macmillan, 1987, pp. 8-9.
14. Gandhi Mahatma; *Selected Works,* Ahmedabad: Navjivan, 1968, Vol. 4, pp. 188-91.
15. Same *Hindu Dharma,* Delhi: Orient, 2005, pp.20-1.
16. Aurobindo Sri; 'Sri Aurobindo on Science', *AIM*, July 2006, p.15.
17. Same *A Call To The Youth of India,* ed. Vijay, Pondicherry: Sri Aurobindo Society, 1993, p.14.
18. Samuelson P. A: 'The Fable of Recovery', *Business World*, August 3, 2009, p.44.
19. Toynbee, op.cit., p. 342.
20. Brown D. M ; *The White Umbrella,* Berkeley: University of California Press, 1964, pp. 49-51.
21. Chakraborty S. K. and Chakraborty D : *Spirituality In Management, Delhi*: Oxford University Press, 2008.
22. Danino M., and Nahar S.; *The Invasion That Never Was*, The Mother's Insitute of Research, Delhi, 2001, p. 27.
23. Agarwal D.; 'How True is the Aryan Invasion?', *Samvit*, March 2009, pp. 24-9.
24. Vivekananda Swami: *Complete Works,* Vol. 5, p. 534-5.
25. *Ibid. p.210.*
26. Tagore Rabindranath: *The Centre of Indian Culture,* op.cit, pp.19, 23, 24, 34.
27. Bose Subhas Chandra: *Complete Works,* Kolkata: Netaji Research Bureau, Vol. 2, p. 131.
28. Vivekananda S. W.; *Complete Works,* Kolkata: Advaita Ashrama, 2005, *Vol. 3, p. 299.*
29. *Ibid.;* p. 301.
30. *Ibid.;* p. 289.
31. *Ibid.;* p. 277.
32. *Ibid.;* pp. 245, 277, 284.
33. *Ibid.;* p. 317.
34. *Ibid.;* p. 227.
35. *Chanakya Niti*, Verse XVI-5.

INDEX

K

L

M

S

V

W

Y

Z